NAACL-HLT 2007/AMTA Workshop on Syntax and Structure in Statistical Translation

(SSST)

Held at NAACL-HLT 2007

Rochester, New York, USA
26 April 2007

Editors:

Dekai Wu **David Chiang**

ISBN: 978-1-61738-515-5

Printed from e-media with permission by:

Curran Associates, Inc.
57 Morehouse Lane
Red Hook, NY 12571
www.proceedings.com

Some format issues inherent in the e-media version may also appear in this print version.

Printed by Curran Associates, Inc. (2010)

Association for Computational Linguistics
209 N. Eighth Street
Stroudsburg, Pennsylvania 18360

Phone: 1-570-476-8006
Fax: 1-570-476-0860

acl@aclweb.org

Introduction

The NAACL-HLT 2007 / AMTA Workshop on Syntax and Structure in Statistical Translation (SSST) took place on 26 April 2007 following the NAACL-HLT conference hosted by the University of Rochester in New York. It was organized in response to growing interest in statistical, tree structured models of relations between natural languages. Our hope was to bring together researchers working on various aspects of this subject, and coming from various traditions. One way that the diversity of these traditions can be seen is in their nomenclature: transduction grammars originated in formal language theory (Lewis and Stearns 1968, Aho and Ullman 1969), and as interest in them was renewed in the computational linguistics literature in the 1990s, they came to be also known as synchronous grammars. Pushdown transducers and tree transducers, also introduced in the late 1960s, embody a less declarative, rather more procedural view, but, in many cases, have transduction-grammar equivalents.

Another dimension of diversity is the variety of applications of synchronous/transduction grammars, which is richly reflected in our workshop program. We selected fourteen papers, which include papers on formal properties of synchronous/transduction grammars from both theoretical (Shieber) and comparative experimental (Zhang and Gildea; Huang; Dreyer, Hall and Khudanpur) perspectives, and papers applying synchronous/transduction grammars to machine translation as well as generation (Hall and Němec) and semantic interpretation (Nesson and Shieber). The invited speaker for the workshop was William C. Rounds of the University of Michigan, a pioneer of tree-transducer theory who was one of the first to explore the usefulness of tree transducers for natural language.

The papers included a wide spectrum of experiments trying different tradeoffs between representational adequacy versus efficiency. Some models adopted binary-rank ITG or inversion transduction grammar constraints (Cherry and Lin; Huang; Dreyer, Hall and Khudanpur), while others permitted up to STAG or synchronous tree-adjoining grammar expressiveness (Nesson and Shieber; Shieber), with others in between at the SDTG or syntax directed transduction grammar a.k.a. SCFG or synchronous context-free grammar level (Zhang, Zens and Ney; Zhang and Gildea). Transduction rules ranged from mildly hierarchical, heavily lexical transduction rules on one hand (Cherry and Lin; Zhang, Zens and Ney; Venkatapathy and Bangalore; Dreyer, Hall and Khudanpur), to abstract transduction rules emphasizing compositional syntax on the other (Nesson and Shieber; Hall and Němec; Shieber).

A number of papers investigated machine learning techniques for inducing synchronous/transduction grammars (Zhang, Zens and Ney; Cherry and Lin). Some of these focused on improving algorithms for binarizing or reducing the rank of synchronous/transduction grammars (Zhang and Gildea; Huang). The workshop also witnessed a number of papers proposing new ways of integrating tree structured models into statistical methods in machine translation (Hopkins and Kuhn; Venkatapathy and Joshi; Bonneau-Maynard, Allauzen, Déchelotte and Schwenk; Font Llitjós and Vogel; Owczarzak, van Genabith and Way; Venkatapathy and Bangalore).

The Association for Machine Translation in the Americas sponsored $1000 in scholarships for several students to attend the workshop. We thank AMTA for their generosity, and we also thank the Program Committee for their extremely quick reviews.

Dekai Wu and David Chiang

Organizers:

Dekai WU, Hong Kong University of Science and Technology (HKUST), Hong Kong
David CHIANG, USC Information Sciences Institute, USA

Program Committee:

Srinivas BANGALORE, AT&T Research, USA
Marine CARPUAT, Hong Kong University of Science and Technology (HKUST), Hong Kong
Daniel GILDEA, University of Rochester, USA
Kevin KNIGHT, USC Information Sciences Institute, USA
Daniel MARCU, USC Information Sciences Institute, USA
Hermann NEY, RWTH Aachen, Germany
Owen RAMBOW, Columbia University, USA
Philip RESNIK, University of Maryland, USA
Giorgio SATTA, University of Padua, Italy
Stuart M. SHIEBER, Harvard University, USA
Christoph TILLMANN, IBM, USA
Enrique VIDAL, Universidad Politécnica de Valencia, Spain
Stephan VOGEL, Carnegie Mellon University, USA
Andy WAY, Dublin City University, Ireland
Taro WATANABE, NTT, Japan
Richard ZENS, RWTH Aachen, Germany

Table of Contents

Conference Program

Thursday, April 26, 2007

9:00–9:05	Opening
9:05–9:30	*Chunk-Level Reordering of Source Language Sentences with Automatically Learned Rules for Statistical Machine Translation* Yuqi ZHANG, Richard ZENS and Hermann NEY
9:30–9:55	*Extraction Phenomena in Synchronous TAG Syntax and Semantics* Rebecca NESSON and Stuart M. SHIEBER
9:55–10:45	Invited Talk by William C. ROUNDS
10:45–11:15	Coffee Break
11:15–11:40	*Inversion Transduction Grammar for Joint Phrasal Translation Modeling* Colin CHERRY and Dekang LIN
11:40–12:05	*Factorization of Synchronous Context-Free Grammars in Linear Time* Hao ZHANG and Daniel GILDEA
12:05–12:30	*Binarization, Synchronous Binarization, and Target-side Binarization* Liang HUANG
12:30–14:00	Lunch
14:00–14:25	*Machine Translation as Tree Labeling* Mark HOPKINS and Jonas KUHN
14:25–14:50	*Discriminative word alignment by learning the alignment structure and syntactic divergence between a language pair* Sriram VENKATAPATHY and Aravind JOSHI
14:50–15:15	*Generation in Machine Translation from Deep Syntactic Trees* Keith HALL and Petr NĚMEC

Thursday, April 26, 2007 (continued)

15:15–16:00 Posters with Coffee

Combining Morphosyntactic Enriched Representation with n-best Reranking in Statistical Translation
Hélène BONNEAU-MAYNARD, Alexandre ALLAUZEN, Daniel DÉCHELOTTE and Holger SCHWENK

A Walk on the Other Side: Using SMT Components in a Transfer-Based Translation System
Ariadna FONT LLITJÓS and Stephan VOGEL

Dependency-Based Automatic Evaluation for Machine Translation
Karolina OWCZARZAK, Josef VAN GENABITH and Andy WAY

Probabilistic Synchronous Tree-Adjoining Grammars for Machine Translation: The Argument from Bilingual Dictionaries
Stuart M. SHIEBER

16:00–16:25 *Three models for discriminative machine translation using Global Lexical Selection and Sentence Reconstruction*
Sriram VENKATAPATHY and Srinivas BANGALORE

16:25–16:50 *Comparing Reordering Constraints for SMT Using Efficient BLEU Oracle Computation*
Markus DREYER, Keith HALL and Sanjeev KHUDANPUR

16:50–17:50 Panel Discussion

17:50–18:00 Closing

Chunk-Level Reordering of Source Language Sentences with Automatically Learned Rules for Statistical Machine Translation

Yuqi Zhang and Richard Zens and Hermann Ney

Human Language Technology and Pattern Recognition
Lehrstuhl für Informatik 6 – Computer Science Department
RWTH Aachen University, D-52056 Aachen, Germany
{yzhang,zens,ney}@cs.rwth-aachen.de

Abstract

In this paper, we describe a source-side reordering method based on syntactic chunks for phrase-based statistical machine translation. First, we shallow parse the source language sentences. Then, reordering rules are automatically learned from source-side chunks and word alignments. During translation, the rules are used to generate a reordering lattice for each sentence. Experimental results are reported for a Chinese-to-English task, showing an improvement of 0.5%–1.8% BLEU score absolute on various test sets and better computational efficiency than reordering during decoding. The experiments also show that the reordering at the chunk-level performs better than at the POS-level.

1 Introduction

In machine translation, reordering is one of the major problems, since different languages have different word order requirements. Many reordering constraints have been used for word reorderings, such as ITG constraints (Wu, 1996), IBM constraints (Berger et al., 1996) and local constraints (Kanthak et al., 2005). These approaches do not make use of any linguistic knowledge.

Several methods have been proposed to use syntactic information to handle the reordering problem, e.g. (Wu, 1997; Yamada and Knight, 2001; Gildea, 2003; Melamed, 2004; Graehl and Knight, 2004; Galley et al., 2006). One approach makes use of bitext grammars to parse both the source and target languages. Another approach makes use of syntactic information only in the target language. Note that these models have radically different structures and parameterizations than phrase-based models for SMT.

Another kind of approaches is to use syntactic information in rescoring methods. (Koehn and Knight, 2003) apply a reranking approach to the sub-task of noun-phrase translation. (Och et al., 2004) and (Shen et al., 2004) describe the use of syntactic features in reranking the output of a full translation system, but the syntactic features give very small gains.

In this paper, we present a strategy to reorder a source sentence using rules based on syntactic chunks. It is possible to integrate reordering rules directly into the search process, but here, we consider a more modular approach: easy to exchange reordering strategy. To avoid hard decisions before SMT, we generate a source-reordering lattice instead of a single reordered source sentence as input to the SMT system. Then, the decoder uses the reordered source language model as an additional feature function. A language model trained on the reordered source-side chunks gives a score for each path in the lattice. The novel ideas in this paper are:

- reordering of the source sentence at the chunk level,
- representing linguistic chunks-reorderings in a lattice.

Proceedings of SSST, NAACL-HLT 2007 / AMTA Workshop on Syntax and Structure in Statistical Translation, pages 1–8,
Rochester, New York, April 2007.

The rest of this paper is organized as follows. Section 2 presents a review of related work. In Sections 3, we review the phrase-based translation system used in this work and propose the framework of the new reordering method. In Section 4, we introduce the details of the reordering rules, how they are defined and how to extract them. In Section 5, we explain how to apply the rules and how to generate reordering lattice. In Section 6, we present some results that show that the chunk-level source reordering is helpful for phrase-based statistical machine translation. Finally, we conclude this paper and discuss future work in Section 7.

2 Related Work

Beside the reordering methods during decoding, an alternative approach is to reorder the input source sentence to match the word order of the target sentence.

Some reordering methods are carried out on syntactic source trees. (Collins et al., 2005) describe a method for reordering German for German-to-English translation, where six transformations are applied to the surface string of the parsed source sentence. (Xia and McCord, 2004) propose an approach for translation from French-to-English. This approach automatically extracts rewrite patterns by parsing the source and target sides of the training corpus. These rewrite patterns can be applied to any input source sentence so that the rewritten source and target sentences have similar word order. Both methods need a parser to generate trees of source sentences and are applied only as a preprocessing step.

Another kind of source reordering methods besides full parsing is based on Part-Of-Speech (POS) tags or word classes. (Costa-jussà and Fonollosa, 2006) view the source reordering as a translation task that translate the source language into a reordered source language. Then, the reordered source sentence is taken as the single input to the standard SMT system.

(Chen et al., 2006) automatically extract rules from word alignments. These rules are defined at the POS level and the scores of matching rules are used as additional feature functions during rescoring. (Crego and Mariño, 2006) integrate source-side reordering into SMT decoding. They automatically learn rewrite patterns from word alignment and represent the patterns with POS tags. To our knowledge no work is reported on the reordering with shallow parsing.

Decoding lattices were already used in (Zens et al., 2002; Kanthak et al., 2005). Those approaches used linguistically uninformed word-level reorderings.

3 System Overview

In this section, we will describe the phrase-based SMT system which we use for the experiments. Then, we will give an outline of the extentions with the chunk-level source reordering model.

3.1 The Baseline Phrase-based SMT System

In statistical machine translation, we are given a source language sentence $f_1^J = f_1 \ldots f_j \ldots f_J$, which is to be translated into a target language sentence $e_1^I = e_1 \ldots e_i \ldots e_I$. Among all possible target language sentences, we will choose the sentence with the highest probability:

$$\hat{e}_1^{\hat{I}} = \underset{I, e_1^I}{\operatorname{argmax}} \left\{ Pr(e_1^I | f_1^J) \right\} \quad (1)$$

$$= \underset{I, e_1^I}{\operatorname{argmax}} \left\{ Pr(e_1^I) \cdot Pr(f_1^J | e_1^I) \right\} \quad (2)$$

This decomposition into two knowledge sources is known as the source-channel approach to statistical machine translation (Brown et al., 1990). It allows an independent modeling of the target language model $Pr(e_1^I)$ and the translation model $Pr(f_1^J | e_1^I)$. The target language model describes the well-formedness of the target language sentence. The translation model links the source language sentence to the target language sentence. The argmax operation denotes the search problem, i.e., the generation of the output sentence in the target language.

A generalization of the classical source-channel approach is the direct modeling of the posterior probability $Pr(e_1^I | f_1^J)$. Using a log-linear model

(Och and Ney, 2002), we obtain:

$$Pr(e_1^I|f_1^J) = \frac{\exp\left(\sum_{m=1}^{M}\lambda_m h_m(e_1^I, f_1^J)\right)}{\sum_{I', e'^{I'}_1} \exp\left(\sum_{m=1}^{M}\lambda_m h_m(e'^{I'}_1, f_1^J)\right)} \quad (3)$$

The denominator represents a normalization factor that depends only on the source sentence f_1^J. Therefore, we can omit it during the search process. As a decision rule, we obtain:

$$\hat{e}_1^{\hat{I}} = \underset{I, e_1^I}{\operatorname{argmax}} \left\{ \sum_{m=1}^{M} \lambda_m h_m(e_1^I, f_1^J) \right\} \quad (4)$$

The log-linear model has the advantage that additional models $h(\cdot)$ can be easily integrated into the overall system. The model scaling factors λ_1^M are trained according to the maximum entropy principle, e.g., using the GIS algorithm. Alternatively, one can train them with respect to the final translation quality measured by an error criterion (Och, 2003).

The log-linear model is a natural framework to integrate many models. The baseline system uses the following models:

- phrase translation model
- phrase count features
- word-based translation model
- word and phrase penalty
- target language model (6-gram)
- distortion model (assigning costs based on the jump width)

All the experiments in the paper are evaluated without rescoring. More details about the baseline system can be found in (Mauser et al., 2006)

3.2 Source Sentence Reordering Framework

Encouraged by the work of (Xia and McCord, 2004) and (Crego and Mariño, 2006), we also reorder the source language side. Compared to reordering on the target language side, one advantage is the efficiency since the reordering lattice can be translated monotonically as in (Zens et al., 2002). Another advantage is that there is correct sentence information for the reordering methods, because the source sentences are always given. Syntactic reordering on target language is difficult, since the methods will degrade much because of the errors in hypothesis.

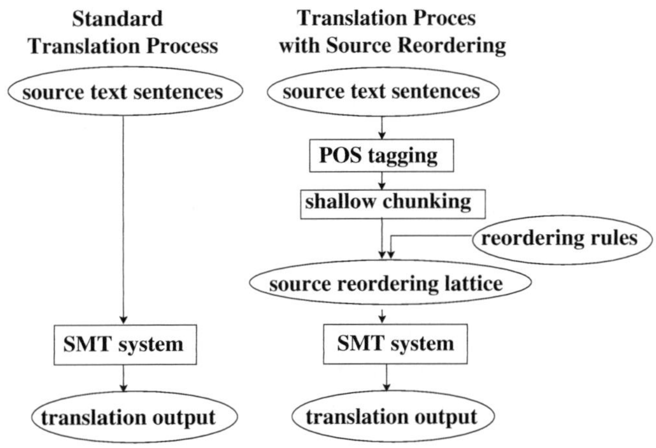

Figure 1: Illustration of the translation process with and without source reordering.

We apply reordering at the syntactic chunk level which can been seen as an intermediate level between full parsing and POS tagging. Figure 1 shows the differences between the new translation framework and the standard translation process. A reordering lattice replaces the original source sentence as the input to the translation system. The use of a lattice avoids hard decisions before translation. To generate the reordering lattice, the source sentence is first POS tagged and chunk parsed. Then, reordering rules are applied to the chunks to generate the reordering lattice.

Reordering rules are the key information for source reordering. They are automatically learned from the training data. The details of these two modules will be introduced in Section 5.

4 Reordering Rules

There has been much work on learning and applying reordering rules on source language, such as (Nießen and Ney, 2001; Xia and McCord, 2004; Collins et al., 2005; Chen et al., 2006; Crego and Mariño, 2006; Popović and Ney, 2006). The reordering rules could be composed of words, POS tags or syntactic tags of phrases. In our work, a rule is composed of chunk tags and POS tags. There is

Table 1: Examples of reordering rules. (lhs: chunk and POS tag sequence, rhs: permutation)

no.	lhs	rhs
1.	$NP_0\, PP_1\, u_2\, n_3$	0 1 2 3
2.	$NP_0\, PP_1\, u_2\, n_3$	3 0 1 2
3.	$DNP_0\, NP_1\, VP_2$	0 1 2
4.	$DNP_0\, NP_1\, VP_2$	1 0 2
5.	$DNP_0\, NP_1\, m_2$	0 1 2
6.	$DNP_0\, NP_1\, m_2\, ad_3$	3 0 1 2
7.	$DNP_0\, NP_1\, m_2\, ad_3\, v_4$	4 3 0 1 2

no hierarchical structure in a rule.

4.1 Definition of Reordering Rules

First, we show some rule examples in Table 1. A reordering rule consists of a left-hand-side (lhs) and a right-hand-side (rhs). The left-hand-side is a syntactic rule (chunk or POS tags), while the right-hand-side is the reordering positions of the rule. Different rules can share the same left-hand-side, such as rules no. 1, 2 and no. 3, 4. The rules record not only the *real* reordered chunk sequence, but also the monotone chunk sequences, like no. 1, 3 and 5. Note that the same tag sequence can appear multiple times according to different contexts, such as $DNP_0\, NP_1\, m_2$ # 0 1 2 in rules no. 5, 6, 7.

4.2 Extraction of Reordering Rules

The extraction of reordering rules is based on the word alignment and the source sentence chunks. Here, we train word alignments in both directions with GIZA++ (Och and Ney, 2003). To get alignment with high accuracy, we use the intersection alignment here.

For a given word-aligned sentence pair (f_1^J, e_1^I, a_1^J), the source word sequence f_1^J is first parsed into a chunk sequence F_1^K. Accordingly, the word-to-word alignment a_1^J is changed to a chunk-to-word alignment $\tilde{a}_1^K$ which is the combination of the target words aligned to the source words in a chunk. It is defined as:

$$\tilde{a}_k = \{i | i = a_j \wedge j \in [j_k, j_{k+1} - 1]\}$$

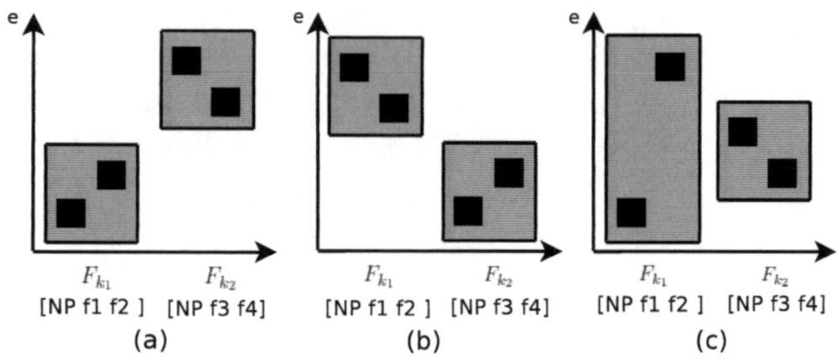

Figure 2: Illustration of three kinds of phrases: (a)monotone phrase, (b)reordering phrase, (c)cross phrase. The black box is a word-to-word alignment. The gray box is a chunk-to-word alignment.

Here, j_k denotes the position of the first source word in k^{th} chunk. The new alignment is $1 : m$ from source chunks to target words. It also means $\tilde{a}_k$ is a set of positions of target words.

We apply the standard phrase extraction algorithm (Zens et al., 2002) to $(F_1^K, e_1^I, \tilde{a}_1^K)$. Discarding the cross phrases, we keep the other phrases as rules. In a cross phrase, at least two chunk-word alignments overlap on the target language side. An example of a cross phrase is illustrated in Figure 2(c). Figure 2(a) and (b) illustrate the phrases for reordering rules, which could be monotone phrases or reordering phrases.

5 Reordering Lattice Generation

5.1 Parsing the Source Sentence

The first step of chunk parsing is word segmentation. Then, a POS tagger is usually needed for further syntactic analysis. In our experiments, we use the tool of "Inst. of Computing Tech., Chinese Lexical Analysis System (ICTCLAS)" (Zhang et al., 2003), which does the two tasks in one pass.

Referring to the description of the chunking task in CoNLL-2000[1], instead of English, a Chinese chunker is processed and evaluated. Each word is assigned a chunk tag, which contains the name of the chunk type and "B" for the first word of the chunk and "I" for each other word in the chunk. The "O" chunk tag is used for tokens which are not part of any chunk. We use the maximum entropy tool YAS-

[1]http://www.cnts.ua.ac.be/conll2000/chunking/

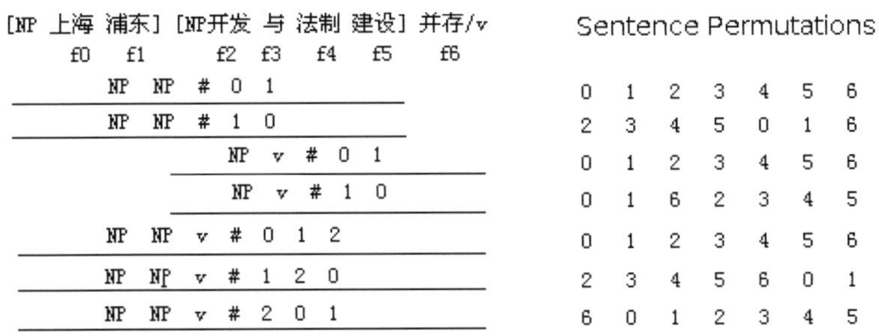

Figure 3: Example of applying rules. The left part is the used rules. The right part is the generated new orders of source words.

MET[2] to learn the chunking model. The model is based on a combination of word and POS tags. Since specific training and test data are not available for Chinese chunking, we convert subtrees of the Chinese treebank (LDC2005T01) into chunks. As there are many ways to choose a subtree, we uses the minimum subtree with the following constraints:

- a subtree has more than one child,
- the children of a subtree are all leaves.

Compared to chunking of English as in CoNLL-2000, there are more chunk types (24 instead of 6) and no single-word chunks. These two aspects make chunking for Chinese harder.

5.2 Applying Reordering Rules

First, we search the reordering rules, in which the chunk sequence matches any tag sequence in the input sentence. A source sentence has many paths generated by the rules . For a word uncovered by any rules, its POS tag is used. Each path corresponds to one sentence permutation.

The left part of the Figure 3 shows seven possible coverages, the right part is the reordering for each coverage. Some of the reorderings are identical, like the permutations in line 1, 3 and 5. That is because one word sequence is memorized by several rules in different contexts.

5.3 Lattice Weighting

All reorderings of an input sentence S are compressed and stored in a lattice. Each path is a possible reordering S' and is given a weight W. In this paper, the weight is computed using a source language model $p(S')$. The weight is used directly in the decoder, integrated into Equation (4). There is also a scaling factor for this weight, which is optimized together with other scaling factors on the development data. The probability of the reordered source sentence is calculated as follows: for a reordered source sentence $w_1 w_2 ... w_n$, the trigram language model is:

$$p(S') = \prod_{n=1}^{N} p(w_n | w_{n-2}, w_{n-1}) \qquad (5)$$

Beside a word N-gram language model, a POS tag N-gram model or a chunk tag N-gram model could be used as well.

In this paper, we use a word trigram model. The model is trained on reordered training source sentences. A training source sentence is parsed into chunks. In the same way as described in Section 4.2, word-to-word alignments is converted to chunk-to-word alignments. We reorder the source chunks to monotonize the chunk-to-word alignments. The chunk boundaries are kept when this reordering is done.

6 Experiments

6.1 Chunking Result

In this section, we report results for chunk parsing. The annotation of the data is derived from the Chinese treebank (LDC2005T01). The corpus is split into two parts: 1000 sentences are randomly se-

[2] http://www-i6.informatik.rwth-aachen.de/web/Software /index.html

Table 2: Statistics of training and test corpus for chunk parsing.

	train	test
sentences	17 785	1 000
words	486 468	21 851
chunks	105 773	4 680
words out of chunks	244 416	10 282

Table 3: Chunk parsing result on 1000 sentences.

accuracy	precision	recall	F-measure
74.51%	65.2%	61.5%	63.3

lected as test data. The remaining part is used for training. The corpus is from the newswire domain.

Table 2 shows the corpus statistics. For the 4 680 chunks in the test set, the chunker has found 4 414 chunks, of which 2 879 are correct. Following the criteria of CoNLL-2000, the chunker is evaluated using the F-score, which is a combination of precision and recall. The result is shown in Table 3.

The accuracy is evaluated at the word level, the other three metrics are evaluated at the chunk level. The results at the chunk level are worse than at the word level, because a chunk is counted as correct only if the chunk tag and the chunk boundaries are both correct.

6.2 Translation Results

For the translation experiments, we report the two accuracy measures BLEU (Papineni et al., 2002) and NIST (Doddington, 2002) as well as the two error rates word error rate (WER) and position-independent word error rate (PER).

We perform translation experiments on the Basic Traveling Expression Corpus (BTEC) for the Chinese-English task. It is a speech translation task in the domain of tourism-related information. We report results on the IWSLT 2004, 2005 and 2006 evaluation test sets. There are 16 reference translations for the IWSLT 2004 and 2005 tasks and 7 reference translations for the IWSLT 2006 task.

Table 4 shows the corpus statistics of the task. A training corpus is used to train the translation model, the language model and to obtain the reordering rules. A development corpus is used to optimize the scaling factors for the BLEU score. The English text is processed using a tokenizer. The Chinese text processing uses word segmentation with the ICTCLAS segmenter (Zhang et al., 2003). The translation is evaluated case-insensitive and without punctuation marks.

Table 4: Statistics of training and test corpora for the IWSLT tasks.

		Chinese	English
Train	Sentences	40k	
	Words	308k	377k
Dev	Sentences	489	
	Words	5 478	6 008
Test IWSLT04	Sentences	500	
	Words	3 866	3 581
Test IWSLT05	Sentences	506	
	Words	3 652	3 579
Test IWSLT06	Sentences	500	
	Words	5 846	–

The translation results are presented in Table 5. The baseline system is a non-monotone translation system, in which the decoder does reordering on the target language side. Compared to the baseline system, the source reordering method improves the BLEU score by $0.5\% - 1.8\%$ absolute. It also achieves a better WER. Note that the used chunker here is out-of-domain [3]. An improvement is achieved even with a low F-measure for chunking. So, we could hope that larger improvement is possible using a high-accuracy chunker.

Though the input is a lattice, the source reordering is still faster than the reordering during decoding, e.g. for the IWSLT 2006 test set, the baseline system took 17.5 minutes and the source reordering system took 12.3 minutes. The result also indicates that the non-monotone decoding hurts the performance in a source reordering framework. A similar conclusion is also presented in (Xia and McCord, 2004).

Additional experiments we carried out to compare POS-level and chunk-level reorderings. We delete the chunk information and keep the POS tags. Then,

[3]The chunker is trained on newswire data, but the test data is from the tourism domain.

Table 5: Translation performance for the Chinese-English IWSLT task

		WER[%]	PER[%]	NIST	BLEU[%]
IWSLT04	baseline	47.3	38.2	7.78	39.1
	source reordering	46.3	37.2	7.70	40.9
IWSLT05	baseline	45.0	37.3	7.40	41.8
	source reordering	44.6	36.8	7.51	42.3
IWSLT06	baseline	67.4	50.0	6.65	22.4
	source reordering	65.6	50.4	6.46	23.3
	source reordering+non-monotone decoder	66.5	50.3	6.52	22.4

Table 6: Translation performance of reordering methods on IWSLT 2004 test set

	WER [%]	PER [%]	NIST	BLEU [%]
Baseline	47.3	38.2	7.78	39.1
POS	46.9	37.5	7.38	39.7
Chunk	46.3	37.2	7.70	40.9

Table 7: Lattice information for the Chinese-English IWSLT 2004 test data

	avg. density pro sent	used rules	translation time [min/sec]
POS	15.7	6 868	7:08
Chunk	8.2	3 685	3:47

we rerun the source reordering system on the IWSLT 2004 test set. The translation results are shown in Table 6. Though the accuracy of chunking is low, the chunk-level method gets better results than POS-level method. With POS tags, we get more reordering rules and more paths in the lattice, since the sentence length is longer than with chunks. The statistics are shown in Table 7.

7 Conclusions and Future Work

This paper presents a source-side reordering method which is based on syntactic chunks. The reordering rules are automatically learned from bilingual data. To avoid hard decision before decoding, a reordering lattice representing all possible reorderings is used instead of single source sentence for decoding. The experiments demonstrate that even with a very poor chunker, the chunk-level source reordering is still helpful for a state-of-the-art statistical translation system and it has better performance than the POS-level source reordering and target-side reordering.

There are some directions for future work. First, we would like to try this method on larger data sets and other language pairs. Second, we are going to improve the chunking accuracy. Third, we would reduce the number of rules and prune the lattice.

Acknowledgments

This material is partly based upon work supported by the Defense Advanced Research Projects Agency (DARPA) under Contract No. HR0011-06-C-0023, and was partially funded by the Deutsche Forschungsgemeinschaft (DFG) under the project "Statistische Textübersetzung" (Ne572/5)

References

A. L. Berger, S. A. Della Pietra, and V. J. Della Pietra. 1996. A maximum entropy approach to natural language processing. *Computational Linguistics*, 22(1):39–72, March.

P. F. Brown, J. Cocke, S. A. Della Pietra, V. J. Della Pietra, F. Jelinek, J. D. Lafferty, R. L. Mercer, and P. S. Roossin. 1990. A statistical approach to machine translation. *Computational Linguistics*, 16(2):79–85, June.

B. Chen, M. Cettolo, and M. Federico. 2006. Reordering rules for phrase-based statistical machine translation. In *Int. Workshop on Spoken Language Translation Evaluation Campaign on Spoken Language Translation*, pages 1–15, Kyoto, Japan, November.

M. Collins, P. Koehn, and I. Kucerova. 2005. Clause restructuring for statistical machine translation. In *Proc. of the 43rd Annual Meeting of the Association for Computational Linguistics (ACL)*, pages 531–540, Ann Arbor, Michigan, June.

M. R. Costa-jussà and J. A. R. Fonollosa. 2006. Statistical machine reordering. In *Proc. of the Conf. on Empirical Methods in Natural Language Processing*, pages 70–76, Sydney, Australia, July.

J. M. Crego and J. B. Mariño. 2006. Integration of postag-based source reordering into SMT decoding by an extended search graph. In *Proc. of AMTA06*, pages 29–36, Massachusetts, USA, August.

G. Doddington. 2002. Automatic evaluation of machine translation quality using n-gram co-occurrence statistics. In *Proc. ARPA Workshop on Human Language Technology*.

M. Galley, J. Graehl, K. Knight, D. Marcu, S. DeNeefe, W. Wang, and I. Thayer. 2006. Scalable inference and training of context-rich syntactic translation models. In *Proc. of the 21st Int. Conf. on Computational Linguistics and 44th Annual Meeting of the Association for Computational Linguistics*, pages 961–968, Sydney, Australia, July.

D. Gildea. 2003. Loosely tree-based alignment for machine translation. In *Proc. of the 41th Annual Meeting of the Association for Computational Linguistics (ACL)*, pages 80–87, Sapporo, Japan, July.

J. Graehl and K. Knight. 2004. Training tree transducers. In *HLT-NAACL 2004: Main Proc.*, pages 105–112, Boston, Massachusetts, USA, May 2 - May 7.

S. Kanthak, D. Vilar, E. Matusov, R. Zens, and H. Ney. 2005. Novel reordering approaches in phrase-based statistical machine translation. In *43rd Annual Meeting of the Assoc. for Computational Linguistics: Proc. Workshop on Building and Using Parallel Texts: Data-Driven Machine Translation and Beyond*, pages 167–174, Ann Arbor, Michigan, June.

P. Koehn and K. Knight. 2003. Empirical methods for compound splitting. In *Proc. 10th Conf. of the Europ. Chapter of the Assoc. for Computational Linguistics (EACL)*, pages 347–354, Budapest, Hungary, April.

A. Mauser, R. Zens, E. Matusov, S. Hasan, and H. Ney. 2006. The RWTH Statistical Machine Translation System for the IWSLT 2006 Evaluation. In *Proc. of the Int. Workshop on Spoken Language Translation*, pages 103–110, Kyoto, Japan.

I. Melamed. 2004. Statistical machine translation by parsing. In *The Companion Volume to the Proc. of 42nd Annual Meeting of the Association for Computational Linguistics*, pages 653–660.

S. Nießen and H. Ney. 2001. Morpho-syntactic analysis for reordering in statistical machine translation. In *Proc. of MT Summit VIII*, pages 247–252.

F. J. Och and H. Ney. 2002. Discriminative training and maximum entropy models for statistical machine translation. In *Proc. of the 40th Annual Meeting of the Association for Computational Linguistics (ACL)*, pages 295–302, Philadelphia, PA, July.

F. J. Och and H. Ney. 2003. A systematic comparison of various statistical alignment models. *Computational Linguistics*, 29(1):19–51, March.

F. J. Och, D. Gildea, S. Khudanpur, A. Sarkar, K. Yamada, A. Fraser, S. Kumar, L. Shen, D. Smith, K. Eng, V. Jain, Z. Jin, and D. Radev. 2004. A smorgasbord of features for statistical machine translation. In *Proc. 2004 Human Language Technology Conf. / North American Chapter of the Association for Computational Linguistics Annual Meeting (HLT-NAACL)*, pages 161–168, Boston,MA.

F. J. Och. 2003. Minimum error rate training in statistical machine translation. In *Proc. of the 41th Annual Meeting of the Association for Computational Linguistics (ACL)*, pages 160–167, Sapporo, Japan, July.

K. Papineni, S. Roukos, T. Ward, and W. J. Zhu. 2002. Bleu: a method for automatic evaluation of machine translation. In *Proc. of the 40th Annual Meeting of the Association for Computational Linguistics (ACL)*, pages 311–318, Philadelphia, PA, July.

M. Popović and H. Ney. 2006. POS-based word reorderings for statistical machine translation. In *Proc. of the Fifth Int. Conf. on Language Resources and Evaluation (LREC)*.

L. Shen, A. Sarkar, and F. J. Och. 2004. Discriminative reranking for machine translation. In *HLT-NAACL 2004: Main Proc.*, pages 177–184, Boston, Massachusetts, USA, May 2 - May 7.

C. Tillmann, S. Vogel, H. Ney, and A. Zubiaga. 1997. A DP-based search using monotone alignments in statistical translation. In *Proc. 35th Annual Conf. of the Association for Computational Linguistics*, pages 289–296, Madrid, Spain, July.

D. Wu. 1996. A polynomial-time algorithm for statistical machine translation. In *Proc. 34th Annual Meeting of the Assoc. for Computational Linguistics*, pages 152–158, Santa Cruz, CA, June.

D. Wu. 1997. Stochastic inversion transduction grammars and bilingual parsing of parallel corpora. *Computational Linguistics*, 23(3):377–403, September.

F. Xia and M. McCord. 2004. Improving a statistical MT system with automatically learned rewrite patterns. In *Proc. of COLING04*, pages 508–514, Geneva, Switzerland, Aug 23–Aug 27.

K. Yamada and K. Knight. 2001. A syntax-based statistical translation model. In *Proc. of the 39th Annual Meeting of the Association for Computational Linguistics (ACL)*, pages 523–530, Toulouse, France, July.

R. Zens, F. J. Och, and H. Ney. 2002. Phrase-based statistical machine translation. In M. Jarke, J. Koehler, and G. Lakemeyer, editors, *25th German Conf. on Artificial Intelligence (KI2002)*, volume 2479 of *Lecture Notes in Artificial Intelligence (LNAI)*, pages 18–32, Aachen, Germany, September. Springer Verlag.

H. P. Zhang, Q. Liu, X. Q. Cheng, H. Zhang, and H. K. Yu. 2003. Chinese lexical analysis using hierarchical hidden markov model. In *Proc. of the second SIGHAN workshop on Chinese language processing*, pages 63–70, Morristown, NJ, USA.

Extraction Phenomena in Synchronous TAG Syntax and Semantics

Rebecca Nesson and Stuart M. Shieber
School of Engineering and Applied Sciences
Harvard University
Cambridge, MA 02138
{nesson,shieber}@deas.harvard.edu

Abstract

We present a proposal for the structure of noun phrases in Synchronous Tree-Adjoining Grammar (STAG) syntax and semantics that permits an elegant and uniform analysis of a variety of phenomena, including quantifier scope and extraction phenomena such as wh-questions with both moved and in-place wh-words, pied-piping, stranding of prepositions, and topicalization. The tight coupling between syntax and semantics enforced by the STAG helps to illuminate the critical relationships and filter out analyses that may be appealing for either syntax or semantics alone but do not allow for a meaningful relationship between them.

1 Introduction

Nesson and Shieber (2006) showed how a now-standard variant of the tree-adjoining grammar (TAG) formalism (multi-component, multiple adjunction, finite-feature-based TAG), when synchronized, leads to a natural analysis of the syntax-semantics relation, including handling of syntactic movement phenomena such as wh questions and relativization, semantic "movement" phenomena such as quantification, quantifier scope ambiguity, and even their interactions as found in pied-piped relative clauses.[1] phenomena were previously viewed as problematic for TAG analyses, leading to the hypothesizing of various extensions to the TAG formalism (Kallmeyer and Romero, 2004, and work cited therein). Independently, Han (2006a) developed a similar synchronous TAG analysis of pied-piping, providing evidence for the naturalness of the analysis.

Here, we update the analyses of noun phrases found in the previous works in one simple way, again with no additional formal TAG innovations, and show that it allows a further coverage of extraction and quantification phenomena as well as in-situ wh-phrases and topicalization. We emphasize that no novel formal devices are postulated to achieve this increased coverage — just a simple, natural and uniform change to the canonical structure of NPs and their semantics.

A word may be useful on the pertinence of this work in a workshop on "syntax and structure in machine translation", above and beyond the intrinsic importance of exploring the "applications of [synchronous/transduction grammars] to related areas including... formal semantics" underlying the workshop. Tree-structured mappings are advocated for machine translation systems because they allow for the expression of generalizations about relationships between languages more accurately and effectively. Evidence for this benefit ought to be found in the ability of the formalisms to characterize the primitive linguistic relationships as well, in particular, the form-meaning relationship for a natural language. The present work is part of a general program to explore the suitability of synchronous grammars for expressing this primary linguistic relationship. Inso-

[1]This work was supported in part by grant IIS-0329089 from the National Science Foundation.

Proceedings of SSST, NAACL-HLT 2007 / AMTA Workshop on Syntax and Structure in Statistical Translation, pages 9–16,
Rochester, New York, April 2007. ©2007 Association for Computational Linguistics

far as it is successful, it lends credence to the use of these formal tools for a variety of language processing tasks, including MT. Insofar as it reveals insufficiencies in the formalism, it may lead to insights in the design or deployment of alternative systems.

We present a proposal for the structure of noun phrases in Synchronous Tree-Adjoining Grammar (STAG) syntax and semantics that permits an elegant and uniform analysis of a variety of phenomena, including quantifier scope and extraction phenomena such as wh-questions with both moved and in-situ wh-words, pied-piping, stranding of prepositions, and topicalization. Furthermore, the tight coupling between syntax and semantics enforced by grammar synchronization helps to illuminate the critical relationships and filter out analyses that may be appealing for either syntax or semantics alone but do not allow for a meaningful relationship between them.

We begin in Section 2 with a brief review of synchronous TAG and its application to English syntax and semantics. In Section 3, we present an analysis of quantifier scope that elucidates the relationship between the syntactic and semantic structures and explains an anomaly of previously proposed analyses. We apply the underlying idea from Section 3 to wh-questions in Section 4, showing that an alteration of the standard TAG syntax analysis of wh-questions produces the same derived trees while also elegantly modeling in-place wh-words. In Section 5 we present a challenging case for STAG syntax and semantics, the stranding of prepositions. This case is particularly difficult because the syntactic analyses suggested by previous work in STAG syntax do not encapsulate the relationships that appear necessary for the semantics. Our proposed analysis falls out naturally from the revision to the syntax of wh-words and respects both Frank's Condition on Elementary Tree Minimality (CETM) and the semantic relationships in the construction. In Section 6 we give an analysis of topicalization that also follows from the underlying ideas of the earlier analyses. We summarize the main ideas of the analysis in Section 7.

2 Introduction to Synchronous TAG

A tree-adjoining grammar (TAG) consists of a set of elementary tree structures of arbitrary depth,

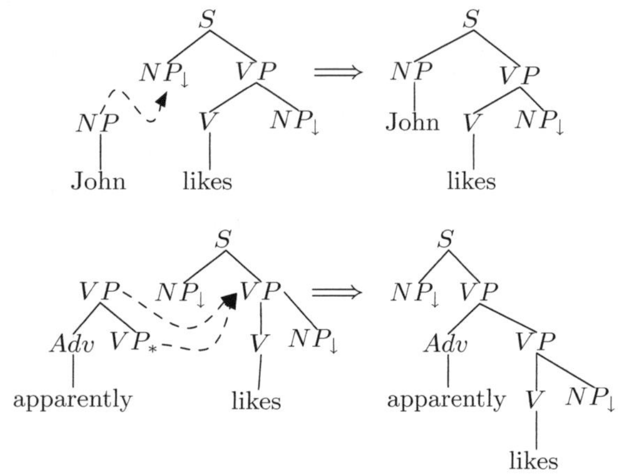

Figure 1: Example TAG substitution and adjunction.

which are combined with two operations, substitution and adjunction. Internal nodes in the elementary trees are labeled with a nonterminal symbol. Frontier nodes may be labeled with either terminal symbols or nonterminal symbols annotated with one of the diacritics $\downarrow$ or $*$. The $\downarrow$ diacritic marks a frontier nonterminal node as a *substitution node*, the target of the substitution operation. The *substitution* operation occurs when an elementary tree rooted in a nonterminal symbol *A* replaces a substitution node with the same nonterminal symbol.

Auxiliary trees are elementary trees in which the root and a frontier node, called the *foot node* and distinguished by the diacritic $*$, are labeled with the same nonterminal *A*. The *adjunction* operation involves splicing an auxiliary tree in at an internal node in an elementary tree also labeled with nonterminal *A*. Trees without a foot node, intended for substitution rather than adjunction into other trees, are called *initial trees*. Examples of the substitution and adjunction operations on sample elementary trees are shown in Figure 1. For further information, refer to Joshi and Schabes (1997).

Synchronous TAG (Shieber, 1994; Shieber and Schabes, 1990) extends TAG by taking the elementary structures to be pairs of TAG trees with links between particular nodes in those trees. Derivation proceeds as in TAG except that all operations must be paired. That is, a tree can only be substituted or adjoined at a node if its pair is simultaneously substituted or adjoined at a linked node. We notate the links by using boxed indices $\boxed{i}$ marking linked nodes.

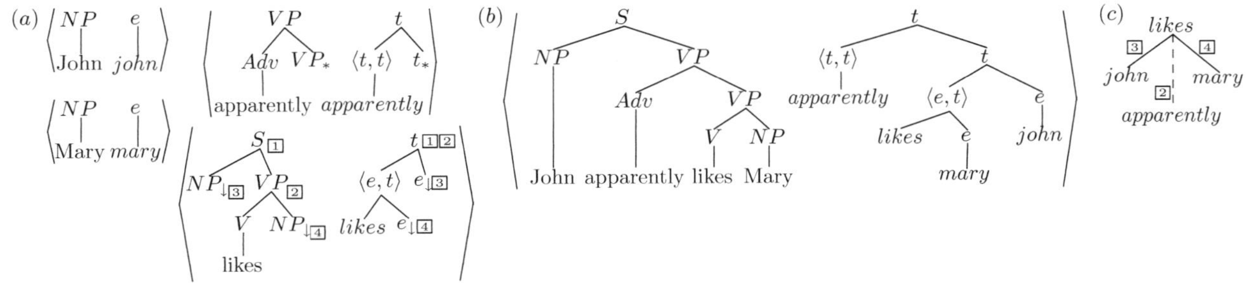

Figure 2: An English syntax/semantics STAG fragment (a), derived tree pair (b), and derivation tree (c) for the sentence "John apparently likes Mary."

As first described by Shieber and Schabes (1990), STAG can be used to provide a semantics for a TAG syntactic analysis by taking the tree pairs to represent a syntactic analysis synchronized with a semantic analysis.

For example, Figure 2(a) contains a sample English syntax/semantics grammar fragment that can be used to analyze the sentence "John apparently likes Mary". The node labels we use in the semantics correspond to the semantic types of the phrases they dominate.

Figure 2(c) shows the derivation tree for the sentence. Substitutions are notated with a solid line and adjunctions are notated with a dashed line. Each link in the derivation tree specifies a link number in the elementary tree pair, providing the location at which the operations take place. In this case, the tree pairs for the noun phrases *John* and *Mary* substitute into the *likes* tree pair at links 3 and 4, respectively. The word *apparently* adjoins at link 2. The tree pair so derived is shown in Figure 2(b). The resulting semantic representation can be read off the right-hand derived tree by treating the leftmost child of a node as a functor and its siblings as its arguments. Our sample sentence thus results in the semantic representation $apparently(likes(john, mary))$.

3 Quantifier Scope

We start by reviewing the prior approach to quantifier semantics in synchronous TAG. Consider the sentence "Everyone likes someone." We would like to allow both the reading where *some* takes scope over *every* and the reading where *every* takes scope over *some*. We start with the proposal of Shieber and Schabes (1990), which used multi-component TAG for the semantic portion of a synchronous TAG. Each quantified noun phrase has a two-component tree set as its semantics. One component introduces the variable quantified over in the scope of the quantifier; the other adjoins over the scope to provide the quantifier and restriction. Williford (1993) explored the use of multiple adjunction (Schabes and Shieber, 1993) to achieve scope ambiguity. Since the scope components of subject and object noun phrases adjoin at the same location in the semantic tree, they give rise to a systematic ambiguity as to which dominates the other in the derived tree, reflecting the semantic scope ambiguity of the sentence; the derivation tree itself is therefore a scope neutral representation. Previous work by Han (2006a; 2006b) and Nesson and Shieber (2006) describe this approach in detail, showing its applicability to a range of semantic phenomena.

A range of research has proceeded in an alternative line of using complex-feature-based TAG — rather than synchronous TAG — for TAG semantics (Kallmeyer and Romero, 2004, and work cited therein). Semantic representations are carried in features associated with nodes. Nonetheless, multi-component TAG with separate trees for bound position and scope is used here too. However, the two trees are syntactic trees, the quantified NP tree and a vestigial S tree, respectively. (An example is shown in Figure 6.) In such analyses, the single-node auxiliary S tree is used for the scope part of the syntax in order to get the desired relationship between the quantifier and the quantified expression in features threaded through the derivation tree and hence in the semantics.

The present analysis marries these two ap-

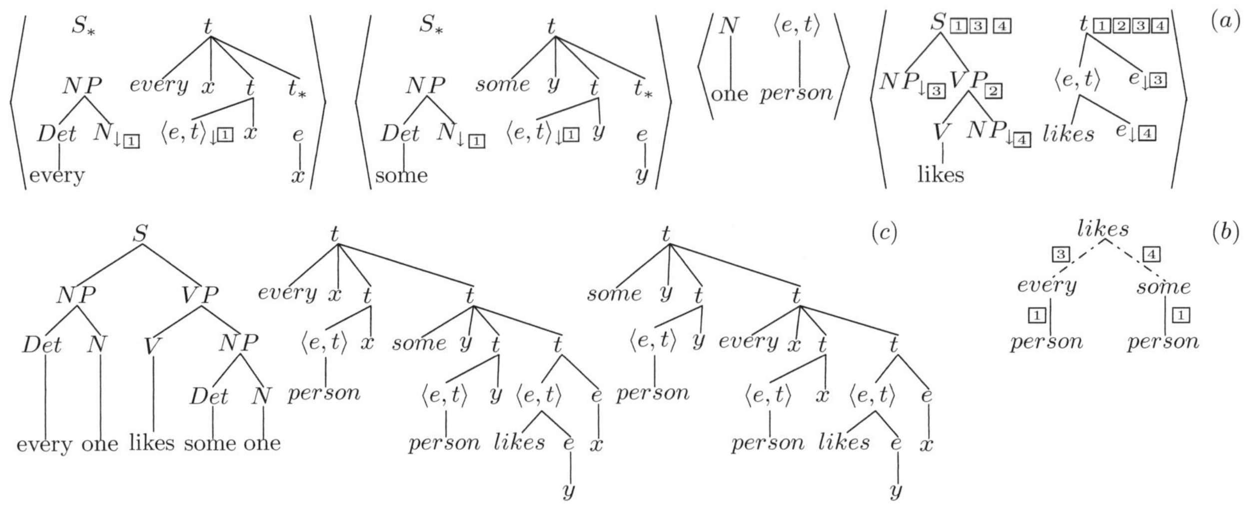

Figure 3: The elementary tree pairs (a), derivation tree (b), and derived trees (c) for the sentence "Everyone likes someone". Note that the derivation tree is a scope neutral representation: depending on whether *every* or *some* adjoins higher, we obtain different semantic derived trees and scope orderings.

proaches. Like the previous STAG work, we propose a solution in which a multi-component tree set provides semantics for quantified phrases, with multiple adjunction providing scope ambiguity. Like the complex-feature-based approach, we reflect the multi-component structure *in the syntax as well.* It is this single change in the analysis that makes possible the coverage of the wide range of phenomena we describe here.

Combining these two approaches, we give both the syntactic and semantic trees for quantifiers two parts, as depicted in Figure 3(a). In the semantics, the top part corresponds to the scope of the quantifier and attaches where the quantifier takes scope. The bottom part corresponds to the bound variable of the quantifier. By multiply adjoining the scope parts of the semantic trees of the quantifiers at the same location in the *likes* tree, we generate both available scope readings of the sentence.[2] Correspondingly on the syntax side, an NP tree provides the content of the noun phrase with a vestigial S tree available as well. Prior to the analyses given in this paper, the use of two trees in the quantifier syntax was an arbitrary stipulation used to make the semantic analysis possible. The pairing of the upper tree in the syntax with the scope tree in the semantics explicitly demonstrates their relationship and leads naturally to the exploration of non-degenerate upper trees in the syntax that we explore in this paper.

In order to use these multi-component quantifiers, we change the links in the elementary trees for verbs to allow a single link to indicate two positions in the syntax and semantics where a tree pair can adjoin, as shown in Figure 3(a). We add four-way links and drop the two-way links used by the unquantified noun phrases in the first example. This choice forces all noun phrase tree pairs to be multi-component in the syntax and semantics. Essentially, all noun phrases are "lifted" à la Montague. We explore the consequences of this in Section 6.

We turn now to the ramifications of this new syntactico-semantic STAG representation, showing its utility for a range of phenomena.

4 Wh-questions

The structure we propose for quantifiers suggests a new possibility for the TAG analysis of wh-words. We propose to simply treat wh-words as regular noun phrases by making them a multi-component tree set with an auxiliary tree that adjoins at the root of the verb tree and contains the lexical content and an initial tree with an empty frontier that substitutes at the argument position. This syntactic tree set can

[2]Nesson and Shieber (2006) provide a more in-depth explanation of the multiple-adjunction-driven approach to scope neutrality in STAG.

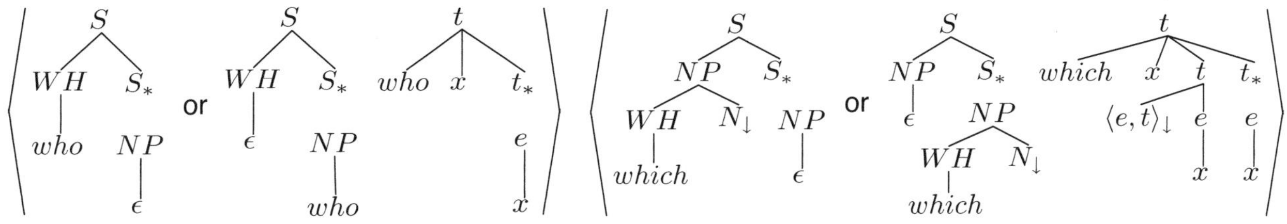

Figure 4: Elementary tree pairs for *who* and *which*. The left and middle tree sets are the syntactic alternatives used to model wh-movement and in-situ wh-words. The tree sets on the right provide the semantics.

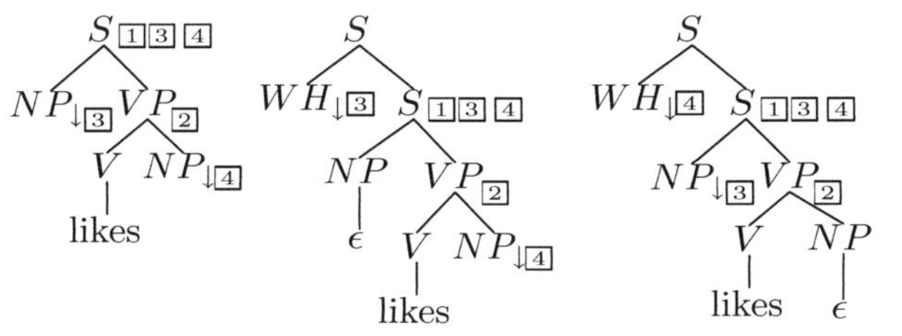

Figure 5: Traditional elementary trees for the verb *likes*. Using a revised, elementary syntax tree set for wh-words like *who*, only the left tree is necessary.

be paired with a multi-component semantic tree set that has an auxiliary tree containing the scope part and an initial tree that contains the bound variable. Wh-questions with the wh-word in place can be elegantly modeled with an alternative syntactic tree set in which the auxiliary tree has no lexical content and the wh-word is on the frontier of the initial tree that substitutes into the argument position. The semantic tree sets for both syntactic variations is the same. These trees are shown in Figure 4.

Besides the incorporation of a semantics, the basic analyses for wh-questions familiar from TAG syntax are otherwise unchanged because the top piece of the syntax tree set still ends up at the root of the main verb in sentences such as the following:

(1) Who likes Mary?
$who(x, likes(mary, x))$

(2) Which person does John like?[3]
$which(x, person(x), likes(x, john))$

(3) Which person does Bill think John likes?
$which(x, person(x), thinks(bill, likes(x, john)))$

(4) Who does each person like?
$who(x, each(y, person(y), likes(x, y)))$
$each(y, person(y), who(x, likes(x, y)))$

Note that in Sentence 3 *thinks* is not constrained to appear to the right of *who* in the syntax, because *thinks* and *who* both adjoin at the same location in the syntax. However, we can use a feature to force embedding verbs to adjoin lower than wh-words. The same situation exists in Sentence 4, though only in the semantics; the order of words in the syntax is well-defined but the multiple adjunction of the scope of *who* and the scope of *each* underspecifies the scope ordering between them. Both scope orderings are indeed arguably valid. Again, the preferences for certain orderings can be regulated using a feature. These issues highlight the many open questions about how to combine quantification and wh-terms, but also provides a first step towards their analysis within a concise STAG construction.

Our approach has several distinct advantages. First, it allows wh-words to be analyzed in a way that is uniform with the analysis of other noun phrases and allows us to simplify the lexical entries for verbs. In the traditional TAG analysis, wh-words substitute into specialized lexical trees for verbs that add an additional frontier node for the wh-word and abstract over one of the arguments of the verb by adding an empty terminal node at the frontier. Our revision to the elementary trees for wh-words allows us to remove several tree pairs from the elementary tree sets for verbs such as *like*. Instead of requiring an elementary tree pair for declarative sentences and an additional elementary tree for each argument

[3]The presence of do-support in wh-questions can be handled independently using a feature on the NP node into which the bottom part of the wh-word tree pair substitutes that governs whether and where a *do* tree adjoins.

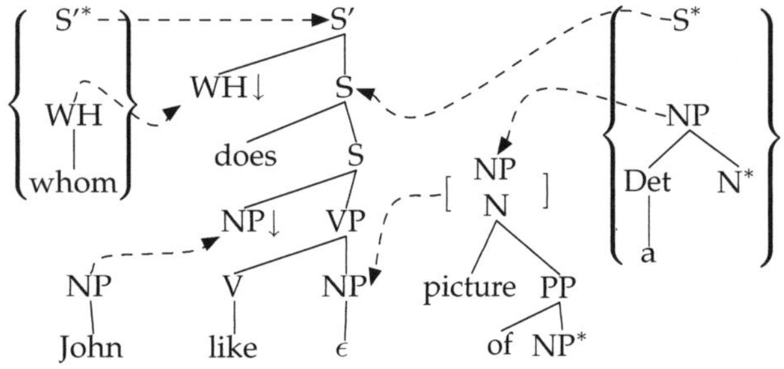

Figure 6: Kallmeyer and Scheffler's syntactic analysis for Sentence 6.

that can be replaced by a fronted wh-word to form a question (as shown in Figure 5), we can use just the single declarative sentence elementary tree.

Second, it provides a simple and elegant characterization of the syntax and semantics of wh-movement and the relationship between fronted and in-place wh-words. Using the alternative syntax tree set given in Figure 4 we model in-place use of wh-words as in Sentence 5 while still maintaining the usual semantic analysis:

(5) John likes who?
who(x, likes(x, john))

5 Stranded Prepositions

Sentence 6 presents a particularly challenging case for TAG semantics. The problem arises because *who* must contribute its bound variable, *x*, to the noun phrase "a picture of *x*". However, in the standard syntactic analysis *who* substitutes into the *likes* tree, and in any reasonable semantic analysis, *who* takes scope at the root of the *likes* tree.

(6) Who does John like a picture of?
$who(x, a(y,\ and(picture(y), of(x,y)),$
$likes(john,y)))$

Kallmeyer and Scheffler (2004) propose a syntactic analysis in which "a picture of" adjoins into the syntactic tree for "likes". The syntax for this analysis is shown for comparison in Figure 6. Associated with the syntactic analysis is a semantic analysis, which differs from ours in that all of the semantic computation is accomplished by use of a flexible set of features that are associated with nodes in the syntactic trees. This analysis maintains Frank's Constraint on Elementary Tree Minimality (CETM) if one analyzes the prepositional phrase as a complement of *picture* but it does so at the expense of a straightforward compositional semantics.[4] The source of the problem is that *who* contributes its bound variable to *likes* to form an intermediate semantics $who(x, likes(john,x))$, then *a picture of* combines non-compositionally to form the complete semantics given in Sentence 6.

Kroch (1989) describes the intuition eschewing this analysis: "The problem is that under such a derivation, the preposed wh-phrase changes its thematic role with each adjunction and the interpretation of the derived tree is not a simple function of the interpretations of its component elementary trees." When we consider the semantics of the two sentences, the anomaly of this analysis becomes apparent. In the first sentence the entity liked by John is referred to by the variable contributed by *who*. In the second sentence John likes an entirely different entity: the entity referred to by the variable contributed by *a*. Kallmeyer and Scheffler obtain the correct semantics by making use of non-local TAG operations to have the scope part of *a* adjoin into *likes* to capture the semantics of the likes proposition and employing a feature-based mechanism for swapping the variables as necessary.

Our revision to the syntax of wh-words provides an alternative way of maintaining the CETM that offers a much simpler semantic analysis. The details of the analysis are given in Figure 7. We adjoin *who* into the preposition *of* at link 1 where it contributes both variable and scope. The tree pair for *of* attaches to *a* at link 1, thus allowing the scope parts of the quantifier *a* and the wh-word *who* to end up taking scope over the main verb as in the analysis of prepositional phrases given by Nesson and Shieber (2006). It also places all the bound variables in the correct propositions without use of non-local operations or additional manipulation. A diagram of the derived syntax and semantics is given in Figure 8.

[4] In addition to suggesting a non-compositional semantics, their syntactic analysis makes use of non-local multi-component TAG in order to achieve the necessary semantic relationships. Although their use of non-local TAG may be benign in terms of complexity, our analysis is set-local. Our proposal therefore simplifies the syntactic analysis while also bringing it in line with a straightforward, compositional semantics.

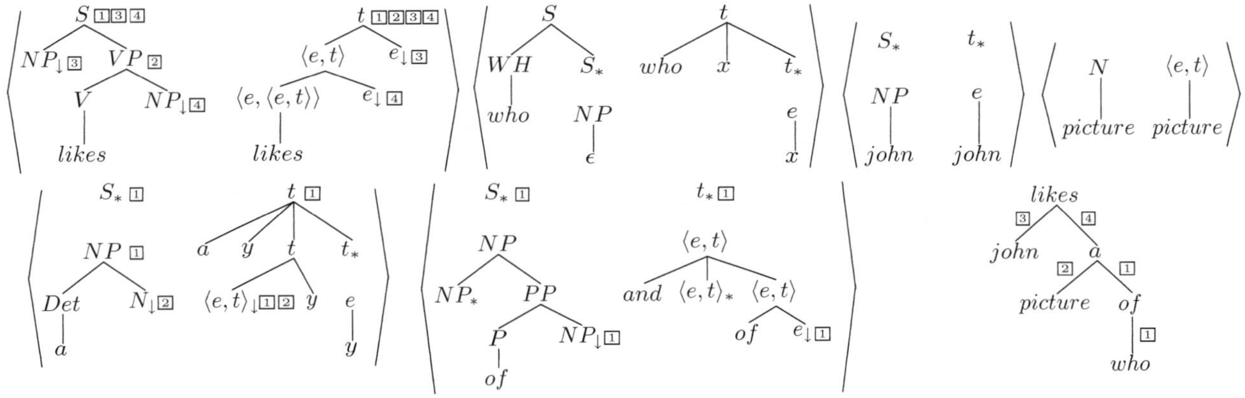

Figure 7: The elementary tree pairs and derivation tree for the sentence "Who does John like a picture of?".

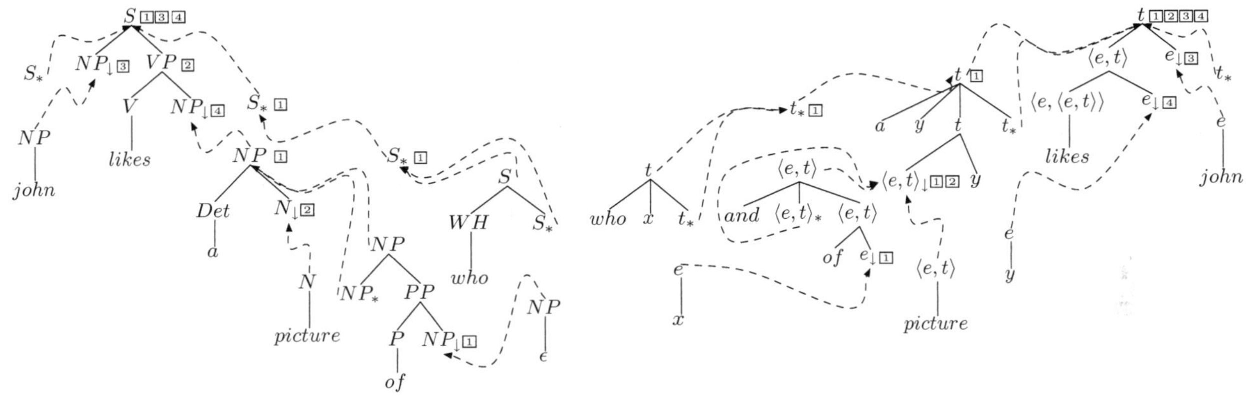

Figure 8: The derived syntax and semantics for Sentence 6.

6 Topicalization

The insight that allows us to model in-place wh-words extends to an elegant analysis of topicalization as well. The vestigial S_* tree that we added to the tree set for the syntax of every noun phrase need not always be contentless. Just as we moved the wh-word *who* from the top tree in its set to the bottom tree to model in-situ wh-words, we can move the lexical content of noun phrases to the top tree in their sets to model topicalization. For instance, the alternative tree pair for *Mary* shown in Figure 9 provides for an analysis of the sentence

(7) Mary, John likes.
likes(mary,john)

The analysis interacts properly with that for preposition stranding, so that the sentence

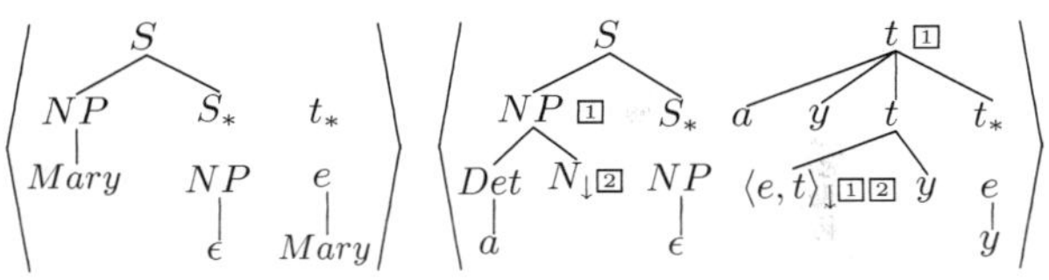

Figure 9: Alternative tree pairs for *Mary* and *a* that model topicalization.

(8) A picture of Mary, John likes.
a(x, and(picture(x), of(mary,x)), likes(x,john))

follows from the tree pair for *a* in the same figure.

7 Conclusion

In this paper we have proposed a uniform change to the structure of noun phrases in the STAG syntactico-semantic grammar. The formal tools we avail ourselves of comprise synchronous TAG with set-local multicomponent adjunction and multiple adjunction. Nothing more is required.

All noun phrases now have a uniform multi-component structure in both the syntax and the semantics. In the semantics the top part corresponds to the scope-giving piece provided by the noun phrase and the bottom part to the bound variable or simple noun-phrase meaning. In the syntax, the top part corresponds to the lexical material that should appear moved to the edge of the sentence or clause; the bottom part corresponds to the lexical material that will fill an argument position of some head. By moving lexical material among the pieces of the multi-component set in the syntax, we can simply model phenomena like in-place wh-words and topicalization.

Making the top parts of wh-word tree sets into auxiliary trees allows them to adjoin not just to the main verb but also to heads of modifying clauses, such as prepositional phrases. This allows us to handle more complex sentences like Sentence 6 without violating either the CETM or going beyond simple compositional semantics. In order to allow the scope-giving part of the wh-word to percolate up to the root of the semantics of the main verb, each tree set that it adjoins into on its way must also have a scope part in the semantics to which it can adjoin. Scope carriers, such as prepositions, are therefore also multi-component in the semantics with a top node to which scope-givers can adjoin. One nice property of this analysis is that it predicts the observed facts about disallowed scope orderings in sentences that have three quantifiers, one of which is in a modifying clause. The scope part of the quantifier of the modified clause and the scope part of the quantifier of the modifying clause form an indivisible set as the derivation proceeds so that when they adjoin multiply with the scope part of the unmodified clause, that quantifier cannot intervene between them.

Our synchronous grammar treatment of the syntax-semantic relation with TAG is at least as simple and arguably more accurate than previous TAG proposals, offering treatments of such phenomena as in-situ wh-words, stranded prepositions, and topicalization.

References

Chung-Hye Han. 2006a. Pied-piping in relative clauses: Syntax and compositional semantics based on synchronous tree adjoining grammar. In *Proceedings of the 8th International Workshop on Tree Adjoining Grammars and Related Formalisms (TAG+ 8)*, pages 41–48, Sydney, Australia.

Chung-Hye Han. 2006b. A tree adjoining grammar analysis of the syntax and semantics of it-clefts. In *Proceedings of the 8th International Workshop on Tree Adjoining Grammars and Related Formalisms (TAG+ 8)*, pages 33–40, Sydney, Australia.

Aravind K. Joshi and Yves Schabes. 1997. Tree-adjoining grammars. In G. Rozenberg and A. Salomaa, editors, *Handbook of Formal Languages*, pages 69–124. Springer.

Laura Kallmeyer and Maribel Romero. 2004. LTAG semantics with semantic unification. In *Proceedings of TAG+7*, pages 155–162, Vancouver, May.

Laura Kallmeyer and Tatjana Scheffler. 2004. LTAG analysis for pied-piping and stranding of wh-phrases. In *Proceedings of TAG+7*, pages 32–39, Vancouver, May.

Anthony Kroch. 1989. Asymmetries in long distance extraction in a tree adjoining grammar. In Mark Baltin and Anthony Kroch, editors, *Alternative Conceptions of Phrase Structure*. University of Chicago Press.

Rebecca Nesson and Stuart M. Shieber. 2006. Simpler TAG semantics through synchronization. In *Proceedings of the 11th Conference on Formal Grammar*, Malaga, Spain, 29–30 July.

Yves Schabes and Stuart M. Shieber. 1993. An alternative conception of tree-adjoining derivation. *Computational Linguistics*, 20(1):91–124.

Stuart M. Shieber and Yves Schabes. 1990. Synchronous tree-adjoining grammars. In *Proceedings of the 13th International Conference on Computational Linguistics*, volume 3, pages 253–258, Helsinki.

Stuart M. Shieber. 1994. Restricting the weak-generative capacity of synchronous tree-adjoining grammars. *Computational Intelligence*, 10(4):371–385, November.

Sean Williford. 1993. Application of synchronous tree-adjoining grammar to quantifier scoping phenomena in English. Undergraduate Thesis, Harvard College.

Inversion Transduction Grammar for Joint Phrasal Translation Modeling

Colin Cherry
Department of Computing Science
University of Alberta
Edmonton, AB, Canada, T6G 2E8
colinc@cs.ualberta.ca

Dekang Lin
Google Inc.
1600 Amphitheatre Parkway
Mountain View, CA, USA, 9403
lindek@google.com

Abstract

We present a phrasal inversion transduction grammar as an alternative to joint phrasal translation models. This syntactic model is similar to its flat-string phrasal predecessors, but admits polynomial-time algorithms for Viterbi alignment and EM training. We demonstrate that the consistency constraints that allow flat phrasal models to scale also help ITG algorithms, producing an 80-times faster inside-outside algorithm. We also show that the phrasal translation tables produced by the ITG are superior to those of the flat joint phrasal model, producing up to a 2.5 point improvement in BLEU score. Finally, we explore, for the first time, the utility of a joint phrasal translation model as a word alignment method.

1 Introduction

Statistical machine translation benefits greatly from considering more than one word at a time. One can put forward any number of non-compositional translations to support this point, such as the colloquial Canadian French-English pair, (*Wo les moteurs*, *Hold your horses*), where no clear word-to-word connection can be drawn. Nearly all current decoding methods have shifted to phrasal representations, gaining the ability to handle non-compositional translations, but also allowing the decoder to memorize phenomena such as monolingual agreement and short-range movement, taking pressure off of language and distortion models.

Despite the success of phrasal decoders, knowledge acquisition for translation generally begins with a word-level analysis of the training text, taking the form of a word alignment. Attempts to apply the same statistical analysis used at the word level in a phrasal setting have met with limited success, held back by the sheer size of phrasal alignment space. Hybrid methods that combine well-founded statistical analysis with high-confidence word-level alignments have made some headway (Birch et al., 2006), but suffer from the daunting task of heuristically exploring a still very large alignment space. In the meantime, synchronous parsing methods efficiently process the same bitext phrases while building their bilingual constituents, but continue to be employed primarily for word-to-word analysis (Wu, 1997). In this paper we unify the probability models for phrasal translation with the algorithms for synchronous parsing, harnessing the benefits of both to create a statistically and algorithmically well-founded method for phrasal analysis of bitext.

Section 2 begins by outlining the phrase extraction system we intend to replace and the two methods we combine to do so: the joint phrasal translation model (JPTM) and inversion transduction grammar (ITG). Section 3 describes our proposed solution, a phrasal ITG. Section 4 describes how to apply our phrasal ITG, both as a translation model and as a phrasal word-aligner. Section 5 tests our system in both these capacities, while Section 6 concludes.

2 Background

2.1 Phrase Table Extraction

Phrasal decoders require a phrase table (Koehn et al., 2003), which contains bilingual phrase pairs and

Proceedings of SSST, NAACL-HLT 2007 / AMTA Workshop on Syntax and Structure in Statistical Translation, pages 17–24,
Rochester, New York, April 2007. ©2007 Association for Computational Linguistics

scores indicating their utility. The **surface heuristic** is the most popular method for phrase-table construction. It extracts all consistent phrase pairs from word-aligned bitext (Koehn et al., 2003). The word alignment provides bilingual links, indicating translation relationships between words. **Consistency** is defined so that alignment links are never broken by phrase boundaries. For each token w in a consistent phrase pair $\bar{p}$, all tokens linked to w by the alignment must also be included in $\bar{p}$. Each consistent phrase pair is counted as occurring once per sentence pair. The scores for the extracted phrase pairs are provided by normalizing these flat counts according to common English or Foreign components, producing the conditional distributions $p(\bar{f}|\bar{e})$ and $p(\bar{e}|\bar{f})$.

The surface heuristic can define consistency according to any word alignment; but most often, the alignment is provided by GIZA++ (Och and Ney, 2003). This alignment system is powered by the IBM translation models (Brown et al., 1993), in which one sentence generates the other. These models produce only one-to-many alignments: each generated token can participate in at most one link. Many-to-many alignments can be created by combining two GIZA++ alignments, one where English generates Foreign and another with those roles reversed (Och and Ney, 2003). Combination approaches begin with the intersection of the two alignments, and add links from the union heuristically. The grow-diag-final (GDF) combination heuristic (Koehn et al., 2003) adds links so that each new link connects a previously unlinked token.

2.2 Joint phrasal translation model

The IBM models that power GIZA++ are trained with Expectation Maximization (Dempster et al., 1977), or EM, on sentence-aligned bitext. A translation model assigns probabilities to alignments; these alignment distributions are used to count translation events, which are then used to estimate new parameters for the translation model. Sampling is employed when the alignment distributions cannot be calculated efficiently. This statistically-motivated process is much more appealing than the flat counting described in Section 2.1, but it does not directly include phrases.

The joint phrasal translation model (Marcu and Wong, 2002), or JPTM, applies the same statistical techniques from the IBM models in a phrasal setting. The JPTM is designed according to a generative process where both languages are generated simultaneously. First, a bag of concepts, or cepts, C is generated. Each $c_i \in C$ corresponds to a bilingual phrase pair, $c_i = (\bar{e}_i, \bar{f}_i)$. These contiguous phrases are permuted in each language to create two sequences of phrases. Initially, Marcu and Wong assume that the number of cepts, as well as the phrase orderings, are drawn from uniform distributions. That leaves a joint translation distribution $p(\bar{e}_i, \bar{f}_i)$ to determine which phrase pairs are selected. Given a lexicon of possible cepts and a predicate $L(E, F, C)$ that determines if a bag of cepts C can be bilingually permuted to create the sentence pair (E, F), the probability of a sentence pair is:

$$p(E, F) \propto \sum_{\{C|L(E,F,C)\}} \left[\prod_{c_i \in C} p(\bar{e}_i, \bar{f}_i) \right] \quad (1)$$

If left unconstrained, (1) will consider every phrasal segmentation of E and F, and every alignment between those phrases. Later, a distortion model based on absolute token positions is added to (1).

The JPTM faces several problems when scaling up to large training sets:

1. The alignment space enumerated by the sum in (1) is huge, far larger than the one-to-many space explored by GIZA++.
2. The translation distribution $p(\bar{e}, \bar{f})$ will cover all co-occurring phrases observed in the bitext. This is far too large to fit in main memory, and can be unwieldy for storage on disk.
3. Given a non-uniform $p(\bar{e}, \bar{f})$, there is no efficient algorithm to compute the expectation of phrase pair counts required for EM, or to find the most likely phrasal alignment.

Marcu and Wong (2002) address point 2 with a **lexicon constraint**; monolingual phrases that are above a length threshold or below a frequency threshold are excluded from the lexicon. Point 3 is handled by hill-climbing to a likely phrasal alignment and sampling around it. However, point 1 remains unaddressed, which prevents the model from scaling to large data sets.

Birch et al. (2006) handle point 1 directly by reducing the size of the alignment space. This is accomplished by constraining the JPTM to only use phrase pairs that are consistent with a high-confidence word alignment, which is provided by GIZA++ intersection. We refer to this constrained JPTM as a C-JPTM. This strikes an interesting middle ground between the surface heuristic described in Section 2.1 and the JPTM. Like the surface heuristic, a word alignment is used to limit the phrase pairs considered, but the C-JPTM reasons about distributions over phrasal alignments, instead of taking flat counts. The consistency constraint allows them to scale their C-JPTM up to 700,000 sentence pairs. With this constraint in place, the use of hill-climbing and sampling during EM training becomes one of the largest remaining weaknesses of the C-JPTM.

2.3 Inversion Transduction Grammar

Like the JPTM, stochastic synchronous grammars provide a generative process to produce a sentence and its translation simultaneously. Inversion transduction grammar (Wu, 1997), or ITG, is a well-studied synchronous grammar formalism. Terminal productions of the form $A \rightarrow e/f$ produce a token in each stream, or a token in one stream with the null symbol $\emptyset$ in the other. To allow for movement during translation, non-terminal productions can be either straight or inverted. Straight productions, with their non-terminals inside square brackets [...], produce their symbols in the given order in both streams. Inverted productions, indicated by angled brackets $\langle \ldots \rangle$, are output in reverse order in the Foreign stream only.

The work described here uses the binary bracketing ITG, which has a single non-terminal:

$$A \rightarrow [AA] \mid \langle AA \rangle \mid e/f \qquad (2)$$

This grammar admits an efficient bitext parsing algorithm, and holds no language-specific biases.

(2) cannot represent all possible permutations of concepts that may occur during translation, because some permutations will require discontinuous constituents (Melamed, 2003). This **ITG constraint** is characterized by the two forbidden structures shown in Figure 1 (Wu, 1997). Empirical studies suggest that only a small percentage of human translations violate these constraints (Cherry and Lin, 2006).

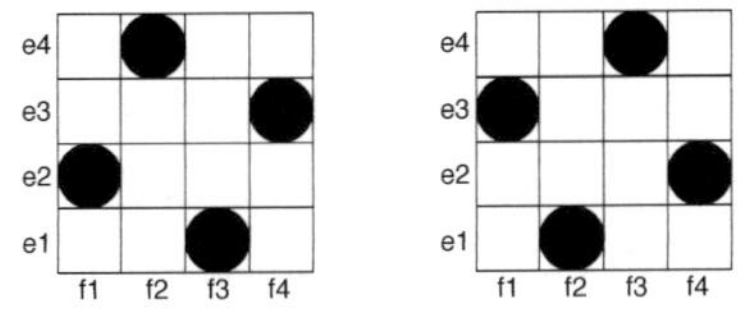

Figure 1: The two ITG forbidden structures.

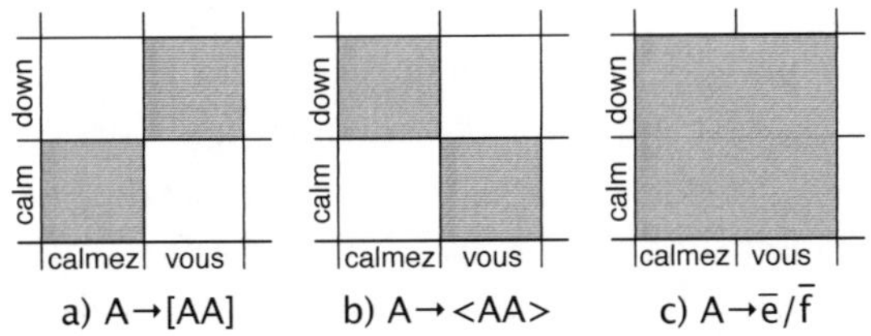

Figure 2: Three ways in which a phrasal ITG can analyze a multi-word span or phrase.

Stochastic ITGs are parameterized like their PCFG counterparts (Wu, 1997); productions $A \rightarrow \mathcal{X}$ are assigned probability $\Pr(\mathcal{X}|A)$. These parameters can be learned from sentence-aligned bitext using the EM algorithm. The expectation task of counting productions weighted by their probability is handled with dynamic programming, using the inside-outside algorithm extended to bitext (Zhang and Gildea, 2004).

3 ITG as a Phrasal Translation Model

This paper introduces a phrasal ITG; in doing so, we combine ITG with the JPTM. ITG parsing algorithms consider every possible two-dimensional span of bitext, each corresponding to a bilingual phrase pair. Each multi-token span is analyzed in terms of how it could be built from smaller spans using a straight or inverted production, as is illustrated in Figures 2 (a) and (b). To extend ITG to a phrasal setting, we add a third option for span analysis: that the span under consideration might have been drawn directly from the lexicon. This option can be added to our grammar by altering the definition of a terminal production to include phrases: $A \rightarrow \bar{e}/\bar{f}$. This third option is shown in Figure 2 (c). The model implied by this extended grammar is trained using inside-outside and EM.

Our approach differs from previous attempts to use ITGs for phrasal bitext analysis. Wu (1997) used a binary bracketing ITG to segment a sentence while simultaneously word-aligning it to its translation, but the model was trained heuristically with a fixed segmentation. Vilar and Vidal (2005) used ITG-like dynamic programming to drive both training and alignment for their recursive translation model, but they employed a conditional model that did not maintain a phrasal lexicon. Instead, they scored phrase pairs using IBM Model 1.

Our phrasal ITG is quite similar to the JPTM. Both models are trained with EM, and both employ generative stories that create a sentence and its translation simultaneously. The similarities become more apparent when we consider the canonical-form binary-bracketing ITG (Wu, 1997) shown here:

$$\begin{array}{rl} S \rightarrow & A \mid B \mid C \\ A \rightarrow & [AB] \mid [BB] \mid [CB] \mid \\ & [AC] \mid [BC] \mid [CC] \\ B \rightarrow & \langle AA \rangle \mid \langle BA \rangle \mid \langle CA \rangle \mid \\ & \langle AC \rangle \mid \langle BC \rangle \mid \langle CC \rangle \\ C \rightarrow & \bar{e}/\bar{f} \end{array} \tag{3}$$

(3) is employed in place of (2) to reduce redundant alignments and clean up EM expectations.[1] More importantly for our purposes, it introduces a preterminal C, which generates all phrase pairs or cepts. When (3) is parameterized as a stochastic ITG, the conditional distribution $p(\bar{e}/\bar{f}|C)$ is equivalent to the JPTM's $p(\bar{e}, \bar{f})$; both are joint distributions over all possible phrase pairs. The distributions conditioned on the remaining three non-terminals assign probability to concept movement by tracking inversions. Like the JPTM's distortion model, these parameters grade each movement decision independently. With terminal productions producing cepts, and inversions measuring distortion, our phrasal ITG is essentially a variation on the JPTM with an alternate distortion model.

Our phrasal ITG has two main advantages over the JPTM. Most significantly, we gain polynomial-time algorithms for both Viterbi alignment and EM expectation, through the use of ITG parsing and inside-outside algorithms. These phrasal ITG algorithms are no more expensive asymptotically than their word-to-word counterparts, since each potential phrase needs to be analyzed anyway during constituent construction. We hypothesize that using these methods in place of heuristic search and sampling will improve the phrasal translation model learned by EM. Also, we can easily incorporate links to $\emptyset$ by including the symbol among our terminals. To minimize redundancy, we allow only single tokens, not phrases, to align to $\emptyset$. The JPTM does not allow links to $\emptyset$.

The phrasal ITG also introduces two new complications. ITG Viterbi and inside-outside algorithms have polynomial complexity, but that polynomial is $O(n^6)$, where n is the length of the longer sentence in the pair. This is too slow to train on large data sets without massive parallelization. Also, ITG algorithms explore their alignment space perfectly, but that space has been reduced by the ITG constraint described in Section 2.3. We will address each of these issues in the following two subsections.

3.1 Pruning Spans

First, we address the problem of scaling ITG to large data. ITG dynamic programming algorithms work by analyzing each bitext span only once, storing its value in a table for future use. There are $O(n^4)$ of these spans, and each analysis takes $O(n^2)$ time. An effective approach to speeding up ITG algorithms is to eliminate unlikely spans as a preprocessing step, assigning them 0 probability and saving the time spent processing them. Past approaches have pruned spans using IBM Model 1 probability estimates (Zhang and Gildea, 2005) or using agreement with an existing parse tree (Cherry and Lin, 2006). The former is referred to as tic-tac-toe pruning because it uses both inside and outside estimates.

We propose a new ITG pruning method that leverages high-confidence links by pruning all spans that are inconsistent with a provided alignment. This is similar to the constraint used in the C-JPTM, but we do not just eliminate those spans as potential phrase-to-phrase links: we never consider any ITG parse that builds a non-terminal over a pruned span.[2] This **fixed-link pruning** will speed up both Viterbi alignment and EM training by reducing the number of analyzed spans, and so long as we trust

[1]If the null symbol $\emptyset$ is included among the terminals, then redundant parses will still occur, but far less frequently.

[2]Birch et al. (2006) re-introduce inconsistent phrase-pairs in cases where the sentence pair could not be aligned otherwise. We allow links to $\emptyset$ to handle these situations, completely eliminating the pruned spans from our alignment space.

our high-confidence links, it will do so harmlessly. We demonstrate the effectiveness of this pruning method experimentally in Section 5.1.

3.2 Handling the ITG Constraint

Our remaining concern is the ITG constraint. There are some alignments that we just cannot build, and sentence pairs requiring those alignments will occur. These could potentially pollute our training data; if the system is unable to build the right alignment, the counts it will collect from that pair must be wrong. Furthermore, if our high-confidence links are not ITG-compatible, our fixed-link pruning will prevent the aligner from forming any alignments at all.

However, these two potential problems cancel each other out. Sentence pairs containing non-ITG translations will tend to have high-confidence links that are also not ITG-compatible. Our EM learner will simply skip these sentence pairs during training, avoiding pollution of our training data. We can use a linear-time algorithm (Zhang et al., 2006) to detect non-ITG movement in our high-confidence links, and remove the offending sentence pairs from our training corpus. This results in only a minor reduction in training data; in our French-English training set, we lose less than 1%. In the experiments described in Section 5, all systems that do not use ITG will take advantage of the complete training set.

4 Applying the model

Any phrasal translation model can be used for two tasks: translation modeling and phrasal word alignment. Previous work on JPTM has focused on only the first task. We are interested in phrasal alignment because it may be better suited to heuristic phrase-extraction than word-based models. This section describes how to use our phrasal ITG first as a translation model, and then as a phrasal aligner.

4.1 Translation Modeling

We can test our model's utility for translation by transforming its parameters into a phrase table for the phrasal decoder Pharaoh (Koehn et al., 2003). Any joint model can produce the necessary conditional probabilities by conditionalizing the joint table in both directions. We use our $p(\bar{e}/\bar{f}|C)$ distribution from our stochastic grammar to produce $p(\bar{e}|\bar{f})$ and $p(\bar{f}|\bar{e})$ values for its phrasal lexicon.

Pharaoh also includes lexical weighting parameters that are derived from the alignments used to induce its phrase pairs (Koehn et al., 2003). Using the phrasal ITG as a direct translation model, we do not produce alignments for individual sentence pairs. Instead, we provide a lexical preference with an IBM Model 1 feature p_{M1} that penalizes unmatched words (Vogel et al., 2003). We include both $p_{\mathrm{M1}}(\bar{e}|\bar{f})$ and $p_{\mathrm{M1}}(\bar{f}|\bar{e})$.

4.2 Phrasal Word Alignment

We can produce a translation model using inside-outside, without ever creating a Viterbi parse. However, we can also examine the maximum likelihood phrasal alignments predicted by the trained model.

Despite its strengths derived from using phrases throughout training, the alignments predicted by our phrasal ITG are usually unsatisfying. For example, the fragment pair (*order of business*, *ordre des travaux*) is aligned as a phrase pair by our system, linking every English word to every French word. This is frustrating, since there is a clear compositional relationship between the fragment's component words. This happens because the system seeks only to maximize the likelihood of its training corpus, and phrases are far more efficient than word-to-word connections. When aligning text, annotators are told to resort to many-to-many links only when no clear compositional relationship exists (Melamed, 1998). If we could tell our phrasal aligner the same thing, we could greatly improve the intuitive appeal of our alignments. Again, we can leverage high-confidence links for help.

In the high-confidence alignments provided by GIZA++ intersection, each token participates in at most one link. Links only appear when two word-based IBM translation models can agree. Therefore, they occur at points of high compositionality: the two words clearly account for one another. We adopt an alignment-driven definition of compositionality: any phrase pair containing two or more high-confidence links is compositional, and can be separated into at least two non-compositional phrases. By removing any phrase pairs that are compositional by this definition from our terminal productions, we can ensure that our aligner never creates such phrases during training or alignment. Doing so produces far more intuitive alignments. Aligned with a model trained using this **non-compositional constraint** (NCC), our example now forms three word-to-word connections, rather than a single phrasal one. The phrases produced with this constraint are very small, and include only non-compositional context. Therefore, we use the constraint only to train models intended for Viterbi alignment, and not when generating phrase tables directly as in Section 4.1.

5 Experiments and Results

In this section, we first verify the effectiveness of fixed-link pruning, and then test our phrasal ITG, both as an aligner and as a translation model. We train all translation models with a French-English Europarl corpus obtained by applying a 25 token sentence-length limit to the training set provided for the HLT-NAACL SMT Workshop Shared Task (Koehn and Monz, 2006). The resulting corpus has 393,132 sentence pairs. 3,376 of these are omitted for ITG methods because their high-confidence alignments have ITG-incompatible constructions. Like our predecessors (Marcu and Wong, 2002; Birch et al., 2006), we apply a lexicon constraint: no monolingual phrase can be used by any phrasal model unless it occurs at least five times. High-confidence alignments are provided by intersecting GIZA++ alignments trained in each direction with 5 iterations each of Model 1, HMM, and Model 4. All GIZA++ alignments are trained with no sentence-length limit, using the full 688K corpus.

5.1 Pruning Speed Experiments

To measure the speed-up provided by fixed-link pruning, we timed our phrasal inside-outside algorithm on the first 100 sentence pairs in our training set, with and without pruning. The results are shown in Table 1. Tic-tac-toe pruning is included for comparison. With fixed-link pruning, on average 95% of the possible spans are pruned, reducing running time by two orders of magnitude. This improvement makes ITG training feasible, even with large bitexts.

5.2 Alignment Experiments

The goal of this experiment is to compare the Viterbi alignments from the phrasal ITG to gold standard human alignments. We do this to validate our non-compositional constraint and to select good alignments for use with the surface heuristic.

Table 1: Inside-outside run-time comparison.

Method	Seconds	Avg. Spans Pruned
No Prune	415	-
Tic-tac-toe	37	68%
Fixed link	5	95%

Table 2: Alignment Comparison.

Method	Prec	Rec	F-measure
GIZA++ Intersect	**96.7**	53.0	68.5
GIZA++ Union	82.5	69.0	75.1
GIZA++ GDF	84.0	68.2	75.2
Phrasal ITG	50.7	**80.3**	62.2
Phrasal ITG + NCC	75.4	78.0	**76.7**

Following the lead of (Fraser and Marcu, 2006), we hand-aligned the first 100 sentence pairs of our training set according to the Blinker annotation guidelines (Melamed, 1998). We did not differentiate between sure and possible links. We report precision, recall and balanced F-measure (Och and Ney, 2003). For comparison purposes, we include the results of three types of GIZA++ combination, including the grow-diag-final heuristic (GDF). We tested our phrasal ITG with fixed link pruning, and then added the non-compositional constraint (NCC). During development we determined that performance levels off for both of the ITG models after 3 EM iterations. The results are shown in Table 2.

The first thing to note is that GIZA++ Intersection is indeed very high precision. Our confidence in it as a constraint is not misplaced. We also see that both phrasal models have significantly higher recall than any of the GIZA++ alignments, even higher than the permissive GIZA++ union. One factor contributing to this is the phrasal model's use of cepts: it completely interconnects any phrase pair, while GIZA++ union and GDF may not. Its global view of phrases also helps in this regard: evidence for a phrase can be built up over multiple sentences. Finally, we note that in terms of alignment quality, the non-compositional constraint is an unqualified success for the phrasal ITG. It produces a 25 point improvement in precision, at the cost of 2 points of recall. This produces the highest balanced F-measure observed on our test set, but the utility of its alignments will depend largely on one's desired precision-recall trade-off.

5.3 Translation Experiments

In this section, we compare a number of different methods for phrase table generation in a French to English translation task. We are interested in answering three questions:

1. Does the phrasal ITG improve on the C-JPTM?
2. Can phrasal translation models outperform the surface heuristic?
3. Do Viterbi phrasal alignments provide better input for the surface heuristic?

With this in mind, we test five phrase tables. Two are conditionalized phrasal models, each EM trained until performance degrades:

- C-JPTM[3] as described in (Birch et al., 2006)
- Phrasal ITG as described in Section 4.1

Three provide alignments for the surface heuristic:

- GIZA++ with grow-diag-final (GDF)
- Viterbi Phrasal ITG with and without the non-compositional constraint

We use the Pharaoh decoder (Koehn et al., 2003) with the SMT Shared Task baseline system (Koehn and Monz, 2006). Weights for the log-linear model are set using the 500-sentence tuning set provided for the shared task with minimum error rate training (Och, 2003) as implemented by Venugopal and Vogel (2005). Results on the provided 2000-sentence development set are reported using the BLEU metric (Papineni et al., 2002). For all methods, we report performance with and without IBM Model 1 features (M1), along with the size of the resulting tables in millions of phrase pairs. The results of all experiments are shown in Table 3.

We see that the Phrasal ITG surpasses the C-JPTM by more than 2.5 BLEU points. A large component of this improvement is due to the ITG's use of inside-outside for expectation calculation, though there are other differences between the two systems.[4] This improvement over search and sampling is demonstrated by the ITG's larger table size; by exploring more thoroughly, it is extracting more phrase pairs from the same amount of data. Both systems improve drastically with the addition of IBM Model 1 features for lexical preference. These features also narrow the gap between the two systems. To help calibrate the contribution of these features, we parameterized the ITG's phrase table using only Model 1 features, which scores 27.17.

Table 3: Translation Comparison.

Method	BLEU	+M1	Size
Conditionalized Phrasal Model			
C-JPTM	26.27	28.98	1.3M
Phrasal ITG	28.85	30.24	2.2M
Alignment with Surface Heuristic			
GIZA++ GDF	30.46	30.61	9.8M
Phrasal ITG	30.31	30.39	5.8M
Phrasal ITG + NCC	**30.66**	**30.80**	9.0M

Although ITG+M1 comes close, neither phrasal model matches the performance of the surface heuristic. Whatever the surface heuristic lacks in sophistication, it makes up for in sheer coverage, as demonstrated by its huge table sizes. Even the Phrasal ITG Viterbi alignments, which over-commit wildly and have horrible precision, score slightly higher than the best phrasal model. The surface heuristic benefits from capturing as much context as possible, while still covering smaller translation events with its flat counts. It is not held back by any lexicon constraints. When GIZA++ GDF+M1 is forced to conform to a lexicon constraint by dropping any phrase with a frequency lower than 5 from its table, it scores only 29.26, for a reduction of 1.35 BLEU points.

Phrases extracted from our non-compositional Viterbi alignments receive the highest BLEU score, but they are not significantly better than GIZA++ GDF. The two methods also produce similarly-sized tables, despite the ITG's higher recall.

[3]Supplied by personal communication. Run with default parameters, but with maximum phrase length increased to 5.

[4]Unlike our system, the Birch implementation does table smoothing and internal lexical weighting, both of which should help improve their results. The systems also differ in distortion modeling and ∅ handling, as described in Section 3.

6 Conclusion

We have presented a phrasal ITG as an alternative to the joint phrasal translation model. This syntactic solution to phrase modeling admits polynomial-time training and alignment algorithms. We demonstrate that the same consistency constraints that allow joint phrasal models to scale also dramatically speed up ITGs, producing an 80-times faster inside-outside algorithm. We show that when used to learn phrase tables for the Pharaoh decoder, the phrasal ITG is superior to the constrained joint phrasal model, producing tables that result in a 2.5 point improvement in BLEU when used alone, and a 1 point improvement when used with IBM Model 1 features. This suggests that ITG's perfect expectation counting does matter; other phrasal models could benefit from either adopting the ITG formalism, or improving their sampling heuristics.

We have explored, for the first time, the utility of a joint phrasal model as a word alignment method. We present a non-compositional constraint that turns the phrasal ITG into a high-recall phrasal aligner with an F-measure that is comparable to GIZA++.

With search and sampling no longer a concern, the remaining weaknesses of the system seem to lie with the model itself. Phrases are just too efficient probabilistically: were we to remove all lexicon constraints, EM would always align entire sentences to entire sentences. This pressure to always build the longest phrase possible may be overwhelming otherwise strong correlations in our training data. A promising next step would be to develop a prior over lexicon size or phrase size, allowing EM to introduce large phrases at a penalty, and removing the need for artificial constraints on the lexicon.

Acknowledgments Special thanks to Alexandra Birch for the use of her code, and to our reviewers for their comments. The first author is funded by Alberta Ingenuity and iCORE studentships.

References

A. Birch, C. Callison-Burch, M. Osborne, and P. Koehn. 2006. Constraining the phrase-based, joint probability statistical translation model. In *HLT-NAACL Workshop on Statistical Machine Translation*, pages 154–157.

P. F. Brown, S. A. Della Pietra, V. J. Della Pietra, and R. L. Mercer. 1993. The mathematics of statistical machine translation: Parameter estimation. *Computational Linguistics*, 19(2):263–312.

C. Cherry and D. Lin. 2006. A comparison of syntactically motivated word alignment spaces. In *EACL*, pages 145–152.

A. P. Dempster, N. M. Laird, and D. B. Rubin. 1977. Maximum likelihood from incomplete data via the EM algorithm. *Journal of the Royal Statistical Society*, 39(1):1–38.

A. Fraser and D. Marcu. 2006. Semi-supervised training for statistical word alignment. In *ACL*, pages 769–776.

P. Koehn and C. Monz. 2006. Manual and automatic evaluation of machine translation. In *HLT-NACCL Workshop on Statistical Machine Translation*, pages 102–121.

P. Koehn, F. J. Och, and D. Marcu. 2003. Statistical phrase-based translation. In *HLT-NAACL*, pages 127–133.

D. Marcu and W. Wong. 2002. A phrase-based, joint probability model for statistic machine translation. In *EMNLP*, pages 133–139.

I. D. Melamed. 1998. Manual annotation of translational equivalence: The blinker project. Technical Report 98-07, Institute for Research in Cognitive Science.

I. D. Melamed. 2003. Multitext grammars and synchronous parsers. In *HLT-NAACL*, pages 158–165.

F. J. Och and H. Ney. 2003. A systematic comparison of various statistical alignment models. *Computational Linguistics*, 29(1):19–52.

F. J. Och. 2003. Minimum error rate training for statistical machine translation. In *ACL*, pages 160–167.

K. Papineni, S. Roukos, T. Ward, and W. J. Zhu. 2002. BLEU: a method for automatic evaluation of machine translation. In *ACL*, pages 311–318.

A. Venugopal and S. Vogel. 2005. Considerations in maximum mutual information and minimum classification error training for statistical machine translation. In *EAMT*.

J. M. Vilar and E. Vidal. 2005. A recursive statistical translation model. In *Proceedings of the ACL Workshop on Building and Using Parallel Texts*, pages 199–207.

S. Vogel, Y. Zhang, F. Huang, A. Tribble, A. Venugopal, B. Zhang, and A. Waibel. 2003. The CMU statistical machine translation system. In *MT Summmit*.

D. Wu. 1997. Stochastic inversion transduction grammars and bilingual parsing of parallel corpora. *Computational Linguistics*, 23(3):377–403.

H. Zhang and D. Gildea. 2004. Syntax-based alignment: Supervised or unsupervised? In *COLING*, pages 418–424.

H. Zhang and D. Gildea. 2005. Stochastic lexicalized inversion transduction grammar for alignment. In *ACL*, pages 475–482.

H. Zhang, L. Huang, D. Gildea, and K. Knight. 2006. Synchronous binarization for machine translation. In *HLT-NAACL*, pages 256–263.

Factorization of Synchronous Context-Free Grammars in Linear Time

Hao Zhang and **Daniel Gildea**
Computer Science Department
University of Rochester
Rochester, NY 14627

Abstract

Factoring a Synchronous Context-Free Grammar into an equivalent grammar with a smaller number of nonterminals in each rule enables synchronous parsing algorithms of lower complexity. The problem can be formalized as searching for the tree-decomposition of a given permutation with the minimal branching factor. In this paper, by modifying the algorithm of Uno and Yagiura (2000) for the closely related problem of finding all common intervals of two permutations, we achieve a linear time algorithm for the permutation factorization problem. We also use the algorithm to analyze the maximum SCFG rule length needed to cover hand-aligned data from various language pairs.

1 Introduction

A number of recent syntax-based approaches to statistical machine translation make use of Synchronous Context Free Grammar (SCFG) as the underlying model of translational equivalence. Wu (1997)'s Inversion Transduction Grammar, as well as tree-transformation models of translation such as Yamada and Knight (2001), Galley et al. (2004), and Chiang (2005) all fall into this category.

A crucial question for efficient computation in approaches based on SCFG is the length of the grammar rules. Grammars with longer rules can represent a larger set of reorderings between languages (Aho and Ullman, 1972), but also require greater computational complexity for word alignment algorithms based on synchronous parsing (Satta and Peserico, 2005). Grammar rules extracted from large parallel corpora by systems such as Galley et al. (2004) can be quite large, and Wellington et al. (2006) argue that complex rules are necessary by analyzing the coverage of gold-standard word alignments from different language pairs by various grammars.

However, parsing complexity depends not only on rule length, but also on the specific permutations represented by the individual rules. It may be possible to factor an SCFG with maximum rule length n into a simpler grammar with a maximum of k nonterminals in any one rule, if not all $n!$ permutations appear in the rules. Zhang et al. (2006) discuss methods for binarizing SCFGs, ignoring the non-binarizable grammars; in Section 2 we discuss the generalized problem of factoring to k-ary grammars for any k and formalize the problem as permutation factorization in Section 3.

In Section 4, we describe an $O(k \cdot n)$ left-to-right shift-reduce algorithm for analyzing permutations that can be k-arized. Its time complexity becomes $O(n^2)$ when k is not specified beforehand and the minimal k is to be discovered. Instead of linearly shifting in one number at a time, Gildea et al. (2006) employ a balanced binary tree as the control structure, producing an algorithm similar in spirit to merge-sort with a reduced time complexity of $O(n \log n)$. However, both algorithms rely on reduction tests on emerging spans which involve redundancies with the spans that have already been tested.

Proceedings of SSST, NAACL-HLT 2007 / AMTA Workshop on Syntax and Structure in Statistical Translation, pages 25–32,
Rochester, New York, April 2007.

Uno and Yagiura (2000) describe a clever algorithm for the problem of finding all common intervals of two permutations in time $O(n+K)$, where K is the number of common intervals, which can itself be $\Omega(n^2)$. In Section 5, we adapt their approach to the problem of factoring SCFGs, and show that, given this problem definition, running time can be improved to $O(n)$, the optimum given the time needed to read the input permutation.

The methodology in Wellington et al. (2006) measures the complexity of word alignment using the number of gaps that are necessary for their synchronous parser which allows discontinuous spans to succeed in parsing. In Section 6, we provide a more direct measurement using the minimal branching factor yielded by the permutation factorization algorithm.

2 Synchronous CFG and Synchronous Parsing

We begin by describing the synchronous CFG formalism, which is more rigorously defined by Aho and Ullman (1972) and Satta and Peserico (2005).

We adopt the SCFG notation of Satta and Peserico (2005). Superscript *indices* in the right-hand side of grammar rules:

$$X \rightarrow X_1^{(1)} ... X_n^{(n)},\ X_{\pi(1)}^{(\pi(1))} ... X_{\pi(n)}^{(\pi(n))}$$

indicate that the nonterminals with the same index are linked across the two languages, and will eventually be rewritten by the same rule application. Each X_i is a variable which can take the value of any nonterminal in the grammar.

We say an SCFG is n-ary if and only if the maximum number of co-indexed nonterminals, i.e. the longest permutation contained in the set of rules, is of size n.

Given a synchronous CFG and a pair of input strings, we can apply a generalized CYK-style bottom up chart parser to build synchronous parse trees over the string pair. Wu (1997) demonstrates the case of binary SCFG parsing, where six string boundary variables, three for each language as in monolingual CFG parsing, interact with each other, yielding an $O(N^6)$ dynamic programming algorithm, where N is the string length, assuming the two paired strings are comparable in length. For an n-ary SCFG, the parsing complexity can be as high as $O(N^{n+4})$. The reason is even if we binarize on one side to maintain 3 indices, for many unfriendly permutations, at most $n+1$ boundary variables in the other language are necessary.

The fact that this bound is exponential in the rule length n suggests that it is advantageous to reduce the length of grammar rules as much as possible. This paper focuses on converting an SCFG to the equivalent grammar with smallest possible maximum rule size. The algorithm processes each rule in the input grammar independently, and determines whether the rule can be factored into smaller SCFG rules by analyzing the rule's permutation π.

As an example, given the input rule:

$$[X \rightarrow A^{(1)}B^{(2)}C^{(3)}D^{(4)}E^{(5)}F^{(6)}G^{(7)},\ X \rightarrow E^{(5)}G^{(7)}D^{(4)}F^{(6)}C^{(3)}A^{(1)}B^{(2)}] \quad (1)$$

we consider the associated permutation:

$$(5, 7, 4, 6, 3, 1, 2)$$

We determine that this permutation can be factored into the following **permutation tree**:

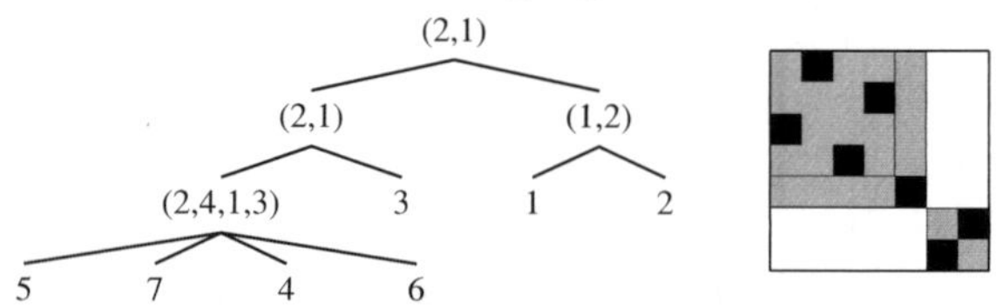

We define permutation trees formally in the next section, but note here that nodes in the tree correspond to subsets of nonterminals that form a single continuous span in both languages, as shown by the shaded regions in the permutation matrix above. This tree can be converted into a set of output rules that are generatively equivalent to the original rule:

$$[X \rightarrow X_1^{(1)}X_2^{(2)},\ X \rightarrow X_2^{(2)}X_1^{(1)}]$$
$$[X_1 \rightarrow A^{(1)}B^{(2)},\ X_1 \rightarrow A^{(1)}B^{(2)}]$$
$$[X_2 \rightarrow C^{(1)}X_3^{(2)},\ X_2 \rightarrow X_3^{(2)}C^{(1)}]$$
$$[X_3 \rightarrow D^{(1)}E^{(2)}F^{(3)}G^{(4)},\ X_3 \rightarrow E^{(2)}G^{(4)}D^{(1)}F^{(3)}]$$

where X_1, X_2 and X_3 are new nonterminals used to represent the intermediate states in which the synchronous nodes are combined. The factorized grammar is only larger than the original grammar by a constant factor.

3 Permutation Trees

We define the notion of permutation structure in this section. We define a **permuted sequence** as a permutation of n ($n \geq 1$) consecutive natural numbers.

A permuted sequence is said to be **k-ary parsable** if either of the following conditions holds:

1. The permuted sequence only has one number.
2. It has more than one number and can be segmented into k' ($k \geq k' \geq 2$) permuted sequences each of which is k-ary parsable, and the k' subsequences are arranged in an order identified by one of the $k'!$ permutations of k'.

This is a recursive definition, and we call the corresponding recursive structure over the entire sequence a **k-ary permutation tree**.

Our goal is to find out the k-ary permutation tree for a given permutation, where k is minimized.

4 Shift-reduce on Permutations

In this section, we present an $O(n \cdot k)$ algorithm which can be viewed as a need-to-be-optimized version of the linear time algorithm to be presented in the next section.

The algorithm is based on a shift-reduce parser, which maintains a stack for subsequences that have been discovered so far and loops over shift and reduce steps:

1. Shift the next number in the input permutation onto the stack.
2. Go down the stack from the top to the bottom. Whenever the top m subsequences satisfy the **partition property**, which says the total length of the m ($k \geq m \geq 2$) subsequences minus 1 is equal to the difference between the smallest number and the largest number contained in the m segments, make a reduction by gluing the m segments into one subsequence and restart reducing from the top of the new stack. Stop when no reduction is possible.
3. If there are remaining numbers in the input permutation, go to 1.

When we exit from the loop, if the height of the stack is 1, the input permutation of n has been reduced to a linear sequence of 1 to n, and parsing is successful. Otherwise, the input permutation of n cannot be parsed into a k-ary permutation tree.

Stack	Input	Operation
	5, 7, 4, 6, 3, 1, 2	shift
5	7, 4, 6, 3, 1, 2	shift
5, 7	4, 6, 3, 1, 2	shift
5, 7, 4	6, 3, 1, 2	shift
5, 7, 4, 6	3, 1, 2	reduce by (2,4,1,3)
[4...7]	3, 1, 2	shift
[4...7], 3	1, 2	reduce by (2,1)
[3...7]	1, 2	shift
[3...7], 1	2	shift
[3...7], 1, 2		reduce by (1,2)
[3...7], [1...2]		reduce by (2,1)
[1...7]		

Table 1: The execution trace of the shift-reduce parser on the input permutation $5, 7, 4, 6, 3, 1, 2$.

An example execution trace of the algorithm is shown in Table 1.

The partition property is a sufficient and necessary condition for the top m subsequences to be reducible. In order to check if the property holds, we need to compute the sum of the lengths of subsequences under consideration and the difference between the largest and smallest number in the covered region. We can incrementally compute both along with each step going down the stack. If m is bounded by k, we need $O(k)$ operations for each item shifted onto the stack. So, the algorithm runs in $O(n \cdot k)$.

We might also wish to compute the minimum k for which k-arization can be successful on an input permutation of n. We can simply keep doing reduction tests for every possible top region of the stack while going deeper in the stack to find the minimal reduction. In the worst case, each time we go down to the bottom of the increasingly higher stack without a successful reduction. Thus, in $O(n^2)$, we can find the minimum k-arization.

5 Linear Time Factorization

In this section, we show a linear time algorithm which shares the left-to-right and bottom-up control structure but uses more book-keeping operations to reduce unnecessary reduction attempts. The reason that our previous algorithm is asymptotically $O(n^2)$

is that whenever a new number is shifted in, we have to try out every possible new span ending at the new number. Do we need to try every possible span? Let us start with a motivating example. The permuted sequence $(5, 7, 4, 6)$ in Table 1 can only be reduced as a whole block. However, in the last algorithm, when 4 is shifted in, we make an unsuccessful attempt for the span on $(7, 4)$, knowing we are missing 5, which will not appear when we expand the span no matter how much further to the right. Yet we repeat the same mistake to try on 7 when 6 is scanned in by attempting on $(7, 4, 6)$. Such wasteful checks result in the quadratic behavior of the algorithm. The way the following algorithm differs from and outperforms the previous algorithm is exactly that it crosses out impossible candidates for reductions such as 7 in the example as early as possible.

Now we state our problem mathematically. We define a function whose value indicates the reducibility of each pair of positions (x, y) $(1 \leq x \leq y \leq n)$:

$$f(x, y) = u(x, y) - l(x, y) - (y - x)$$

where

$$l(x, y) = \min_{i \in [x,y]} \pi(i)$$
$$u(x, y) = \max_{i \in [x,y]} \pi(i)$$

l records the minimum of the numbers that are permuted to from the positions in the region $[x, y]$. u records the maximum. Figure 1 provides the visualization of u, l, and f for the example permutation $(5, 7, 4, 6, 3, 1, 2)$. u and l can be visualized as stairs. u goes up from the right end to the left. l goes down. f is non-negative, but not monotonic in general. We can make a reduction on (x, y) if and only if $f(x, y) = 0$. This is the mathematical statement of the partition property in step 2 of the shift-reduce algorithm. u and l can be computed incrementally from smaller spans to larger spans to guarantee $O(1)$ operations for computing f on each new span of $[x, y]$ as long as we go bottom up. In the new algorithm, we will reduce the size of the search space of candidate position pairs (x, y) to be linear in n so that the whole algorithm is $O(n)$.

The algorithm has two main ideas:

- We filter x's to maintain the invariant that $f(x, y)$ $(x \leq y)$ is monotonically decreasing with respect to x, over iterations on y (from 1 to n), so that any remaining values of x corresponding to valid reductions are clustered at the point where f tails off to zero. To put it another way, we never have to test invalid reductions, because the valid reductions have been sorted together for us.

- We make greedy reductions as in the shift-reduce algorithm.

In the new algorithm, we use a doubly linked list, instead of a stack, as the data structure that stores the candidate x's to allow for more flexible maintaining operations. The steps of the algorithm are as follows:

1. Increase the left-to-right index y by one and append it to the right end of the list.
2. Find the *pivot* x^* in the list which is minimum (leftmost) among x satisfying either $u(x, y - 1) < u(x, y)$ (exclusively) or $l(x, y - 1) > l(x, y)$.
3. Remove those x's that yield even smaller $u(x, y - 1)$ than $u(x^*, y - 1)$ or even larger $l(x, y - 1)$ than $l(x^*, y - 1)$. Those x's must be on the right of x^* if they exist. They must form a sub-list extending to the right end of the original x list.
4. Denote the x which is immediately to the left of x^* as x'. Repeatedly remove all x's such that $f(x, y) > f(x', y)$ where x is at the left end of the sub-list of x's starting from x^* extending to the right.
5. Go down the pruned list from the right end, output (x, y) until $f(x, y) > 0$. Remove x's such that $f(x, y) = 0$, sparing the smallest x which is the leftmost among all such x's on the list.
6. If there are remaining numbers in the input permutation, go to 1.

The tricks lie in step 3 and step 4, where bad candidate x's are filtered out. We use the following diagram to help readers understand the parts of x-list that the two steps are filtering on.

$$x_1, ..., x', \overbrace{x^*, ..., x_i}^{step\ 4}, ..., \underbrace{x_j, ..., x_k}_{step\ 3}, y$$

The steps from 2 to 4 are the operations that maintain the monotonic invariant which makes the reductions in step 5 as trivial as performing output. The stack-based shift-reduce algorithm has the same top-level structure, but lacks steps 2 to 4 so that in step 5 we have to winnow the entire list. Both algorithms scan left to right and examine potential reduction spans by extending the left endpoint from right to left given a right endpoint.

5.1 Example Execution Trace

An example of the algorithm's execution is shown in Figure 1. The evolution of $u(x, y)$, $l(x, y)$, and $f(x, y)$ is displayed for increasing y's (from 2 to 7). To identify reducible spans, we can check the plot of $f(x, y)$ to locate the (x, y) pairs that yield zero. The pivots found by step 2 of the algorithm are marked with $*$'s on the x-axis in the plot for u and l. The x's that are filtered out by step 3 or 4 are marked with horizontal bars across. We want to point out the interesting steps. When $y = 3$, $x^* = 1$, $x = 2$ needs to be crossed out by step 3 in the algorithm. When $y = 4$, $x^* = 3$, $x = 3$ itself is to be deleted by step 4 in the algorithm. $x = 4$ is removed at step 5 because it is the right end in the first reduction. On the other hand, $x = 4$ is also a bad starting point for future reductions. Notice that we also remove $x = 5$ at step 6, which can be a good starting point for reductions. But we exclude it from further considerations, because we want left-most reductions.

5.2 Correctness

Now we explain why the algorithm works. Both algorithms are greedy in the sense that at each scan point we exhaustively reduce all candidate spans to the leftmost possible point. It can be shown that greediness is safe for parsing permutations.

What we need to show is how the monotonic invariant holds and is valid. Now we sketch the proof. We want to show for all x_i remaining on the list, $f(x_i, y) \geq f(x_{i+1}, y)$. When $y = 1$, it is trivially true. Now we do the induction on y step by case analysis:

Case 1: If $x_i < x_{i+1} < x^*$, then $f(x_i, y) - f(x_i, y - 1) = -1$. The reason is if x_i is on the left of x^*, both $u(x_i, y)$ and $l(x_i, y)$ are not changed from the $y - 1$-th step, so the only difference is that $y - x_i$ has increased by one. Graphically, the f curve extending to the left of x^* shifts down a unit of 1. So, the monotonic property still holds to the left of x^*.

Case 2: If $x^* \leq x_i < x_{i+1}$, then $f(x_i, y) - f(x_i, y - 1) = c$ $(c \geq 0)$. The reason is that after executing step 3 in the algorithm, the remaining x_i's have either their $u(x_i, y)$ shifted up uniformly with $l(x_i, y)$ being unchanged, or the symmetric case that $l(x_i, y)$ is shifted down uniformly without changing $u(x_i, y)$. In both cases, the difference between u and l increases by at least one unit to offset the one unit increase of $y - x_i$. The result is that the f curve extending from x^* to the right shifts up or remains the same.

Case 3: So the half curve of f on the left of x^* is shifting down and the half right curve on the right is shifting up, making it necessary to consider the case that x_i is on the left and x_{i+1} on the right. Fortunately, step 4 in the algorithm deals with this case explicitly by cutting down the head of the right half curve to smooth the whole curve into a monotonically decreasing one.

We still need one last piece for the proof, i.e., the validity of pruning. Is it possible we winnow off good x's that will become useful in later stages of y? The answer is no. The values we remove in step 3 and 4 are similar to the points indexing into the second and third numbers in the permuted sequence $(5, 7, 4, 6)$. Any span starting from these two points will not be reducible because the element 5 is missing.[1]

To summarize, we remove impossible left boundaries and keep good ones, resulting in the monotonicity of f function which in turn makes safe greedy reductions fast.

5.3 Implementation and Time Analysis

We use a doubly linked list to implement both the u and l functions, where list element includes a span of x values (shaded rectangles in Figure 1). Both lists can be doubly linked with the list of x's so that

[1] Uno and Yagiura (2000) prove the validity of step 3 and step 4 rigorously.

we can access the u function and l function at $O(1)$ time for each x. At the same time, if we search for x based on u or l, we can follow the stair functions, skipping many intermediate x's.

The total number of operations that occur at step 4 and step 5 is $O(n)$ since these steps just involve removing nodes on the x list, and only n nodes are created in total over the entire algorithm. To find x^*, we scan back from the right end of u list or l list. Due to step 3, each u (and l) element that we scan over is removed at this iteration. So the total number of operations accountable to step 2 and step 3 is bounded by the maximum number of nodes ever created on the u and l lists, which is also n.

5.4 Related Work

Our algorithm is based on an algorithm for finding all common intervals of two permutations (Uno and Yagiura, 2000). The difference[2] is in step 5, where we remove the embedded reducible x's and keep only the leftmost one; their algorithm will keep all of the reducible x's for future considerations so that in the example the number 3 will be able to involve in both the reduction $([4-7], 3)$ and $(3, [1-2])$. In the worst case, their algorithm will output a quadratic number of reducible spans, making the whole algorithm $O(n^2)$. Our algorithm is $O(n)$ in the worst case. We can also generate all common intervals by transforming the permutation tree output by our algorithm.

However, we are not the first to specialize the Uno and Yagiura algorithm to produce tree structures for permutations. Bui-Xuan et al. (2005) reached a linear time algorithm in the definition framework of PQ trees. PQ trees represent families of permutations that can be created by composing operations of scrambling subsequences according to any permutation (P nodes) and concatenating subsequences in order (Q nodes). Our definition of permutation tree can be thought of as a more specific version of a PQ tree, where the nodes are all labeled with a specific permutation which is not decomposable.

[2]The original Uno and Yagiura algorithm also has the minor difference that the scan point goes from right to left.

6 Experiments on Analyzing Word Alignments

We apply the factorization algorithm to analyzing word alignments in this section. Wellington et al. (2006) indicate the necessity of introducing discontinuous spans for synchronous parsing to match up with human-annotated word alignment data. The number of discontinuous spans reflects the structural complexity of the synchronous rules that are involved in building the synchronous trees for the given alignments. However, the more direct and detailed analysis would be on the branching factors of the synchronous trees for the aligned data.

Since human-aligned data has many-to-one word links, it is necessary to modify the alignments into one-to-one. Wellington et al. (2006) treat many-to-one word links disjunctively in their synchronous parser. We also commit to one of the many-one links by extracting a maximum match (Cormen et al., 1990) from the bipartite graph of the alignment. In other words, we abstract away the alternative links in the given alignment while capturing the backbone using the maximum number of word links.

We use the same alignment data for the five language pairs Chinese/English, Romanian/English, Hindi/English, Spanish/English, and French/English (Wellington et al., 2006). In Table 2, we report the number of sentences that are k-ary parsable but not $k-1$-ary parsable for increasing k's. Our analysis reveals that the permutations that are accountable for non-ITG alignments include higher order permutations such as $(3, 1, 5, 2, 4)$, albeit sparsely seen.

We also look at the number of terminals the non-binary synchronous nodes can cover. We are interested in doing so, because this can tell us how general these unfriendly rules are. Wellington et al. (2006) did a similar analysis on the English-English bitext. They found out the majority of non-ITG parsable cases are not local in the sense that phrases of length up to 10 are not helpful in covering the gaps. We analyzed the translation data for the five language pairs instead. Our result differs. The rightmost column in Table 2 shows that only a tiny percent of the non-ITG cases are significant in the sense that we can not deal with them through phrases or tree-flattening within windows of size 10.

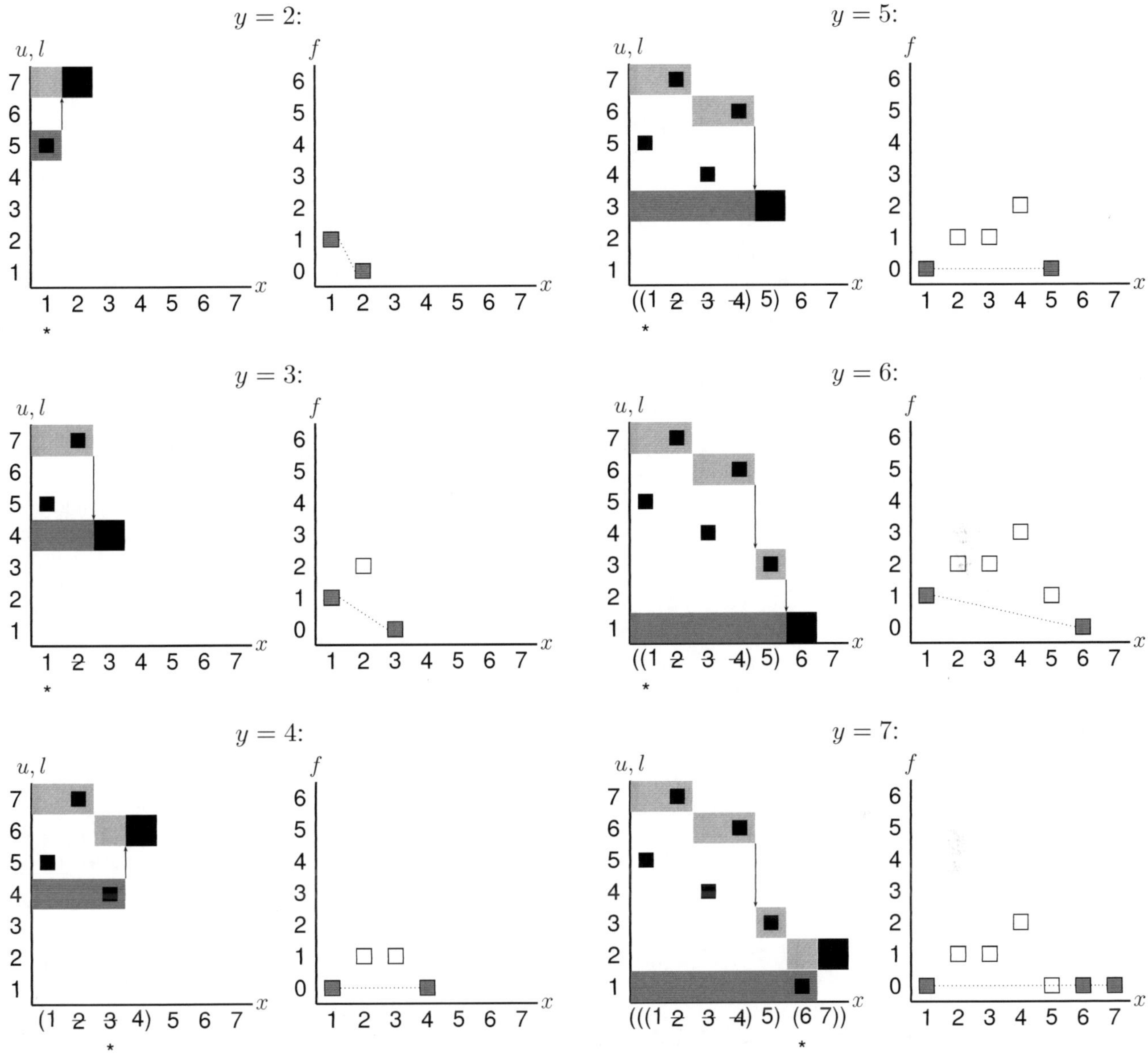

Figure 1: Evolution of $u(x, y)$, $l(x, y)$, and $f(x, y)$ as y goes from 2 to 7 for the permutation $(5, 7, 4, 6, 3, 1, 2)$. We use $*$ under the x-axis to indicate the x^*'s that are pivots in the algorithm. Useless x's are crossed out. x's that contribute to reductions are marked with either (on its left or) on its right. For the f function, we use solid boxes to plot the values of remaining x's on the list but also show the other f values for completeness.

	Branching Factor							
	1	2	4	5	6	7	10	≥ 4 (and covering > 10 words)
Chinese/English		451	30	4	5	1		7(1.4%)
Romanian/English		195	4					0
Hindi/English	3	85	1	1				0
Spanish/English		195	4					1(0.5%)
French/English		425	9	9	3		1	6(1.3%)

Table 2: Distribution of branching factors for synchronous trees on various language pairs.

7 Conclusion

We present a linear time algorithm for factorizing any n-ary SCFG rule into a set of k-ary rules where k is minimized. The algorithm speeds up an easy-to-understand shift-reduce algorithm, by avoiding unnecessary reduction attempts while maintaining the left-to-right bottom-up control structure. Empirically, we provide a complexity analysis of word alignments based on the concept of minimal branching factor.

References

Albert V. Aho and Jeffery D. Ullman. 1972. *The Theory of Parsing, Translation, and Compiling*, volume 1. Prentice-Hall, Englewood Cliffs, NJ.

Binh Minh Bui-Xuan, Michel Habib, and Christophe Paul. 2005. Revisiting T. Uno and M. Yagiura's algorithm. In *The 16th Annual International Symposium on Algorithms and Computation (ISAAC'05)*, pages 146–155.

David Chiang. 2005. A hierarchical phrase-based model for statistical machine translation. In *Proceedings of the 43rd Annual Conference of the Association for Computational Linguistics (ACL-05)*, pages 263–270, Ann Arbor, Michigan.

Thomas H. Cormen, Charles E. Leiserson, and Ronald L. Rivest. 1990. *Introduction to algorithms*. MIT Press, Cambridge, MA.

Michel Galley, Mark Hopkins, Kevin Knight, and Daniel Marcu. 2004. What's in a translation rule? In *Proceedings of the Human Language Technology Conference/North American Chapter of the Association for Computational Linguistics (HLT/NAACL)*.

Daniel Gildea, Giorgio Satta, and Hao Zhang. 2006. Factoring synchronous grammars by sorting. In *Proceedings of the International Conference on Computational Linguistics/Association for Computational Linguistics (COLING/ACL-06) Poster Session*, Sydney.

Giorgio Satta and Enoch Peserico. 2005. Some computational complexity results for synchronous context-free grammars. In *Proceedings of Human Language Technology Conference and Conference on Empirical Methods in Natural Language Processing (HLT/EMNLP)*, pages 803–810, Vancouver, Canada, October.

Takeaki Uno and Mutsunori Yagiura. 2000. Fast algorithms to enumerate all common intervals of two permutations. *Algorithmica*, 26(2):290–309.

Benjamin Wellington, Sonjia Waxmonsky, and I. Dan Melamed. 2006. Empirical lower bounds on the complexity of translational equivalence. In *Proceedings of the International Conference on Computational Linguistics/Association for Computational Linguistics (COLING/ACL-06)*.

Dekai Wu. 1997. Stochastic inversion transduction grammars and bilingual parsing of parallel corpora. *Computational Linguistics*, 23(3):377–403.

Kenji Yamada and Kevin Knight. 2001. A syntax-based statistical translation model. In *Proceedings of the 39th Annual Conference of the Association for Computational Linguistics (ACL-01)*, Toulouse, France.

Hao Zhang, Liang Huang, Daniel Gildea, and Kevin Knight. 2006. Synchronous binarization for machine translation. In *Proceedings of the Human Language Technology Conference/North American Chapter of the Association for Computational Linguistics (HLT/NAACL)*.

Binarization, Synchronous Binarization, and Target-side Binarization*

Liang Huang
University of Pennsylvania
3330 Walnut Street, Levine Hall
Philadelphia, PA 19104
lhuang3@cis.upenn.edu

Abstract

Binarization is essential for achieving polynomial time complexities in parsing and syntax-based machine translation. This paper presents a new binarization scheme, *target-side binarization*, and compares it with source-side and synchronous binarizations on both string-based and tree-based systems using synchronous grammars. In particular, we demonstrate the effectiveness of target-side binarization on a large-scale tree-to-string translation system.

1 Introduction

Several recent syntax-based models for machine translation (Chiang, 2005; Galley et al., 2006) can be seen as instances of the general framework of synchronous grammars and tree transducers. In this framework, decoding can be thought of as parsing problems, whose complexity is in general exponential in the number of nonterminals on the right hand side of a grammar rule. To alleviate this problem, one can borrow from parsing the technique of binarizing context-free grammars (into Chomsky Normal Form) to reduce the complexity. With synchronous context-free grammars (SCFG), however, this problem becomes more complicated with the additional dimension of target-side permutation.

The simplest method of binarizing an SCFG is to binarize (left-to-right) on the source-side as if treating it as a monolingual CFG for the source-langauge. However, this approach does not guarantee contiguous spans on the target-side, due to the arbitrary re-ordering of nonterminals between the two languages. As a result, decoding with an integrated language model still has an exponential complexity.

Synchronous binarization (Zhang et al., 2006) solves this problem by simultaneously binarizing both source and target-sides of a synchronous rule, making sure of contiguous spans on both sides whenever possible. Neglecting the small amount of non-binarizable rules, the decoding complexity with an integrated language model becomes polynomial and translation quality is significantly improved thanks to the better search. However, this method is more sophisticated to implement than the previous method and binarizability ratio decreases on freer word-order languages (Wellington et al., 2006).

This paper presents a third alternative, *target-side binarization*, which is the symmetric version of the simple source-side variant mentioned above. We compare it with the other two schemes in two popular instantiations of MT systems based on SCFGs: the *string-based systems* (Chiang, 2005; Galley et al., 2006) where the input is a string to be parsed using the source-side of the SCFG; and the *tree-based systems* (Liu et al., 2006; Huang et al., 2006) where the input is a parse tree and is recursively converted into a target string using the SCFG as a tree-transducer. While synchronous binarization is the best strategy for string-based systems, we show that target-side binarization can achieve the same performance of synchronous binarization for tree-based systems, with much simpler implementation and 100% binarizability.

2 Synchronous Grammars and Binarization Schemes

In this section, we define synchronous context-free grammars and present the three binarization

*This work is partially supported by NSF ITR grants IIS-0428020 (while I was visiting USC/ISI) and EIA-0205456. I also wish to thank Jonathan Graehl, Giorgio Satta, Hao Zhang, and the three anonymous reviewers for helpful comments.

Proceedings of SSST, NAACL-HLT 2007 / AMTA Workshop on Syntax and Structure in Statistical Translation, pages 33–40,
Rochester, New York, April 2007.

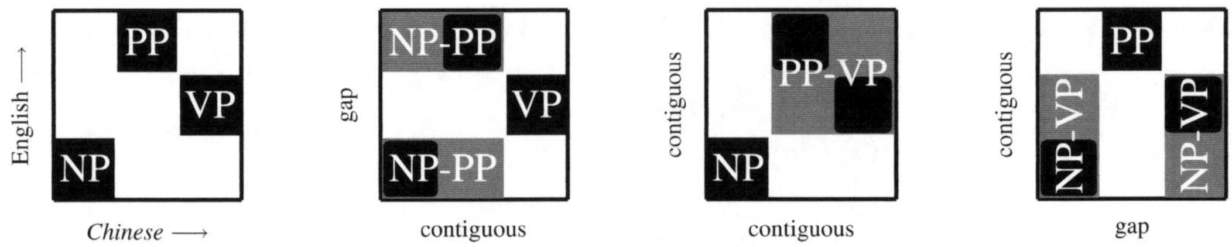

(a) example rule (b) source-side (c) synchronous (d) target-side

Figure 1: Illustration of the three binarization schemes, with virtual nonterminals in gray.

schemes through a motivational example.

A **synchronous CFG** (SCFG) is a context-free rewriting system for generating string pairs. Each rule (*synchronous production*) rewrites a nonterminal in two dimensions subject to the constraint that the sequence of nonterminal children on one side is a permutation of the nonterminal sequence on the other side. Each co-indexed child nonterminal pair will be further rewritten as a unit. The **rank** of a rule is defined as the number of its synchronous nonterminals. We also define the source and target projections of an SCFG to be the CFGs for the source and target languages, respectively.

For example, the following SCFG[1]

$$(1)\quad \begin{array}{rcll} \text{S} & \to & \text{NP}^{\boxed{1}}\ \text{PP}^{\boxed{2}}\ \text{VP}^{\boxed{3}}, & \text{NP}^{\boxed{1}}\ \text{VP}^{\boxed{3}}\ \text{PP}^{\boxed{2}} \\ \text{NP} & \to & \textit{Baoweier}, & \text{Powell} \\ \text{VP} & \to & \textit{juxing le huitan}, & \text{held a meeting} \\ \text{PP} & \to & \textit{yu Shalong}, & \text{with Sharon} \end{array}$$

captures the re-ordering of PP and VP between Chinese (source) and English (target). The source-projection of the first rule, for example, is

$$\text{S} \to \text{NP PP VP}.$$

Decoding with an SCFG (e.g., translating from Chinese to English using the above grammar) can be cast as a parsing problem (see Section 3 for details), in which case we need to binarize a synchronous rule with more than two nonterminals to achieve polynomial time algorithms (Zhang et al., 2006). We will next present the three different binarization schemes using Example 1.

[1]An alternative notation, used by Satta and Peserico (2005), allows co-indexed nonterminals to take different symbols across languages, which is convenient in describing syntactic divergences (see Figure 2).

2.1 Source-side Binarization

The first and simplest scheme, *source-side binarization*, works left-to-right on the source projection of the SCFG without respecting the re-orderings on the target-side. So it will binarize the first rule as:

$$(2)\quad \begin{array}{rcl} \text{S} & \to & \text{NP-PP VP} \\ \text{NP-PP} & \to & \text{NP PP} \end{array}$$

which corresponds to Figure 1 (b). Notice that the *virtual nonterminal* NP-PP representing the intermediate symbol is *discontinuous* with two spans on the target (English) side, because this binarization scheme completely ignores the reorderings of nonterminals. As a result, the binarized grammar, with a gap on the target-side, is no longer an SCFG, but can be represented in the more general formalism of Multi-Text Grammars (MTG) (Melamed, 2003):

$$(3)\quad \begin{pmatrix} \text{S} \\ \text{S} \end{pmatrix} \to_{\bowtie} \begin{array}{c} [1,2] \\ [1,2,1] \end{array} \begin{pmatrix} \text{NP-PP} & \text{VP} \\ \text{NP-PP (2)} & \text{VP} \end{pmatrix}$$

here $[1, 2, 1]$ denotes that on that target-side, the first nonterminal NP-PP has two discontinuous spans, with the second nonterminal VP in the gap.

Intuitively speaking, the gaps on the target-side will lead to exponential complexity in decoding with integrated language models (see Section 3), as well as synchronous parsing (Zhang et al., 2006).

2.2 Synchronous Binarization

A more principled method is *synchronous binarization*, which simultaneously binarizes both source and target sides, with the constraint that virtual nonterminals always have contiguous spans on both sides. The resulting grammar is thus another SCFG, the binary branching equivalent of the original grammar, which can be thought of as an extension of the

[*jinyibu*]$_1$ [*jiu zhongdong weiji*]$_2$ [*juxing*]$_3$ [*huitan*]$_4$
further on Mideast crisis hold talk

'[hold]$_3$ [further]$_1$ [talks]$_4$ [on the Mideast crisis]$_2$'

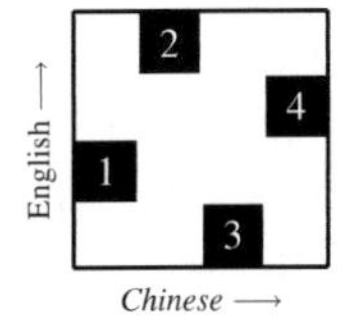

Figure 2: An example of non-binarizable rule from the hand-aligned Chinese-English data in Liu et al. (2005). The SCFG rule is VP $\rightarrow$ ADVP$^{\boxed{1}}$ PP$^{\boxed{2}}$ VB$^{\boxed{3}}$ NN$^{\boxed{4}}$, VP $\rightarrow$ VB$^{\boxed{3}}$ JJ$^{\boxed{1}}$ NNS$^{\boxed{4}}$ PP$^{\boxed{2}}$ in the notatoin of Satta and Peserico (2005).

Chomsky Normal Form in synchronous grammars. The example rule is now binarized into:

$$(4)\quad \begin{array}{rcll} \text{S} & \rightarrow & \text{NP}^{\boxed{1}}\ \text{PP-VP}^{\boxed{2}}, & \text{NP}^{\boxed{1}}\ \text{PP-VP}^{\boxed{2}} \\ \text{PP-VP} & \rightarrow & \text{PP}^{\boxed{1}}\ \text{VP}^{\boxed{2}}, & \text{VP}^{\boxed{2}}\ \text{PP}^{\boxed{1}} \end{array}$$

which corresponds to Figure 1 (c). This representation, being contiguous on both sides, successfully reduces the decoding complexity to a low polynomial and significantly improved the search quality (Zhang et al., 2006).

However, this scheme has the following drawbacks. First, synchronous binarization is *not* always possible with an arbitrary SCFG. Some reorderings, for example, the permutation $(2, 4, 1, 3)$, is non-binarizable. Although according to Zhang et al. (2006), the vast majority (99.7%) of rules in their Chinese-English dataset are binarizable, there do exist some interesting cases that are not (see Figure 2 for a real-data example). More importantly, the ratio of binarizability, as expected, decreases on freer word-order languages (Wellington et al., 2006). Second, synchronous binarization is significantly more complicated to implement than the straightforward source-side binarization.

2.3 Target-side Binarization

We now introduce a novel scheme, target-side binarization, which is the symmetric version of the source-side variant. Under this method, the target-side is always contiguous, while leaving some gaps on the source-side. The example rule is binarized into the following MTG form:

$$(5)\quad \begin{pmatrix} \text{S} \\ \text{S} \end{pmatrix} \rightarrow_{\bowtie} \begin{array}{c} [1, 2, 1] \\ [1, 2] \end{array} \begin{pmatrix} \text{NP-VP (2)} & \text{PP} \\ \text{NP-VP} & \text{PP} \end{pmatrix}$$

which corresponds to Figure 1 (d).

scheme	$s(\mathbf{b})$	$t(\mathbf{b})$
source-side	1	$\leq n/2$
synchronous	1	1
target-side	$\leq n/2$	1

Table 1: Source and target arities of the three binarization schemes of an SCFG rule of rank n.

Although the discontinuity on the source-side in this new scheme causes exponential complexity in string-based systems (Section 3.1), the continuous spans on the target-side will ensure polynomial complexity in tree-based systems (Section 3.2).

Before we move on to study the effects of various binarization schemes in decoding, we need some formal machineries of discontinuities.

We define the **source** and **target arities** of a virtual nonterminal V, denoted $s(V)$ and $t(V)$, to be the number of (consecutive) spans of V on the source and target sides, respectively. This definition extends to a binarization $\mathbf{b}$ of an SCFG rule of rank n, where arities $s(\mathbf{b})$ and $t(\mathbf{b})$ are defined as the maximum source and target arities over all virtual nonterminals in $\mathbf{b}$, respectively. For example, the source and target arities of the three binarizations in Figure 1 are 1 and 2 for (b), 1 and 1 for (c), and 2 and 1 for (d). In general, the arities for the three binarization schemes are summarized in Table 1.

3 Theoretical Analysis

We now compare the algorithmic complexities of the three binarization schemes in a central problem of machine translation: decoding with an integrated n-gram language model. Depending on the input being a string or a parse-tree, we divide MT systems based on synchronous grammars into two broad categories: string-based and tree-based.

3.1 String-based Approaches

String-based approaches include both string-to-string (Chiang, 2005) and string-to-tree systems (Galley et al., 2006).[2] To simplify the presentation we will just focus on the former but the analysis also applies to the latter. We will first discuss decoding with a pure SCFG as the translation model (henceforth *−LM decoding*), and then extend it to include an n-gram model (+LM decoding).

3.1.1 Translation as Parsing

The −LM decoder can be cast as a (monolingual) parser on the source language: it takes the source-language string as input and parses it using the source-projection of the SCFG while building the corresponding target-language sub-translations in parallel. For source-side and synchronous binarizations, since the resulting grammar has contiguous source spans, we can apply the CKY algorithm which guarantees cubic time complexity.

For example, a deduction along the virtual rule in the synchronously binarized grammar (4) is notated

$$\frac{(\mathrm{PP}_{j,k}) : (w_1, t_1) \qquad (\mathrm{VP}_{k,l}) : (w_2, t_2)}{(\mathrm{PP\text{-}VP}_{j,l}) : (w_1 + w_2, t_2 t_1)} \tag{6}$$

where i, j, k are free indices in the source string, w_1, w_2 are the scores of the two antecedent items, and t_1, t_2 are the corresponding sub-translations.[3] The resulting translation $t_2 t_1$ is the inverted concatenation as specified by the target-side of the SCFG rule.

The case for a source-side binarized grammar (3) is slightly more complicated than the above, because we have to keep track of gaps on the target side. For example, we first combine NP with PP

$$\frac{(\mathrm{NP}_{i,j}) : (w_1, t_1) \qquad (\mathrm{PP}_{j,k}) : (w_2, t_2)}{(\mathrm{NP\text{-}PP}_{i,k}) : (w_1 + w_2, t_1 \sqcup t_2)} \tag{7}$$

[2]Our notation of *X-to-Y systems* is defined as follows: X denotes the input, either a string or a tree; while Y represents the RHS structure of an individual rule: Y is *string* if the RHS is a flat one-level tree (as in SCFGs), and Y is *tree* if the RHS is multi-level as in (Galley et al., 2006). This convention also applies to tree-based approaches.

[3]The actual system does not need to store the translations since they can be recovered from backpointers and they are *not* considered part of the state. We keep them here only for presentation reasons.

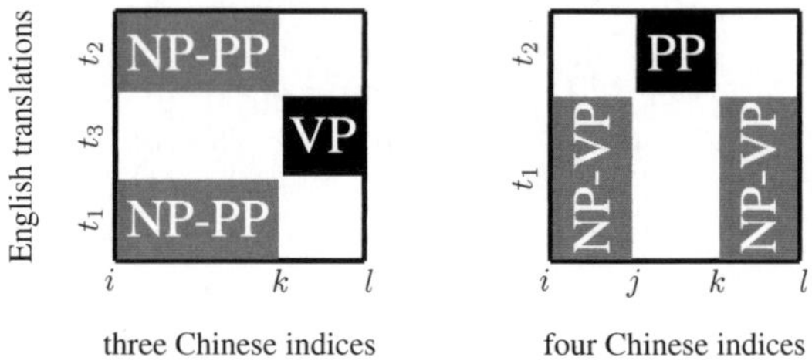

(a): Deduction (8) (b): Deduction (10)

Figure 3: Illustrations of two deductions with gaps.

leaving a gap ($\sqcup$) on the target-side resulting item, because NP and PP are not contiguous in the English ordering. This gap is later filled in by the sub-translation t_3 of VP (see also Figure 3 (a)):

$$\frac{(\mathrm{NP\text{-}PP}_{i,k}) : (w_1, t_1 \sqcup t_2) \qquad (\mathrm{VP}_{k,l}) : (w_2, t_3)}{(\mathrm{S}_{i,l}) : (w_1 + w_2, t_1 t_3 t_2)} \tag{8}$$

In both cases, there are still only three free indices on the source-side, so the complexity remains cubic. The gaps on the target-side do not require any extra computation in the current −LM setting, but as we shall see shortly below, will lead to exponential complexity when integrating a language model.

For a target-side binarized grammar as in (5), however, the source-side spans are discontinuous where CKY can not apply, and we have to enumerate more free indices on the source side. For example, the first deduction

$$\frac{(\mathrm{NP}_{i,j}) : (w_1, t_1) \qquad (\mathrm{VP}_{k,l}) : (w_2, t_2)}{(\mathrm{NP\text{-}VP}_{i,j \sqcup k,l}) : (w_1 + w_2, t_1 t_2)} \tag{9}$$

leaves a gap in the source-side span of the resulting item, which is later filled in when the item is combined with a PP (see also Figure 3 (b)):

$$\frac{(\mathrm{NP\text{-}VP}_{i,j \sqcup k,l}) : (w_1, t_1) \qquad (\mathrm{PP}_{j,k}) : (w_2, t_2)}{(\mathrm{S}_{i,l}) : (w_1 + w_2, t_1 t_2)} \tag{10}$$

Both of the above deductions have four free indices, and thus of complexity $\mathcal{O}(|w|^4)$ instead of cubic in the length of the input string w.

More generally, the complexity of a binarization scheme depends on its source arity. In the worst-case, a binarized grammar with a source arity of s will require at most $(2s + 1)$ free indices in a deduction, because otherwise if one rule needs $(2s + 2)$

indices, then there are $s+1$ spans, which contradicts the definition of arity (Huang et al., 2005).[4]

These deductive systems represent the search space of decoding without a language model. When one is instantiated for a particular input string, it defines a set of derivations, called a *forest*, represented in a compact structure that has a structure of a hypergraph. Accordingly we call items like $(\text{PP}_{1,3})$ *nodes* in the forest, and an instantiated deduction like

$$(\text{PP-VP}_{1,6}) \rightarrow (\text{PP}_{1,3})(\text{VP}_{3,6})$$

we call a *hyperedge* that connects one or more antecedent nodes to a consequent node. In this representation, the time complexity of $-$LM decoding, which we refer to as *source-side complexity*, is proportional to the size of the forest F, i.e., the number of hyperedges (instantiated deductions) in F. To summarize, the source-side complexity for a binarized grammar of source arity s is

$$|F| = \mathcal{O}(|w|^{2s+1}).$$

3.1.2 Adding a Language Model

To integrate with a bigram language model, we can use the dynamic-programming algorithm of Wu (1996), which we may think of as proceeding in two passes. The first pass is as above, and the second pass traverses the first-pass forest, assigning to each node v a set of augmented items, which we call *+LM items*, of the form $(v^{a\star b})$, where a and b are target words and $\star$ is a placeholder symbol for an elided part of a target-language string. This item indicates that a possible translation of the part of the input spanned by v is a target string that starts with a and ends with b.

Here is an example deduction in the synchronously binarized grammar (4), for a +LM item for the node $(\text{PP-VP}_{1,6})$ based on the $-$LM Deduction (6):

$$\frac{(\text{PP}\,^{\text{with} \star \text{Sharon}}_{1,3})\!: (w_1, t_1) \quad (\text{VP}\,^{\text{held} \star \text{talk}}_{3,6})\!: (w_2, t_2)}{(\text{PP-VP}\,^{\text{held} \star \text{Sharon}}_{1,6})\!: (w', t_2 t_1)} \tag{11}$$

where $w' = w_1 + w_2 - \log P_{lm}(\text{with} \mid \text{talk})$ is the score of the resulting +LM item: the sum of the scores of the antecedent items, plus a *combination cost* which is the negative log probability of the bigrams formed in combining adjacent boundary words of antecedents.

Now that we keep track of target-side boundary words, an additional complexity, called *target-side complexity*, is introduced. In Deduction (11), four target words are enumerated, and each +LM item stores two boundary words; this is also true in general for synchronous and target-side binarized grammars where we always combine two consecutive target strings in a deduction. More generally, this scheme can be easily extended to work with an m-gram model (Chiang, 2007) where m is usually ≥ 3 (trigram or higher) in practice. The target-side complexity for this case is thus

$$\mathcal{O}(|V|^{4(m-1)})$$

where V is the target language vocabulary. This is because each constituent must store its initial and final $(m-1)$-grams, which yields four $(m-1)$-grams in a binary combination. In practice, it is often assumed that there are only a constant number of translations for each input word, which reduces this complexity into $\mathcal{O}(|w|^{4(m-1)})$.

However, for source-side binarization which leaves gaps on the target-side, the situation becomes more complicated. Consider Deduction (8), where the sub-translation for the virtual node NP-PP is gapped $(t_1 \sqcup t_2)$. Now if we integrate a bigram model based on that deduction, we have to maintain the boundary words of both t_1 and t_2 in the +LM node of NP-PP. Together with the boundary words in node VP, there are a total of six target words to enumerate for this +LM deduction:

$$\frac{(\text{NP-PP}^{a\star b \sqcup e\star f}_{i,k}) : (w_1, t_1 \sqcup t_2) \quad (\text{VP}^{c\star d}_{k,l}) : (w_2, t_3)}{(\text{S}^{a\star f}_{i,l}) : (w', t_1 t_3 t_2)} \tag{12}$$

where $w' = w_1 + w_2 - \log P_{lm}(\text{c} \mid \text{b}) P_{lm}(\text{e} \mid \text{d})$.

With an analysis similar to that of the source-side, we state that, for a binarized grammar with target arity t, the target-side complexity, denoted $\mathcal{T}$, is

$$\mathcal{T} = \mathcal{O}(|w|^{2(t+1)(m-1)})$$

[4] Actually this is true only if in any binarization scheme, a non-contiguous item is always combined with a contiguous item. We define both source and target binarizations to be *incremental* (i.e., left-to-right or right-to-left), so this assumption trivially holds. More general binarization schemes are possible to have even higher complexities, but also possible to achieve better complexities. Full discussion is left for a separate paper.

scheme	string-based	tree-based
source-side	$\lvert w\rvert^{3+2(t+1)(m-1)}$	$\lvert w\rvert^{1+2(t+1)(m-1)}$
synchronous	$\lvert w\rvert^{3+4(m-1)}$	$\lvert w\rvert^{1+4(m-1)}$
target-side	$\lvert w\rvert^{(2s+1)+4(m-1)}$	$\lvert w\rvert^{1+4(m-1)}$

Table 2: Worst-case decoding complexities of the three binarization schemes in the two approaches (excluding the $O(|w|^3)$ time for source-side parsing in tree-based approaches).

because in the worst-case, there are $t+1$ spans involved in a +LM deduction (t of them from one virtual antecedent and the other one non-virtual), and for each span, there are $m-1$ target words to enumerate at both left and right boundaries, giving a total of $2(t+1)(m-1)$ words in this deduction. We now conclude that, in a string-based system, the combined complexities for a binarized grammar with source arity s and target arity t is

$$\mathcal{O}(|F|\mathcal{T}) = \mathcal{O}(|w|^{(2s+1)+2(t+1)(m-1)}).$$

The results for the three specific binarization schemes are summarized in Table 2. Although both source-side and target-side binarizations lead to exponential complexities, it is likely that language model combinations (target-side complexity) dominate the computation, since m is larger than 2 in practice. In this sense, target-side binarization is still preferable to source-side binarization.

It is also worth noting that with the hook trick of Huang et al. (2005), the target-side complexity can be reduced to $\mathcal{O}(|w|^{(2t+1)(m-1)})$, making it more analogous to its source-side counterpart: if we consider the decoding problem as intersecting the SCFG with a source-side DFA which has $|S| = |w|+1$ states, and a target-side DFA which has $|T| = O(|w|^{m-1})$ states, then the intersected grammar has a parsing complexity of $\mathcal{O}(|S|^{2s+1}|T|^{2t+1})$, which is symmetric from both sides.

3.2 Tree-based Approaches

The *tree-based approaches* include the tree-to-string (also called *syntax-directed*) systems (Liu et al., 2006; Huang et al., 2006). This approach takes a source-language parse tree, instead of the plain string, as input, and tries to find the best derivation that recursively rewrites the input tree into a target

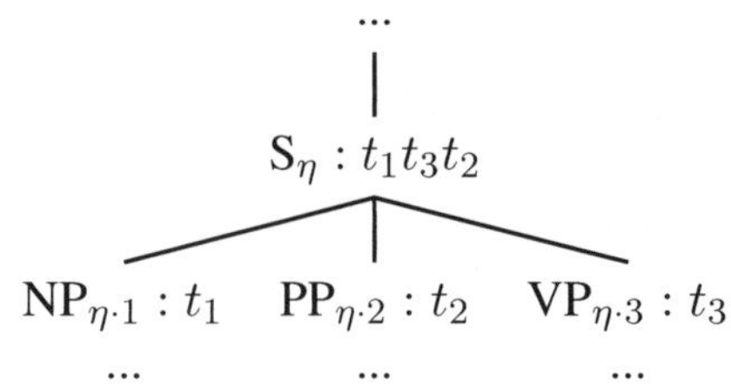

Figure 4: Illustration of tree-to-string deduction.

string, using the SCFG as a tree-transducer. In this setting, the −LM decoding phase is a *tree-parsing* problem (Eisner, 2003) which aims to cover the entire tree by a set of rules. For example, a deduction of the first rule in Example 1 would be:

$$\frac{(\mathrm{NP}_{\eta\cdot 1}) : (w_1, t_1) \quad (\mathrm{PP}_{\eta\cdot 2}) : (w_2, t_2) \quad (\mathrm{VP}_{\eta\cdot 3}) : (w_3, t_3)}{(\mathrm{S}_\eta) : (w_1 + w_2 + w_3, t_1 t_3 t_2)} \tag{13}$$

where η and $\eta \cdot i (i = 1, 2, 3)$ are tree addresses (Shieber et al., 1995), with $\eta \cdot i$ being the ith child of η (the address of the root node is ϵ). The nonterminal labels at these tree nodes must match those in the SCFG rule, e.g., the input tree must have a PP at node $\eta \cdot 2$.

The semantics of this deduction is the following: if the label of the current node in the input tree is S, and its three children are labeled NP, PP, and VP, with corresponding sub-translations t_1, t_2, and t_3, then a possible translation for the current node S is $t_1 t_3 t_2$ (see Figure 4). An alternative, top-down version of this bottom-up deductive system is, at each node, try all SCFG rules that *pattern-match* the current subtree, and recursively solve sub-problems indicated by the variables, i.e., synchronous nonterminals, of the matching rule (Huang et al., 2006).

With the input tree completely given, this setting has some fundamental differences from its string-based counterpart. First, we do *not* need to binarize the SCFG grammar before −LM decoding. In fact, it will be much harder to do the tree-parsing (pattern-matching) with a binarized grammar. Second, regardless of the number of nonterminals in a rule, building the −LM forest always costs time linear in the size of the input tree (times a grammar constant, see (Huang et al., 2006, Sec. 5.1) for details), which is in turn linear in the length of the input string. So we have:

$$\mathcal{O}(|F|) = \mathcal{O}(|w|).$$

This fast $-$LM decoding is a major advantage of tree-based approaches.

Now in $+$LM decoding, we still need binarization of the hyperedges, as opposed to rules, in the forest, but the analysis is almost identical to that of string-based approach. For example, the tree-based version of Deduction (12) for source-side binarization is now notated

$$\frac{(\mathrm{NP}_{\eta\cdot 1}\text{-}\mathrm{PP}_{\eta\cdot 2}{}^{a\star b\sqcup e\star f}) : (w_1, t_1 \sqcup t_2) \quad (\mathrm{VP}_{\eta\cdot 3}{}^{c\star d}) : (w_2, t_3)}{(\mathrm{S}_{\eta}{}^{a\star f}) : (w', t_1 t_3 t_2)} \tag{14}$$

In general, the target-side complexity of a binarized grammar with target arity t is still $\mathcal{T} = \mathcal{O}(|w|^{2(t+1)(m-1)})$ and the combined decoding complexity of the tree-based approach is

$$\mathcal{O}(|F|\mathcal{T}) = \mathcal{O}(|w|^{1+2(t+1)(m-1)}).$$

Table 2 shows that in this tree-based setting, target-side binarization has exactly the same performance with synchronous binarization while being much simpler to implement and does not have the problem of non-binarizability. The fact that simple binarization works (at least) equally well, which is not possible in string-based systems, is another advantage of the tree-based approaches.

4 Experiments

Section 3 shows that target-side binarization achieves the same polynomial decoding complexity as the more sophisticated synchronous binarization in the tree-based systems. We now empirically compare target-side binarization with an even simpler variant, *on-the-fly generation*, where the only difference is that the latter does target-side left-to-right binarization during $+$LM decoding on a hyperedge-per-hyperedge basis, without sharing common virtual nonterminals across hyperedges, while the former binarizes the whole $-$LM forest before the $+$LM decoding.

Our experiments are on English-to-Chinese translation in the tree-to-string system of Huang et al. (2006), which takes a source-language parse tree as input and tries to recursively convert it to a target-language string according to transfer rules in a synchronous grammar (Galley et al., 2006). For instance, the following rule

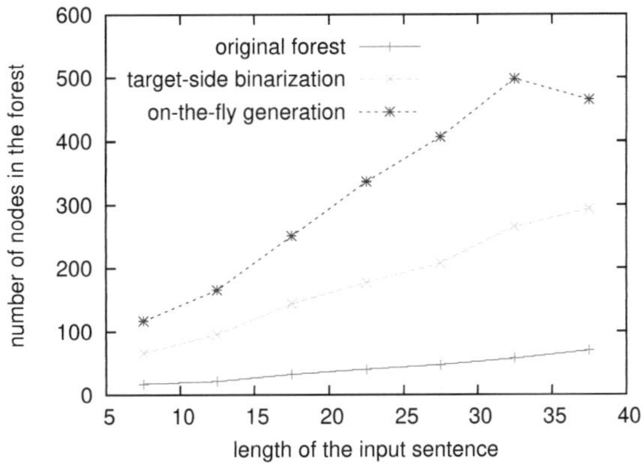

Figure 5: Number of nodes in the forests. Input sentences are grouped into bins according to their lengths (5-9, 10-14, 15-20, etc.).

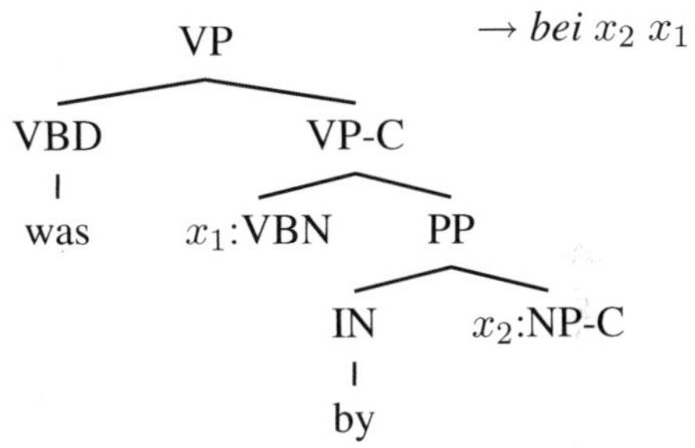

translates an English passive construction into Chinese. Although the rules are actually in a synchronous tree-substitution grammar (STSG) instead of an SCFG, its derivation structure is still a hypergraph and all the analysis in Section 3.2 still applies. This system performs slightly better than the state-of-the-art phrase-based system Pharaoh (Koehn, 2004) on English to Chinese translation. A very similar system for the reverse direction is described in (Liu et al., 2006).

Our data preparation follows (Huang et al., 2006): the training data is a parallel corpus of 28.3M words on the English side, from which we extracted 24.7M tree-to-string rules using the algorithm of (Galley et al., 2006), and trained a Chinese trigram model on the Chinese side. We test our methods on the same test-set as in (Huang et al., 2006) which is a 140 sentence subset of NIST 2003 MT evaluation with 9–36 words on the English side. The weights for the log-linear model is tuned on a separate development set.

Figure 5 compares the number of nodes in the binarized forests against the original forest. On-the-fly generation essentially works on a larger forest with

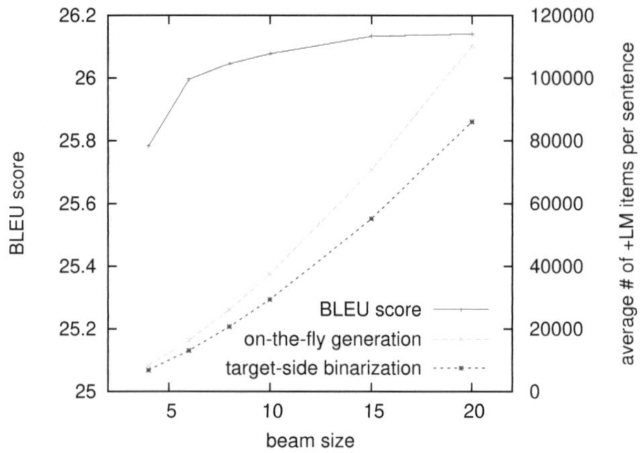

Figure 6: Decoding speed and BLEU scores under beam search.

duplicate nodes due to the lack of sharing, which is on average 1.85 times bigger than the target-side binarized forest. This difference is also reflected in the decoding speed, which is illustrated in Figure 6 under various beam settings and where the amount of computation is measured by the number of +LM items generated. At each individual beam setting, the two methods produce exactly the same set of translations (i.e., there is no relative search error), but the target-side binarization is consistently 1.3 times faster thanks to the sharing. In terms of translation quality, the final BLEU score at the largest beam setting is 0.2614, significantly higher than Pharaoh's 0.2354 as reported in (Huang et al., 2006).

5 Conclusion

This paper introduces a simple binarization scheme, *target-side binarization*, and presents a systematic study of the theoretical properties of the three binarization schemes in both string-based and tree-based systems using syncrhonous grammars. In particular, we show that target-side binarization achieves the same polynomial complexity as synchronous binarization while being much simpler to implement and universally applicable to arbitrary SCFGs. We also demonstrate the empirical effectiveness of this new scheme on a large-scale tree-to-string system.

References

David Chiang. 2005. A hierarchical phrase-based model for statistical machine translation. In *Proceedings of ACL*.

David Chiang. 2007. Hierarchical phrase-based translation. In *Computational Linguistics*, volume 33. To appear.

Jason Eisner. 2003. Learning non-isomorphic tree mappings for machine translation. In *Proceedings of ACL (poster)*, pages 205–208.

Michel Galley, Jonathan Graehl, Kevin Knight, Daniel Marcu, Steve DeNeefe, Wei Wang, and Ignacio Thayer. 2006. Scalable inference and training of context-rich syntactic translation models. In *Proceedings of COLING-ACL*.

Liang Huang, Hao Zhang, and Daniel Gildea. 2005. Machine translation as lexicalized parsing with hooks. In *Proceedings of the Ninth International Workshop on Parsing Technologies (IWPT-2005)*.

Liang Huang, Kevin Knight, and Aravind Joshi. 2006. Statistical syntax-directed translation with extended domain of locality. In *Proc. of AMTA*.

Philipp Koehn. 2004. Pharaoh: a beam search decoder for phrase-based statistical machine translation models. In *Proceedings of AMTA*, pages 115–124.

Yang Liu, Qun Liu, and Shouxun Lin. 2005. Log-linear models for word alignment. In *Proceedings of ACL*.

Yang Liu, Qun Liu, and Shouxun Lin. 2006. Tree-to-string alignment template for statistical machine translation. In *Proceedings of COLING-ACL*.

I. Dan Melamed. 2003. Multitext grammars and synchronous parsers. In *Proceedings of NAACL*.

Giorgio Satta and Enoch Peserico. 2005. Some computational complexity results for synchronous context-free grammars. In *Proc. of HLT-EMNLP 2005*.

Stuart Shieber, Yves Schabes, and Fernando Pereira. 1995. Principles and implementation of deductive parsing. *Journal of Logic Programming*, 24:3–36.

Benjamin Wellington, Sonjia Waxmonsky, and I. Dan Melamed. 2006. Empirical lower bounds on the complexity of translational equivalence. In *Proceedings of COLING-ACL*.

Dekai Wu. 1996. A polynomial-time algorithm for statistical machine translation. In *Proceedings of ACL*.

Hao Zhang, Liang Huang, Daniel Gildea, and Kevin Knight. 2006. Synchronous binarization for machine translation. In *Proc. of HLT-NAACL*.

Machine Translation as Tree Labeling

Mark Hopkins
Department of Linguistics
University of Potsdam, Germany
hopkins@ling.uni-potsdam.de

Jonas Kuhn
Department of Linguistics
University of Potsdam, Germany
kuhn@ling.uni-potsdam.de

Abstract

We present the main ideas behind a new syntax-based machine translation system, based on reducing the machine translation task to a tree-labeling task. This tree labeling is further reduced to a sequence of decisions (of four varieties), which can be discriminatively trained. The optimal tree labeling (i.e. translation) is then found through a simple depth-first branch-and-bound search. An early system founded on these ideas has been shown to be competitive with Pharaoh when both are trained on a small subsection of the Europarl corpus.

1 Motivation

Statistical machine translation has, for a while now, been dominated by the phrase-based translation paradigm (Och and Ney, 2003). In this paradigm, sentences are translated from a source language to a target language through the repeated substitution of contiguous word sequences ("phrases") from the source language for word sequences in the target language. Training of the phrase translation model builds on top of a standard statistical word alignment over the training corpus for identifying corresponding word blocks, assuming no further linguistic analysis of the source or target language. In decoding, these systems then typically rely on n-gram language models and simple statistical reordering models to shuffle the phrases into an order that is coherent in the target language.

There are limits to what such an approach can ultimately achieve. Machine translation based on a deeper analysis of the syntactic structure of a sentence has long been identified as a desirable objective in principle (consider (Wu, 1997; Yamada and Knight, 2001)). However, attempts to retrofit syntactic information into the phrase-based paradigm have not met with enormous success (Koehn et al., 2003; Och et al., 2003)[1], and purely phrase-based machine translation systems continue to outperform these syntax/phrase-based hybrids.

In this work, we try to make a fresh start with syntax-based machine translation, discarding the phrase-based paradigm and designing a machine translation system from the ground up, using syntax as our central guiding star. Evaluation with BLEU and a detailed manual error analysis of our nascent system show that this new approach might well have the potential to finally realize some of the promises of syntax.

2 Problem Formulation

We want to build a system that can learn to translate sentences from a source language to a destination language. As our first step, we will assume that the system will be learning from a corpus consisting of triples $\langle f, e, a \rangle$, where: (i) f is a sentence from our source language, which is parsed (the words of the sentence and the nodes of the parse tree may or may not be annotated with auxiliary information), (ii) e is a gold-standard translation of sentence f (the words of sentence e may or may not be annotated with auxiliary information), and (iii) a is an automatically-generated word alignment (e.g. via GIZA++) between source sentence f and destination sentence e.

[1](Chiang, 2005) also reports that with his hierarchical generalization of the phrase-based approach, the addition of parser information doesn't lead to any improvements.

Proceedings of SSST, NAACL-HLT 2007 / AMTA Workshop on Syntax and Structure in Statistical Translation, pages 41–48,
Rochester, New York, April 2007.

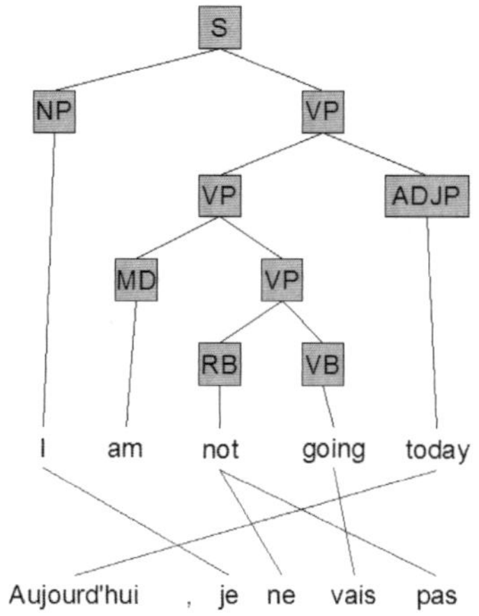

Figure 1: Example translation object.

Let us refer to these triples as *translation objects*. The learning task is: using the training data, produce a scoring function P that assigns a score to every translation object $\langle f, e, a\rangle$, such that this scoring function assigns a high score to good translations, and a low score to poor ones. The decoding task is: given scoring function P and an arbitrary sentence f from the source language, find translation object $\langle f, e, a\rangle$ that maximizes $P(\langle f, e, a\rangle)$.

To facilitate matters, we will map translation objects to an alternate representation. In (Galley et al., 2003), the authors give a semantics to every translation object by associating each with an annotated parse tree (hereafter called a *GHKM tree*) representing a specific theory about how the source sentence was translated into the destination sentence.

In Figure 1, we show an example translation object and in Figure 2, we show its associated GHKM tree. The GHKM tree is simply the parse tree f of the translation object, annotated with rules (hereafter referred to as *GHKM rules*). We will not describe in depth the mapping process from translation object to GHKM tree. Suffice it to say that the alignment induces a set of intuitive translation rules. Essentially, a rule like: "not 1 → ne 1 pas" (see Figure 2) means: if we see the word "not" in English, followed by a phrase already translated into French, then translate the entire thing as the word "ne" + the translated phrase + the word "pas." A parse tree node gets labeled with one of these rules if, roughly speaking, its span is still contiguous when projected (via the alignment) into the target language.

Formally, what is a GHKM tree? Define a *rule element* as a string or an indexed variable (e.g. x_1, x_4, x_{32}). A *GHKM rule of rank* k (where k is a non-negative integer) is a pair $\langle R_s, R_d\rangle$, where *source list* R_s and *destination list* R_d are both lists of rule elements, such that each variable of $X_k \triangleq \{x_1, x_2, ..., x_k\}$ appears exactly once in R_s and exactly once in R_d. Moreover, in R_s, the variables appear in ascending order. In Figure 2, some of the tree nodes are annotated with GHKM rules. For clarity, we use a simplified notation. For instance, rule $\langle\langle x_1, x_2, x_3\rangle, \langle x_3, \text{“,”}, x_1, x_2\rangle\rangle$ is represented as "1 2 3 → 3 , 1 2". We have also labeled the nodes with roman numerals. When we want to refer to a particular node in later examples, we will refer to it, e.g., as $t_{(i)}$ or $t_{(vii)}$.

A *rule node* is a tree node annotated with a GHKM rule (for instance, nodes $t_{(i)}$ or $t_{(v)}$ of Figure 2, but not node $t_{(iv)}$). A tree node t_2 is *reachable* from tree node t_1 iff node t_2 is a proper descendant of node t_1 and there is no rule node (not including nodes t_1, t_2) on the path from node t_1 to node t_2.

Define the *successor list* of a tree node t as the list of rule nodes and leaves reachable from t (ordered in left-to-right depth-first search order). For Figure 2, the successor list of node $t_{(i)}$ is $\langle t_{(ii)}, t_{(v)}, t_{(xiii)}\rangle$, and the successor list of node $t_{(v)}$ is $\langle t_{(vii)}, t_{(viii)}\rangle$. The *rule node successor list* of a tree node is its successor list, with all non-rule nodes removed.

Define the *signature* of a parse tree node t as the result of taking its successor list, replacing the jth rule node with variable x_j, and replacing every non-rule node with its word label (observe that all non-rule nodes in the successor list are parse tree leaves, and therefore they have word labels). For Figure 2, the signature of node $t_{(i)}$ is $\langle x_1, x_2, x_3\rangle$, and the signature of node $t_{(v)}$ is $\langle\text{“am”}, x_1\rangle$.

Notice that the signature of every rule node in Figure 2 coincides with the source list of its GHKM rule. This is no accident, but rather a requirement. Define a *GHKM tree node* as a parse tree node whose children are all GHKM tree nodes, and whose GHKM rule's source list is equivalent to its signature (if the node is a rule node).

Given these definitions, we can proceed to define how a GHKM tree expresses a translation theory. Suppose we have a list $S = \langle s_1, ..., s_k\rangle$ of strings. Define the *substitution* of string list S into rule ele-

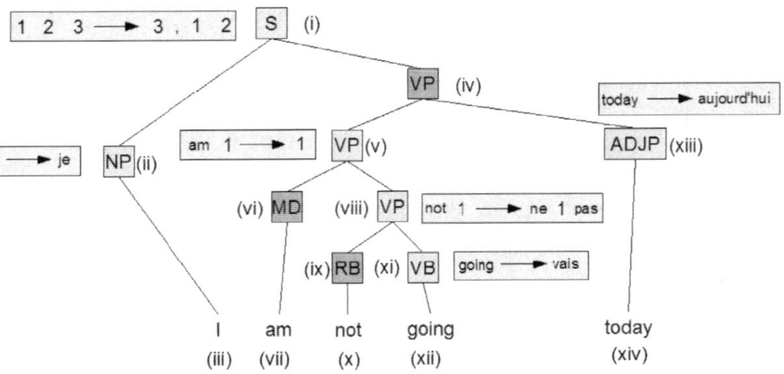

Figure 2: GHKM tree equivalent of example translation object. The light gray nodes are rule nodes of the GHKM tree.

ment r as:

$$r[S] = \begin{cases} s_i & \text{if } r \text{ is indexed var } x_i \\ r & \text{otherwise} \end{cases}$$

Notice that this operation always produces a string. Define the substitution of string list S into rule element list $R = \langle r_1, ..., r_j \rangle$ as:

$$R[S] = \text{concat}(r_1[S], r_2[S], ..., r_j[S])$$

where concat(s_1, ..., s_k) is the spaced concatenation of strings s_1, ..., s_k (e.g., concat("hi", "there") = "hi there"). This operation also produces a string.

Finally, define the *translation* of GHKM tree node t as:

$$\tau(t) \triangleq R_d[\langle \tau(t_1), ..., \tau(t_k) \rangle]$$

where $\langle t_1, ..., t_k \rangle$ is the rule node successor list of GHKM tree node t.

For Figure 2, the rule node successor list of node $t_{(viii)}$ is $\langle t_{(xi)} \rangle$. So:

$$\begin{aligned} \tau(t_{(viii)}) &= \langle \text{"ne"}, x_1, \text{"pas"} \rangle [\langle \tau(t_{(xi)}) \rangle] \\ &= \langle \text{"ne"}, x_1, \text{"pas"} \rangle [\langle \text{"vais"} \rangle] \\ &= \text{"ne vais pas"} \end{aligned}$$

A similar derivation gives us:

$$\tau(t_{(i)}) = \text{"aujourd'hui , je ne vais pas"}$$

In this way, every GHKM tree encodes a translation. Given this interpretation of a translation object, the task of machine translation becomes something concrete: label the nodes of a parsed source sentence with a good set of GHKM rules.

3 Probabilistic Approach

To achieve this "good" labeling of GHKM rules, we will define a probabilistic generative model P of GHKM trees, which will serve as our scoring function. We would like to depart from the standard probabilistic approach of most phrase-based translators, which employ very simple probability models to enable polynomial-time decoding. Instead, we will use an alternative probabilistic approach (an *assignment process*), which sacrifices polynomial-time guarantees in favor of a more flexible and powerful model. This sacrifice of guaranteed polynomial-time decoding does not entail the sacrifice of good running time in practice.

3.1 Assignment Processes

An assignment process builds a sequence of variable assignments (called an *assignment history*) by repeatedly iterating the following steps. First, it requests a variable name (say x_{22}) from a so-named *variable generator*. It takes this variable name and the assignment history built so far and compresses this information into a set of features (say $\{f_2, f_6, f_{80}\}$) using a feature function. These features are then mapped to a probability distribution by a function (say p_7) requested from a so-named *distribution generator*. The iteration ends by assigning to the chosen variable a value (say $v4$) drawn from this distribution. In the above running example, the iteration assigns v_4 to x_{22}, which was drawn according to distribution $p_7(\{f_2, f_6, f_{80}\})$. The process ends when the variable generator produces the reserved token $STOP$ instead of a variable name. At this

Var	Assignment	Distribution	Features
x_{23}	*true*	p_4	$\{\}$
x_7	"the"	p_{10}	$\{f_{12}, f_{102}\}$
x_8	blue	p_2	$\{f_5, f_{55}\}$
x_{51}	red	p_2	$\{f_5, f_{15}, f_{50}\}$
x_{19}	7.29	p_5	$\{f_2\}$
x_{30}	*false*	p_4	$\{f_2, f_5, f_7\}$
x_1	"man"	p_{10}	$\{f_1, f_2, f_{12}\}$
x_{102}	blue	p_2	$\{f_1, f_{55}, f_{56}\}$

Figure 3: A example assignment history generated by an assignment process.

point, the assignment history built so far (like the example in Figure 3) is returned.

Formally, define a *variable signature* as a pair $\Sigma = \langle X, V \rangle$, where X is a set of variable names and V is a set of values. Define a *variable assignment* of signature $\langle X, V \rangle$ as a pair $\langle x, v \rangle$, for variable $x \in X$ and value $v \in V$. Define an *assignment history* of signature Σ as an ordered list of variable assignments of Σ. The notation $H(\Sigma)$ represents the set of all assignment histories of signature Σ.

We define a *feature function* of signature $\Sigma = \langle X, V \rangle$ as a function f that maps every pair of set $X \times H(\Sigma)$ to a set of assignments (called *features*) of an auxiliary variable signature Σ_f.

We define an *assignment process* of signature $\Sigma = \langle X, V \rangle$ as a tuple $\langle f, P, g_x, g_p \rangle$, where: (i) f is a feature function of Σ, (ii) $P = \{p_1, ..., p_k\}$ is a finite set of k functions (called the *feature-conditional distributions*) that map each feature set in $range(f)$ to a probability distribution over V, (iii) g_x is a function (called the *variable generator*) mapping each assignment history in the set $H(\Sigma)$ to either a variable name in X or the reserved token $STOP$, and (iv) g_p is a function (called the *distribution generator*) mapping each assignment history in the set $H(\Sigma)$ to a positive integer between 1 and k.

An assignment process probabilistically generates an assignment history of signature Σ in the following way:

1. $h \leftarrow$ empty list
2. Do until $g_x(h) = STOP$:
   (a) Let $x = g_x(h)$ and let $j = g_p(h)$.
   (b) Draw value v probabilistically from distribution $p_j(f(x, h))$.
   (c) Append assignment $\langle x, v \rangle$ to history h.
3. Return history h.

3.2 Training

Given all components of an assignment process of signature Σ except for the set P of feature-conditional distributions, the training task is to learn P from a training corpus of assignment histories of signature Σ. This can be achieved straightforwardly by taking the feature vectors generated by a particular distribution and using them to discriminatively learn the distribution. For instance, say that our corpus consists of the single history given in Figure **??**. To learn distribution p_2, we simply take the three variable assignments produced by p_2 and feed these feature vectors to a generic discriminative learner. We prefer learners that produce distributions (rather than hard classifiers) as output, but this is not required.

3.3 Decoding

Notice that an assignment process of signature Σ induces a probability distribution over the set $H(\Sigma)$ of all assignment histories of Σ. The decoding question is: given a partial assignment history h, what is the most probable completion of the history, according to this induced distribution? We will use the natural naive search space for this question. The nodes of this search space are the assignment histories of $H(\Sigma)$. The children of the search node representing history h are those histories that can be generated from h in one iteration of the assignment process. The value of a search node is the probability of its assignment history (according to the assignment process). To decode, we begin at the node representing history h, and search for the highest-value descendant that represents a complete assignment history (i.e. an assignment history terminated by the $STOP$ token).

This is, potentially, a very large and intractible search space. However, if most assignment decisions can be made with relative confidence, then the great majority of search nodes have values which are inferior to those of the best solutions. The standard search technique of *depth-first branch-and-bound search* takes advantage of search spaces with this particular characteristic by first finding greedy good-quality solutions and using their values to optimally prune a significant portion of the search space.

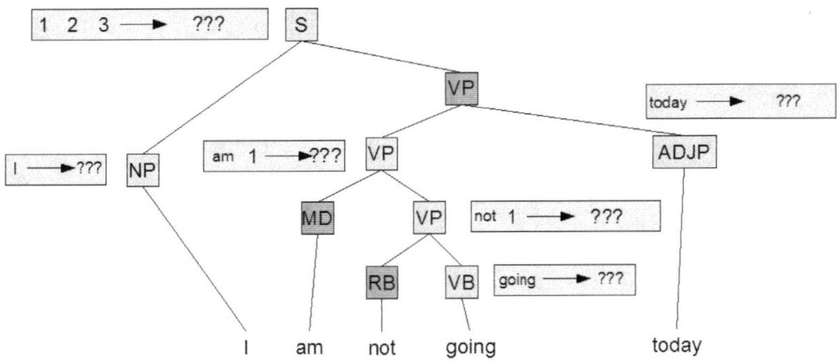

Figure 4: Partial GHKM tree, after rule nodes have been identified (light gray). Notice that once we identify the rule node, the rule left-hand sides are already determined.

Depth-first branch-and-bound search has the following advantage: it finds a good (suboptimal) solution in linear time and continually improves on this solution until it finds the optimal. Thus it can be run either as an optimal decoder or as a heuristic decoder, since we can interrupt its execution at any time to get the best solution found so far. Additionally, it takes only linear space to run.

4 Generative Model

We now return to where we left off at the end of Section 2, and devise an assignment process that produces a GHKM tree from an unlabeled parse tree. This will give us a quality measure that we can use to produce a "good" labeling of a given parse tree with GHKM rules (i.e., the probability of such a labeling according to the assignment process).

The simplest assignment process would have a variable for each node of the parse tree, and these variables would all be assigned by the same feature-conditional distribution over the space of all possible GHKM rules. The problem with such a formulation is that such a distribution would be inachievably difficult to learn. We want an assignment process in which all variables can take only a very small number of possible values, because it will be much easier to learn distributions over such variables. This means we need to break down the process of constructing a GHKM rule into simpler steps.

Our assignment process will begin by sequentially assigning a set of boolean variables (which we will call *rule node indicator variables*), one for each node in the parse tree. For parse tree node t, we denote its corresponding rule node indicator variable x_t^r. Variable x_t^r is assigned $true$ iff the parse tree node t will be a rule node in the GHKM tree.

In Figure 3.3, we show a partial GHKM tree after these assignments are made. The key thing to observe is that, after this sequence of boolean decisions, the LHS of every rule in the tree is already determined! To complete the tree, all we need to do is to fill in their right-hand sides.

Again, we could create variables to do this directly, i.e. have a variable for each rule whose domain is the space of possible right-hand sides for its established left-hand sides. But this is still a wide-open decision, so we will break it down further.

For each rule, we will begin by choosing the *template* of its RHS, which is a RHS in which all sequences of variables are replaced with an empty slot into which variables can later be placed. For instance, the template of $\langle$"ne"$, x_1,$ "pas"$\rangle$ is $\langle$"ne"$, X,$ "pas"$\rangle$ and the template of $\langle x_3,$ ","$, x_1, x_2\rangle$ is $\langle X,$ ","$, X\rangle$, where X represents the empty slots.

Once the template is chosen, it simply needs to be filled with the variables from the LHS. To do so, we process the LHS variables, one by one. By default, they are placed to the right of the previously placed variable (the first variable is placed in the first slot). We repeatedly offer the option to push the variable to the right until the option is declined or it is no longer possible to push it further right. If the variable was not pushed right at all, we repeatedly offer the option to push the variable to the left until the option is declined or it is no longer possible to push it further left. Figure 4 shows this generative story in action for the rule RHS $\langle x_3,$ ","$, x_1, x_2\rangle$.

These are all of the decisions we need to make

Decision to make	Decision	RHS so far
RHS template?	X , X	X , X
default placement of var 1		1 , X
push var 1 right?	yes	X , 1
default placement of var 2		X , 1 2
push var 2 left?	no	X , 1 2
default placement of var 3		X , 1 2 3
push var 3 left?	yes	X , 1 3 2
push var 3 left?	yes	X , 3 1 2
push var 3 left?	yes	3 , 1 2

Figure 5: Trace of the generative story for the right-hand side of a GHKM rule.

in order to label a parse tree with GHKM rules. Notice that, aside from the template decisions, all of the decisions are binary (i.e. feasible to learn discriminatively). Even the template decisions are not terribly large-domain, if we maintain a separate feature-conditional distribution for each LHS template. For instance, if the LHS template is $\langle$"not", $X\rangle$, then RHS template $\langle$"ne", X, "pas"$\rangle$ and a few other select candidates should bear most of the probability mass.

5 Evaluation

In this section, we evaluate a preliminary English-to-German translation system based on the ideas outlined in this paper. We first present a quantiative comparison with the phrase-based approach, using the BLEU metric; then we discuss two concrete translation examples as a preliminary qualitative evaluation. Finally, we present a detailed manual error analysis.

Our data was a subset of the Europarl corpus consisting of sentences of lengths ranging from 8 to 17 words. Our training corpus contained 50000 sentences and our test corpus contained 300 sentences. We also had a small number of reserved sentences for development. The English sentences were parsed using the Bikel parser (Bikel, 2004), and the sentences were aligned with GIZA++ (Och and Ney, 2000). We used the WEKA machine learning package (Witten and Frank, 2005) to train the distributions (specifically, we used model trees).

For comparison, we also trained and evaluated Pharaoh (Koehn, 2005) on this limited corpus, using Pharaoh's default parameters. Pharaoh achieved a BLEU score of 11.17 on the test set, whereas our system achieved a BLEU score of 11.52. What is notable here is not the scores themselves (low due to the size of the training corpus). However our system managed to perform comparably with Pharaoh in a very early stage of its development, with rudimentary features and without the benefit of an n-gram language model.

Let's take a closer look at the sentences produced by our system, to gain some insight as to its current strengths and weaknesses.

Starting with the English sentence (note that all data is lowercase):

i agree with the spirit of those amendments .

Our system produces:

ich	stimme	die	geist	dieser
I	vote	the.FEM	spirit.MASC	these

änderungsanträge zu .
change-proposals to .

The GHKM tree is depicted in Figure 5. The key feature of this translation is how the English phrase "agree with" is translated as the German "stimme ... zu" construction. Such a feat is difficult to produce consistently with a purely phrase-based system, as phrases of arbitrary length can be placed between the words "stimme" and "zu", as we can see happening in this particular example. By contrast, Pharaoh opts for the following (somewhat less desirable) translation:

ich	stimme	mit	dem	geist	dieser
I	vote	with	the.MASC	spirit.MASC	these

änderungsanträge .
change-proposals .

A weakness in our system is also evident here. The German noun "Geist" is masculine, thus our system uses the wrong article (a problem that Pharaoh, with its embedded n-gram language model, does not encounter).

In general, it seems that our system is superior to Pharaoh at figuring out the proper way to arrange the words of the output sentence, and inferior to Pharaoh at finding what the actual translation of those words should be.

Consider the English sentence:

we shall submit a proposal along these lines before the end of this year .

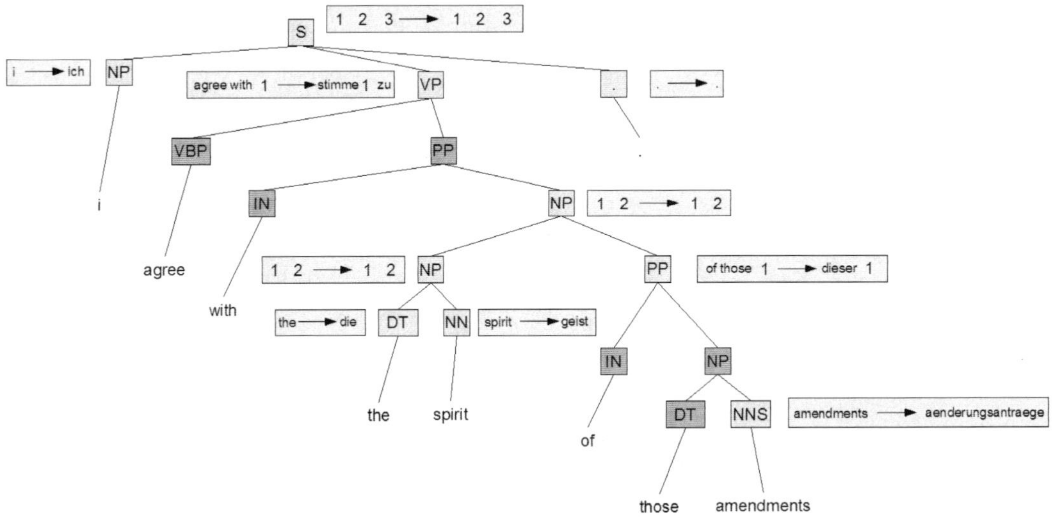

Figure 6: GHKM tree output for the first test sentence.

Here we have an example of a double verb: "shall submit." In German, the second verb should go at the end of the sentence, and this is achieved by our system (translating "shall" as "werden", and "submit" as "vorlegen").

wir	werden	eine	vorschlag	in	dieser
we	will	a.FEM	proposal.MASC	in	these

haushaltslinien	vor	die	ende	
budget-lines	before	the.FEM	end.NEUT	

dieser	jahres	vorlegen	.
this.FEM	year.NEUT	submit	.

Pharaoh does not manage this (translating "submit" as "unterbreiten" and placing it mid-sentence).

werden	wir	unterbreiten	eine	vorschlag	in	dieser
will	we	submit	a	proposal	in	these

haushaltslinien	vor	ende	dieser	jahr	.
budget-lines	before	end	this.FEM	year.NEUT	.

It is worth noting that while our system gets the word order of the output system right, it makes several agreement mistakes and (like Pharaoh) doesn't get the translation of "along these lines" right.

To have a more systematic basis for comparison, we did a manual error analysis for 100 sentences from the test set. A native speaker of German (in the present pilot study one of the authors) determined the editing steps required to transform the system output into an acceptable translation – both in terms of fluency and adequacy of translation. In order to avoid a bias for our system, we randomized the presentation of output from one of the two systems.

We defined the following basic types of edits, with further subdistinctions depending on the word type: ADD, DELETE, CHANGE and MOVE. A special type TRANSLATE-untranslated was assumed for untranslated source words in the output. For the CHANGE, more fine-grained distinctions were made.[2] A single MOVE operation was assumed to displace an entire phrase; the distance of the movement in terms of the number of words was calculated. The table in Figure 7 shows the edits required for correcting the output of the two systems on 100 sentences.

We again observe that our system, which is at an early stage of development and contrary to the Pharaoh system does not include an n-gram language model trained on a large corpus, already yields promising results. The higher proportion of CHANGE operations, in particular CHANGE-inflection and CHANGE-function-word edits is presumably a direct consequence of providing a language model or not. An interesting observation is that our system currently tends to overtranslate, i.e., redundantly produce several translations for a word, which leads to the need of DELETE operations. The Pharaoh system had a tendency to undertranslate, often with crucial words missing.

[2] CHANGE-inflection: keeping the lemma and category the same, e.g. *taken* → *takes*; CHANGE-part-of-speech: choosing a different derivational form, e.g., *judged* → *judgement*; CHANGE-function-word: e.g., *in* → *from*; CHANGE-content-word: e.g., *opinion* → *consensus*.

	TL-MT	Pharaoh
ADD-function-word	40	49
ADD-content-word	17	35
ADD-punctuation	12	13
ADD (total)	69	97
DELETE-function-word	37	18
DELETE-content-word	22	10
DELETE-punctuation	13	15
DELETE-untranslated	2	1
DELETE (total)	74	44
CHANGE-content-word	24	19
CHANGE-function-word	44	26
CHANGE-inflection	101	80
CHANGE-part-of-speech	4	10
CHANGE (total)	173	135
TRANSLATE-untranslated	34	1
MOVE (distance)		
1	16	17
2	12	16
3	13	11
4	3	6
≥ 5	7	5
MOVE (total)	51	55
TOTAL # EDITS	401	332
edits-per-word ratio	0.342	0.295

Figure 7: Edits required for an acceptable system output, based on 100 test sentences.

6 Discussion

In describing this pilot project, we have attempted to give a "big picture" view of the essential ideas behind our system. To avoid obscuring the presentation, we have avoided many of the implementation details, in particular our choice of features. There are exactly four types of decisions that we need to train: (1) whether a parse tree node should be a rule node, (2) the RHS template of a rule, (3) whether a rule variable should be pushed left, and (4) whether a rule variable should be pushed right. For each of these decisions, there are a number of possible features that suggest themselves. For instance, recall that in German, typically the second verb of a double verb (such as "shall submit" or "can do") gets placed at the end of the sentence or clause. So when the system is considering whether to push a rule's noun phrase to the left, past an existing verb, it would be useful for it to consider (as a feature) whether that verb is the first or second verb of its clause.

This system was designed to be very flexible with the kind of information that it can exploit as features. Essentially any aspect of the parse tree, or of previous decisions that have been taken by the assignment process, can be used. Furthermore, we can mark-up the parse tree with any auxiliary information that might be beneficial, like noun gender or verb cases. The current implementation has hardly begun to explore these possibilities, containing only features pertaining to aspects of the parse tree.

Even in these early stages of development, the system shows promise in using syntactic information flexibly and effectively for machine translation. We hope to develop the system into a competitive alternative to phrase-based approaches.

References

Daniel M. Bikel. 2004. Intricacies of Collins' parsing model. *Computational Linguistics*, 30(4):479–511.

David Chiang. 2005. A hierarchical phrase-based model for statistical machine translation. In *Proceedings of ACL*, pages 263–270.

Michel Galley, Mark Hopkins, Kevin Knight, and Daniel Marcu. 2003. What's in a translation rule? In *Proc. NAACL*.

Philipp Koehn, Franz Josef Och, and Daniel Marcu. 2003. Statistical phrase-based translation. In *Proceedings of the Human Language Technology Conference 2003 (HLT-NAACL 2003)*, Edmonton, Canada.

Philipp Koehn. 2005. Pharaoh: a beam search decoder for phrase-based statistical machine translation models. In *Proceedings of the Sixth Conference of the Association for Machine Translation in the Americas*, pages 115–124.

F. J. Och and H. Ney. 2000. Improved statistical alignment models. In *Proc. ACL*, pages 440–447, Hongkong, China, October.

Franz Josef Och and Hermann Ney. 2003. A systematic comparison of various statistical alignment models. *Computational Linguistics*, 29(1):19–51.

F. J. Och, D. Gildea, S. Khudanpur, A. Sarkar, K. Yamada, A. Fraser, S. Kumar, L. Shen, D. Smith, K. Eng, Viren Jain, Z.Jin, and D. Radev. 2003. Syntax for statistical machine translation. Technical report, Center for Language and Speech Processing, Johns Hopkins University, Baltimore. Summer Workshop Final Report.

Ian H. Witten and Eibe Frank. 2005. *Data Mining: Practical machine learning tools and techniques*. Morgan Kaufmann.

Dekai Wu. 1997. Stochastic inversion transduction grammars and bilingual parsing of parallel corpora. *Computational Linguistics*, 23(3):377–403.

Kenji Yamada and Kevin Knight. 2001. A syntax-based statistical translation model. In *Proceedings of the 39th Annual Meeting of the Association for Computational Linguistics*, pages 523–530.

Discriminative word alignment by learning the alignment structure and syntactic divergence between a language pair

Sriram Venkatapathy[1]
Language Technologies Research Centre, IIIT -Hyderabad
Hyderabad - 500019, India.
sriram@research.iiit.ac.in

Aravind K. Joshi
Department of Computer and Information Science and Institute for Research in Cognitive Science,
University of Pennsylvania, PA, USA.
joshi@linc.cis.upenn.edu

Abstract

Discriminative approaches for word alignment have gained popularity in recent years because of the flexibility that they offer for using a large variety of features and combining information from various sources. But, the models proposed in the past have not been able to make much use of features that capture the likelihood of an alignment structure (the set of alignment links) and the syntactic divergence between sentences in the parallel text. This is primarily because of the limitation of their search techniques. In this paper, we propose a generic discriminative re-ranking approach for word alignment which allows us to make use of structural features effectively. These features are particularly useful for language pairs with high structural divergence (like English-Hindi, English-Japanese). We have shown that by using the structural features, we have obtained a decrease of 2.3% in the absolute value of alignment error rate (AER). When we add the cooccurence probabilities obtained from IBM model-4 to our features, we achieved the best AER (50.50) for the English-Hindi parallel corpus.

1 Introduction

In this paper, we propose a discriminative reranking approach for word alignment which allows us to make use of structural features effectively. The alignment algorithm first generates a list of k-best alignments using local features. Then it re-ranks this list of k-best alignments using global features which consider the entire alignment structure (set of alignment links) and the syntactic divergence that exists between the sentence pair. Use of structural information associated with the alignment can be particularly helpful for language pairs for which a large amount of unsupervised data is not available to measure accurately the word cooccurence values but which do have a small set of supervised data to learn the structure and divergence across the language pair. We have tested our model on the English-Hindi language pair. Here is an example of an alignment between English-Hindi which shows the complexity of the alignment task for this language pair.

Figure 1: An example of an alignment between an English and a Hindi sentence

To learn the weights associated with the parameters used in our model, we have used a learning framework called MIRA (The Margin Infused Relaxed Algorithm) (McDonald et al., 2005; Crammer and Singer, 2003). This is an online learning algorithm which looks at one sentence pair at a time and compares the k-best predictions of the alignment algorithm with the gold alignment to update the parameter weights appropriately.

In the past, popular approaches for doing word alignment have largely been generative (Och and Ney, 2003; Vogel et al., 1996). In the past couple of years, the discriminative models for doing word alignment have gained popularity because of

[1] 1Part of the work was done at Institute for Research in Cognitive Science (IRCS), University of Pennsylvania, Philadelphia, PA 19104, USA, when he was visiting IRCS as a Visiting Scholar, February to December, 2006.

Proceedings of SSST, NAACL-HLT 2007 / AMTA Workshop on Syntax and Structure in Statistical Translation, pages 49–56,
Rochester, New York, April 2007.

the flexibility they offer in using a large variety of features and in combining information from various sources.

(Taskar et al., 2005) cast the problem of alignment as a maximum weight bipartite matching problem, where nodes correspond to the words in the two sentences. The link between a pair of words, (e_p,h_q) is associated with a score (score(e_p,h_q)) reflecting the desirability of the existence of the link. The matching problem is solved by formulating it as a linear programming problem. The parameter estimation is done within the framework of large margin estimation by reducing the problem to a quadratic program (QP). The main limitation of this work is that the features considered are local to the alignment links joining pairs of words. The score of an alignment is the sum of scores of individual alignment links measured independently i.e., it is assumed that there is no dependence between the alignment links. (Lacoste-Julien et al., 2006) extend the above approach to include features for fertility and first-order correlation between alignment links of consecutive words in the source sentence. They solve this by formulating the problem as a quadratic assignment problem (QAP). But, even this algorithm cannot include more general features over the entire alignment. In contrast to the above two approaches, our approach does not impose any constraints on the feature space except for fertility ($\leq$1) of words in the source language. In our approach, we model the one-to-one and many-to-one links between the source sentence and target sentence. The many-to-many alignment links are inferred in the post-processing stage using simple generic rules. Another positive aspect of our approach is the application of MIRA. It, being an online approach, converges fast and still retains the generalizing capability of the large margin approach.

(Moore, 2005) has proposed an approach which does not impose any restrictions on the form of model features. But, the search technique has certain heuristic procedures dependent on the types of features used. For example, there is little variation in the alignment search between the LLR (Log-likelihood ratio) based model and the CLP (Conditional-Link Probability) based model. LLR and CLP are the word association statistics used in Moore's work (Moore, 2005). In contrast to the above approach, our search technique is more general. It achieves this by breaking the search into two steps, first by using local features to get the k-best alignments and then by using structural features to re-rank the list. Also, by using all the k-best alignments for updating the parameters through MIRA, it is possible to model the entire inference algorithm but in Moore's work, only the best alignment is used to update the weights of parameters. (Fraser and Marcu, 2006) have proposed an algorithm for doing word alignment which applies a discriminative step at every iteration of the traditional Expectation-Maximization algorithm used in IBM models. This model still relies on the generative story and achieves only a limited freedom in choosing the features. (Blunsom and Cohn, 2006) do word alignment by combining features using conditional random fields. Even though their approach allows one to include overlapping features while training a discriminative model, it still does not allow us to use features that capture information of the entire alignment structure.

In Section 2, we describe the alignment search in detail. Section 3 describes the features that we have considered in our paper. Section 4 talks about the Parameter optimization. In Section 5, we present the results of our experiments. Section 6 contains the conclusion and our proposed future work.

2 Alignment Search

The goal of the word alignment algorithm is to link words in the source language with words in the target language to get the alignments structure. The best alignment structure between a source sentence and a target sentence can be predicted by considering three kinds of information, (1) Properties of alignment links taken independently, (2) Properties of the entire alignment structure taken as a unit, and (3) The syntactic divergence between the source sentence and the target sentence, given the alignment structure. Using the set of alignment links, the syntactic structure of the source sentence is first projected onto the target language to observe the divergence.

Let e_p and h_q denote the source and target words respectively. Let n be the number of words in source sentence and m be the number of words in target sentence. Let S be the source sentence and T be the target sentence.

2.1 Populate the Beam

The task in this step is to obtain the k-best candidate alignment structures using the local features. The local features mainly contain the cooccurence information between a source and a target word and are independent of other alignment links in the sentence pair. Let the local feature vector be denoted as $f_L(e_p, h_q)$. The score of a particular alignment link is computed by taking a dot product of the weight vector W with the local feature vector of the alignment link. More formally, the local score of an alignment link is

$$score_L(e_p, h_q) = W.f_L(e_p, h_q)$$

The total score of an alignment structure is computed by adding the scores of individual alignment links present in the alignment. Hence, the score of an alignment structure $\bar{a}$ is,

$$score_{La}(\bar{a}, S, T) = \sum_{(e_p, h_q) \in \bar{a}} score_L(e_p, h_q)$$

We have proposed a dynamic programming algorithm of worst case complexity $O(nm^2 + nk^2)$ to compute the k-best alignments. First, the local score of each source word with every target word is computed and stored in local beams associated with the source words. The local beams corresponding to all the source words are sorted and the top-k alignment links in each beam are retained. This operation has the worst-case complexity of $O(nm^2)$.

Now, the goal is to get the k-best alignments in the global beam. The global beam initially contains no alignments. The k best alignment links of the first source word e_0 are added to the global beam. To add the alignment links of the next source word to the global beam, the k^2 (if $k < m$) combinations of the alignments in the global beam and alignments links in the local beam are taken and the best k are retained in the global beam. If $k > m$, then the total combinations taken are mk. This is repeated till the entries in all the local beams are considered, the overall worst case complexity being $O(nk^2)$ (or $O(nmk)$ if $k > m$).

2.2 Reorder the beam

We now have the k-best alignments using the local features from the last step. We then use global features to reorder the beam. The global features look at the properties of the entire alignment structure instead of the alignment links locally.

Let the global feature vector be represented as $f_G(\bar{a})$. The global score is defined as the dot product of the weight vector and the global feature vector.

$$score_G(\bar{a}) = W.f_G(\bar{a})$$

The overall score is calculated by adding the local score and the global score.

$$score(\bar{a}) = score_{La}(\bar{a}) + score_G(\bar{a})$$

The beam is now sorted based on the overall scores of each alignment. The alignment at the top of the beam is the best possible alignment between source sentence and the target sentence.

2.3 Post-processing

The previous two steps produce alignment structures which contain one-to-one and many-to-one links. In this step, the goal is to extend the best alignment structure obtained in the previous step to include the other alignments links of one-to-many and many-to-many types.

The majority of the links between the source sentence and the target sentence are one-to-one. Some of the cases where this is not true are the instances of idioms, alignment of verb groups where auxiliaries do not correspond to each other, the alignment of case-markers etc. Except for the cases of idioms in target language, most of the many-to-many links between a source and target sentences can be inferred from the instances of one-to-one and many-to-one links using three language language specific rules (Hindi in our case) to handle the above cases. Figure 1, Figure 2 and Figure 3 depict the three such cases where many-to-many alignments can be inferred. The alignments present at the left are those which can be predicted by our alignment model. The alignments on the right side are those which can be inferred in the post-processing stage.

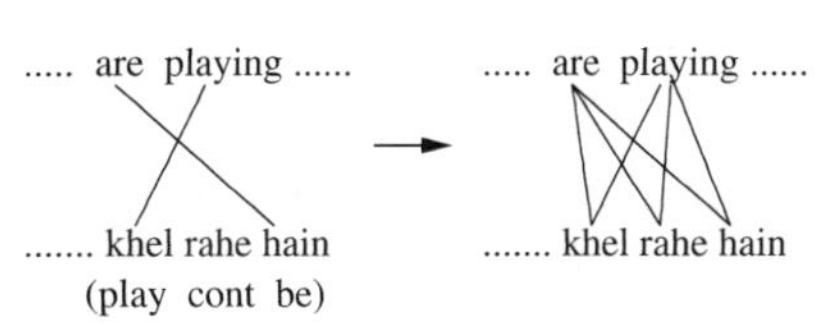

Figure 2: Inferring the many-to-many alignments of verb and auxiliaries

After applying the language specific rules, the dependency structure of the source sentence is traversed to ensure the consistency of the alignment

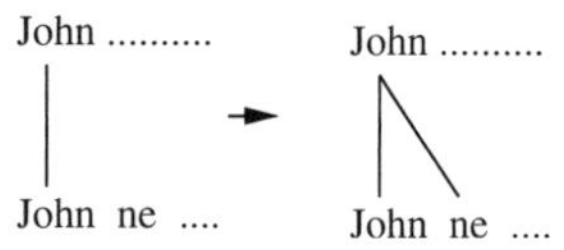

Figure 3: Inferring the one-to-many alignment to case-markers in Hindi

Figure 4: Inferring many-to-many alignment for source idioms

structure. If there is a dependency link between two source words e_o and e_p, where e_o is the head and e_p is the modifier and if e_o and e_p are linked to one or more common target word(s), it is logical to imagine that the alignment should be extended such that both e_o and e_p are linked to the same set of target words. For example, in Figure 4, new alignment link is first formed between 'kick' and 'gayA' using the language specific rule, and as 'kick' and 'bucket' are both linked to 'mara', 'bucket' is also now linked to 'gayA'. Similarity, 'the' is linked to both 'mara' and 'gayA'. Hence, the rules are applied by traversing through the dependency tree associated with the source sentence words in depth-first order. The dependency parser used by us was developed by (Shen, 2006). The following summarizes this step,

- Let w be the next word considered in the dependency tree, let pw be the parent of w.
  - If w and pw are linked to one or more common word(s) in target language, align w to all target words which are aligned to pw.
  - Else, Use the target-specific rules (if they match) to extend the alignments of w.
- Recursively consider all the children of w

3 Parameters

As the number of training examples is small, we chose to use features (both local and structural) which are generic. Some of the features which we used in this experiment are as follows:

3.1 Local features (F_L)

The local features which we consider are mainly co-occurrence features. These features estimate the likelihood of a source word aligning to a target word based on the co-occurrence information obtained from a large sentence aligned corpora[1].

3.1.1 DiceWords

Dice Coefficient of the source word and the target word (Taskar et al., 2005).

$$DCoeff(e_p, h_q) = \frac{2 * Count(e_p, h_q)}{Count(e_p) + Count(h_q)}$$

where $Count(e_p, h_q)$ is the number of times the word h_q was present in the translation of sentences containing the word e_p in the parallel corpus.

3.1.2 DiceRoots

Dice Coefficient of the lemmatized forms of the source and target words. It is important to consider this feature for language pairs which do not have a large unsupervised sentence aligned corpora. Co-occurrence information can be learnt better after we lemmatize the words.

3.1.3 Dict

This feature tests whether there exists a dictionary entry from the source word e_p to the target word h_q. For English-Hindi, we used a medium-coverage dictionary (25000 words) available from IIIT - Hyderabad, India [2].

3.1.4 Null_POS

These parameters measures the likelihood of a source word with a particular part of speech tag[3] to be aligned to no word (Null) on the target language side. This feature was extremely useful because it models the cooccurence information of words with nulls which is not captured by the features *DiceWords* and *DiceRoots*. Here are some of the features of this type with extreme estimated parameter weights.

3.2 Lemmatized word pairs

The word pairs themselves are a good indicator of whether an alignment link exists between the word pair or not. Also, taking word-pairs as feature helps in the alignment of some of the most common words in both the languages. A variation of this feature was used by (Moore, 2005) in his paper.

[1] 50K sentence pairs originally collected as part of TIDES MT project and later refined at IIIT-Hyderabad, India.

[2] http://ltrc.iiit.ac.in/onlineServices/Dictionaries/Dict_Frame.html

[3] We have limited the number of POS tags by considering only the first alphabets of Penn Tags as our POS tag categories

Param.	*weight*		*Param.*	*weight*
Null_‘	0.2737		null_C	-0.7030
Null_U	0.1969		null_D	-0.6914
Null_L	0.1814		null_V	-0.6360
Null_.	0.0383		null_N	-0.5600
Null_:	0.0055		null_I	-0.4839

Table 1: Top Five Features each with Maximum and Minimum weights

Other parameters like the relative distance between the source word e_p and the target word h_q, $RelDist(e_p, h_q) = abs(j/|e| - k/|h|)$, which are mentioned as important features in the previous literature, did not perform well for the English-Hindi language pair. This is because of the predominant word-order variation between the sentences of English and Hindi (Refer Figure 1).

3.3 Structural Features (F_G)

The global features are used to model the properties of the entire alignment structure taken as a unit, between the source and the target sentence. In doing so, we have attempted to exploit the syntactic information available on both the source and the target sides of the corpus. The syntactic information on the target side is obtained by projecting the syntactic information of the source using the alignment links. Some of the features which we have used in our work are in the following subsection.

3.3.1 Overlap

This feature considers the instances in a sentence pair where a source word links to a target word which is a participant in more than one alignment links (has a fertility greater than one). This feature is used to encourage the source words to be linked to different words in the target language. For example, we would prefer the alignment in Figure 6 when compared to the alignment in Figure 5 even before looking at the actual words. This parameter captures such prior information about the alignment structure.

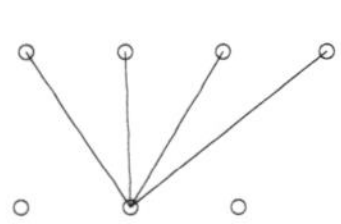

Figure 5: Alignment where many source words are linked to one target word

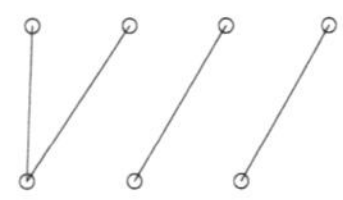

Figure 6: Alignment where the source words are aligned to many different target words

Formally, it is defined as

$$Overlap(\bar{a}) = \frac{\sum_{h_q \in T, Fert(h_q)>1} Fert^2(h_q)}{\sum_{h \in T} Fert(h)}$$

where T is the Hindi sentence. $\sum Fert^2(h_q)$ is measured in the numerator so that a more uniform distribution of target word fertilities be favored in comparison to others. The weight of *overlap* as estimated by our model is -6.1306 which indicates the alignments having a low overlap value are preferred.

3.3.2 NullPercent

This feature measures the percentage of words in target language sentence which are not aligned to any word in the source language sentence. It is defined as

$$NullPercent = \frac{|h_q|_{h_q \in T, Fertility(h_q)==0}}{|h|_{h \in T}}$$

3.3.3 Direction_DepPair

The following feature attempts to capture the first order interdependence between the alignment links of pairs of source sentence words which are connected by dependency relations. One way in which such an interdependence can be measured is by noting the order of the target sentence words linked to the child and parent of a source sentence dependency relation. Figures 7, 8 and 9 depict the various possibilities. The words in the source sentence are represented using their part-of-speech tags. These part-of-speech tags are also projected onto the target words. In the figures p is the parent and c is the part-of-speech of the child.

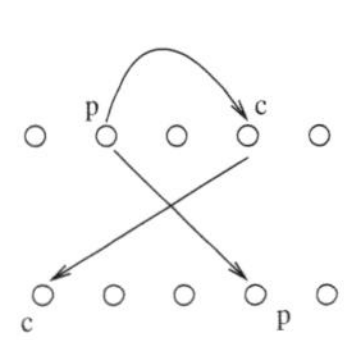

Figure 7: Target word linked to a child precedes the target word linked to a parent

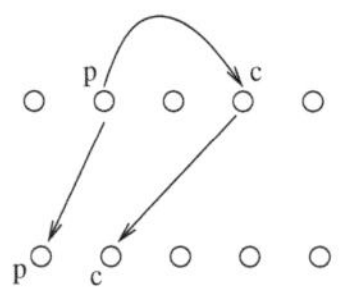

Figure 8: Target word linked to a parent precedes the target word linked to a child

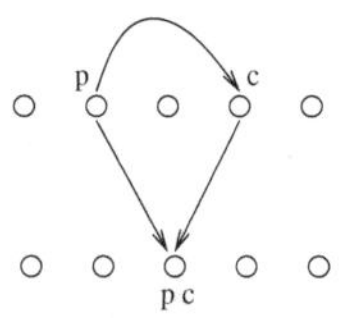

Figure 9: Parent and the child are both linked to same target word

The situation in Figure 9 is an indicator that the parent and child dependency pair might be part or whole of a multi-word expression on the source side. This feature thus captures the divergence between the source sentence dependency structure and the target language dependency structure (induced by taking the alignment as a constraint). Hence, in the test data, the alignments which do not express this divergence between the dependency trees are penalized. For example, the alignment in Figure 10 will be heavily penalized by the model during re-ranking step primarily for two reasons, 1) The word aligned to the preposition 'of' does not precede the word aligned to the noun 'king' and 2) The word aligned to the preposition 'to' does not succeed the word aligned to the noun 'king'.

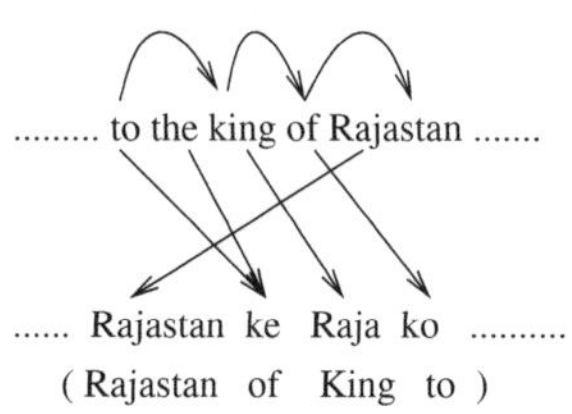

Figure 10: A simple example of an alignment that would be penalized by the feature Direction_DepPair

3.3.4 Direction_Bigram

This feature is a variation of the previous feature. In the previous feature, the dependency pair on the source side was projected to the target side to observe the divergence of the dependency pair. In this feature, we take a bigram instead of a dependency pair and observe its order in the target side. This feature is equivalent to the first-order features used in the related work.

There are three possibilities here, (1) The words of the bigram maintain their order when projected onto the target words, (2) The words of the bigram are reversed when projected, (3) Both the words are linked to the same word of the target sentence.

4 Online large margin training

For parameter optimization, we have used an online large margin algorithm called MIRA (McDonald et al., 2005) (Crammer and Singer, 2003). We will briefly describe the training algorithm that we have used. Our training set is a set of English-Hindi word aligned parallel corpus. Let the number of sentence pairs in the training data be t. We have $\{S_r, T_r, \hat{a}_r\}$ for training where $r \leq t$ is the index number of the sentence pair $\{S_r, T_r\}$ in the training set and $\hat{a}_r$ is the gold alignment for the pair $\{S_r, T_r\}$. Let W be the weight vector which has to be learnt, W_i be the weight vector after the end of ith update. To avoid over-fitting, W is obtained by averaging over all the weight vectors W_i.

A generic large margin algorithm is defined follows for the training instances $\{S_r, T_r, \hat{a}_r\}$,

Initialize W_0, W, i
for $p = 1$ to *Iterations* **do**
  for $r = 1$ to t **do**
    Get K-Best predictions $\alpha_r = \{a_1, a_2 ... a_k\}$ for the training example $(S_r, T_r, \hat{a_r})$ using the current model W^i and applying step 1 and 2 of section 4. Compute W^{i+1} by updating W^i based on $(S_r, T_r, \hat{a_r}, \alpha_r)$.
    i = i + 1
    $W = W + W^{i+1}$
    $W = \frac{W}{Iterations * m}$
  end for
end for

The goal of MIRA is to minimize the change in W^i such that the score of the gold alignment $\hat{a}$ exceeds the score of each of the predictions in α by a margin which is equal to the number of mistakes in the predictions when compared to the gold alignment. One could choose a different loss function which assigns greater penalty for certain kinds of mistakes when compared to others.

Step 4 (*Get K-Best predictions*) in the algorithm mentioned above can be substituted by the following optimization problem,

$$\begin{aligned} &\text{minimize } \|(W^{i+1} - W^{i})\| \\ &\text{s.t. } \forall k, score(\hat{a}_r, S_r, T_r) - score(a_{q,k}, S_r, T_r) \\ &\qquad >= Mistakes(a_k, \hat{a}_r, S_r, T_r) \end{aligned}$$

For optimization of the parameters, ideally, we need to consider all the possible predictions and assign margin constraints based on every prediction. But, here the number of such classes is exponential and therefore we restrict ourselves to the $k - best$ predictions.

We estimate the parameters in two steps. In the first step, we estimate only the weights of the local parameters. After that, we keep the weights of local parameters constant and then estimate the weights of global parameters. It is important to decouple the parameter estimation to two steps. We also experimented estimating the parameters in one stage but as expected, it had an adverse impact on the parameter weights of local features which resulted in generation of poor k-best list after the first step while testing.

5 Experiments and Results

5.1 Data

We have used English-Hindi unsupervised data of 50000 sentence pairs[4]. This data was used to obtain the cooccurence statistics such as *DiceWords* and *DiceRoots* which we used in our model. This data was also used to obtain the predictions of GIZA++ (Implements the IBM models and the HMM model). We take the alignments of GIZA++ as baseline and evaluate our model for the English-Hindi language pair.

The supervised training data which is used to estimate the parameters consists of 4252 sentence pairs. The development data consists of 100 sentence pairs and the test data consists of 100 sentence pairs. This supervised data was obtained from IRCS, University of Pennsylvania. For training our model, we need to convert the many-to-many alignments in the corpus to one-to-one or may-to-one alignments. This is done by applying inverse operations of those performed during the post-processing step (section 2.3).

[4]Originally collected as part of TIDES MT project and later refined at IIIT-Hyderabad, India.

5.2 Experiments

We first obtain the predictions of GIZA++ to obtain the baseline accuracies. GIZA++ was run in four different modes 1) English to Hindi, 2) Hindi to English, 3) English to Hindi where the words in both the languages are lemmatized and 4) Hindi to English where the words are lemmatized. We then take the intersections of the predictions run from both the directions (English to Hindi and Hindi to English). Table 2 contains the results of experiments with GIZA++. As the recall of the alignment links of the intersection is very low for this dataset, further refinements of the alignments as suggested by (Och and Ney, 2003) were not performed.

Mode	*Prec.*	*Rec.*	*F-meas.*	*AER*
Normal: Eng-Hin	47.57	40.87	43.96	**56.04**
Normal: Hin-Eng	47.97	38.50	42.72	57.28
Normal: Inter.	88.71	27.52	42.01	57.99
Lemma.: Eng-Hin	53.60	44.58	48.67	**51.33**
Lemma.: Hin-Eng	53.83	42.68	47.61	52.39
Lemma.: Inter.	86.14	32.80	47.51	52.49

Table 2: GIZA++ Results

In Table 3, we observe that the best result (**51.33**) is obtained when GIZA++ is run after lemmatizing the words on the both sides of the unsupervised corpus. The best results obtained without lemmatizing is **56.04** when GIZA++ is run from English to Hindi.

The table 4 summarizes the results when we used only the local features in our model.

Features	*Prec.*	*Rec.*	*F-meas.*	*AER*
DiceRoots + *DiceWords*	41.49	38.71	40.05	**59.95**
+ *Null_POS*	42.82	38.29	40.43	59.57
+ *Dict.*	43.94	39.30	41.49	58.51
+ *Word pairs*	46.27	41.07	43.52	56.48

Table 3: Results using local features

We now add the global features. While estimating the parameter weights associated with the global features, we keep the weights of local features constant. We choose the appropriate beam size as 50 after testing with several values on the development set. We observed that the beam sizes (between 10 and 100) did not affect the alignment error rates very much.

Features	*Prec.*	*Rec.*	*F-meas.*	*AER*
Local feats.	46.27	41.07	43.52	56.48
Local feats. + Overlap	48.17	42.76	45.30	54.70
Local feats. + Direc._Deppair	47.93	42.55	45.08	54.92
Local feats. + Direc._Bigram	48.31	42.89	45.44	54.56
Local feats. + All Global feats.	48.81	43.31	45.90	**54.10**

Table 4: Results after adding global features

We see that by adding global features, we obtained an absolute increase of about 2.3 AER suggesting the usefulness of structural features which we considered. Also, the new AER is much better than that obtained by GIZA++ run without lemmatizing the words.

We now add the IBM Model-4 parameters (co-occurrence probabilities between source and target words) obtained using GIZA++ and our features, and observe the results (Table 6). We can see that structural features resulted in a significant decrease in AER. Also, the AER that we obtained is slightly better than the best AER obtained by the GIZA++ models.

Features	*Prec.*	*Rec.*	*F-meas.*	*AER*
IBM Model-4 Pars. + LocalFeats	48.85	43.98	46.29	52.71
IBM Model-4 Pars. + All feats.	48.95	50.06	49.50	**50.50**

Table 5: Results after combining IBM model-4 parameters with our features

6 Conclusion and Future Work

In this paper, we have proposed a discriminative re-ranking approach for word alignment which allows us to make use of structural features effectively. We have shown that by using the structural features, we have obtained a decrease of 2.3% in the absolute value of alignment error rate (AER). When we combine the prediction of IBM model-4 with our features, we have achieved an AER which is slightly better than the best AER of GIZA++ for the English-Hindi parallel corpus (a language pair with significant structural divergences). We expect to get large improvements when we add more number of relevant local and structural features. We also plan to design an appropriate dependency based decoder for machine translation to make good use of the parameters estimated by our model.

References

Phil Blunsom and Trevor Cohn. 2006. Discriminative word alignment with conditional random fields. In *Proceedings of the 21st COLING and 44th Annual Meeting of the ACL*, Sydney, Australia, July. ACL.

Koby Crammer and Yoram Singer. 2003. Ultraconservative online algorithms for multiclass problems. In *Journal of Machine Learning Research*.

Alexander Fraser and Daniel Marcu. 2006. Semi-supervised training for statistical word alignment. In *Proceedings of the 21st COLING and 44th Annual Meeting of the ACL*, Sydney, Australia, July. Association for Computational Linguistics.

Simon Lacoste-Julien, Ben Taskar, Dan Klein, and Michael I. Jordan. 2006. Word alignment via quadratic assignment. In *Proceedings of the Human Language Technology Conference of the NAACL, Main Conference*, pages 112–119, New York City, USA, June. Association for Computational Linguistics.

Ryan McDonald, Fernando Pereira, Kiril Ribarov, and Jan Hajic. 2005. Non-project dependency parsing using spanning tree algorithms. In *Proceedings of Human Language Technology Conference and Conference on Empirical Methods in Natural Language Processing*, pages 523–530, Vancouver, British Columbia, Canada, October. Association of Computational Linguistics.

Robert C. Moore. 2005. A discriminative framework for bilingual word alignment. In *Proceedings of Human Language Technology Conference and Conference on Empirical Methods in Natural Language Processing*, pages 81–88, Vancouver, British Columbia, Canada, October. Association of Computational Linguistics.

F. Och and H. Ney. 2003. A systematic comparisoin of various statistical alignment models. In *Computational Linguistics*.

Libin Shen. 2006. *Statistical LTAG Parsing*. Ph.D. thesis.

Ben Taskar, Simon Lacoste-Julien, and Dan Klein. 2005. A discriminative machine approach to word alignment. In *Proceedings of HLT-EMNLP*, pages 73–80, Vancouver, British Columbia, Canada, October. Association of Computational Linguistics.

Stefan Vogel, Hermann Ney, and Christoph Tillmann. 1996. Hmm-based word alignment in statistical translation. In *Proceedings of the 16th International Conference on Computational Linguistics*.

Generation in Machine Translation from Deep Syntactic Trees

Keith Hall
Center for Language and Speech Processing
Johns Hopkins University
Baltimore, MD 21218
keith_hall@jhu.edu

Petr Němec
Institute of Formal and Applied Linguistics
Charles University
Prague, Czech Republic
nemec@ufal.mff.cuni.cz

Abstract

In this paper we explore a generative model for recovering surface syntax and strings from deep-syntactic tree structures. Deep analysis has been proposed for a number of language and speech processing tasks, such as machine translation and paraphrasing of speech transcripts. In an effort to validate one such formalism of deep syntax, the Praguian Tectogrammatical Representation (TR), we present a model of synthesis for English which generates surface-syntactic trees as well as strings. We propose a generative model for function word insertion (prepositions, definite/indefinite articles, etc.) and subphrase reordering. We show by way of empirical results that this model is effective in constructing acceptable English sentences given impoverished trees.

1 Introduction

Syntactic models for language are being reintroduced into language and speech processing systems thanks to the success of sophisticated statistical models of parsing (Charniak and Johnson, 2005; Collins, 2003). Representing deep syntactic relationships is an open area of research; examples of such models are exhibited in a variety of grammatical formalisms, such as Lexical Functional Grammars (Bresnan and Kaplan, 1982), Head-driven Phrase Structure Grammars (Pollard and Sag, 1994) and the Tectogrammatical Representation (TR) of the Functional Generative Description (Sgall et al., 1986). In this paper we do not attempt to analyze the differences of these formalisms; instead, we show how one particular formalism is sufficient for automatic analysis and synthesis. Specifically, in this paper we provide evidence that TR is sufficient for synthesis in English.

Augmenting models of machine translation (MT) with syntactic features is one of the main fronts of the MT research community. The Hiero model has been the most successful to date by incorporating syntactic structure amounting to simple tree structures (Chiang, 2005). Synchronous parsing models have been explored with moderate success (Wu, 1997; Quirk et al., 2005). An extension to this work is the exploration of deeper syntactic models, such as TR. However, a better understanding of the synthesis of surface structure from the deep syntax is necessary.

This paper presents a generative model for surface syntax and strings of English given tectogrammatical trees. Sentence generation begins by inserting auxiliary words associated with autosemantic nodes; these include prepositions, subordinating conjunctions, modal verbs, and articles. Following this, the linear order of nodes is modeled by a similar generative process. These two models are combined in order to synthesize a sentence.

The Amalgam system provides a similar model for generation from a *logical form* (Corston-Oliver et al., 2002). The primary difference between our approach and that of the Amalgam system is that we focus on an impoverished deep structure (akin to

Proceedings of SSST, NAACL-HLT 2007 / AMTA Workshop on Syntax and Structure in Statistical Translation, pages 57–64,
Rochester, New York, April 2007.

logical form); we restrict the deep analysis to contain only the features which transfer directly across languages; specifically, those that transfer directly in our Czech-English machine translation system. Amalgam targets different issues. For example, Amalgam's generation of prepositions and subordinating conjunctions is severely restricted as most of these are considered part of the logical form.

The work of Langkilde-Geary (2002) on the Halogen system is similar to the work we present here. The differences that distinguish their work from ours stem from the type of deep representation from which strings are generated. Although their syntactic and semantic representations appear similar to the Tectogrammatical Representation, more explicit information is preserved in their representation. For example, the Halogen representation includes markings for determiners, voice, subject position, and dative position which simplifies the generation process. We believe their *minimally specified* results are based on input which most closely resembles the input from which we generate in our experiments.

Amalgam's reordering model is similar to the one presented here; their model reorders constituents in a similar way that we reorder subtrees. Both the model of Amalgam and that presented here differ considerably from the n-gram models of Langkilde and Knight (1998), the TAG models of Bangalore and Rambow (2000), and the *stochastic generation from semantic representation* approach of Soricut and Marcu (2006). In our work, we order the local-subtrees[1] of an augmented deep-structure tree based on the syntactic features of the nodes in the tree. By factoring these decisions to be independent for each local-subtree, the set of strings we consider is only constrained by the projective strucutre of the input tree and the local permutation limit described below.

In the following sections we first provide a brief description of the Tectogrammatical Representation as used in our work. Both manually annotated and synthetic TR trees are utilized in our experiments; we present a description of each type of tree as well as the motivation for using it. We then describe the generative statistical process used to model the synthesis of analytical (surface-syntactic) trees based on the TR trees. Details of the model's features are presented in the following section. Finally we present empirical results for experiments using both the manually annotated and automatically generated data.

[1]A local subtree consists of a parent node (governor) and it's immediate children.

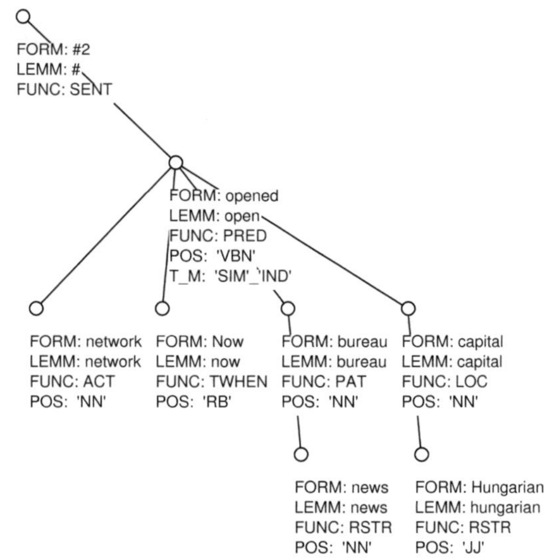

Figure 1: Example of a manually annotated, Synthetic TR tree (see Section 2.2).
Reference: **Now the network has opened a news bureau in the Hungarian capital**
Each sentence has an artificial root node labeled #. Verbs contain their tense and mood (labeled T_M).

2 Tectogrammatical (Deep) Syntax

The Tectogrammatical Representation (TR) comes out of the Praguian linguistic theory known as the Functional Generative Description of language (Sgall et al., 1986). TR attempts to capture deep syntactic relationships based on the valency of predicates (i.e., function-argument structure) and modification of participants (i.e., nouns used as actors, patients, etc.). A key feature of TR is that dependency relationships are represented only for autosemantic words (content words), meaning that synsemantic words (syntactic function words) are encoded as features of the grammatical relationships rather than the actual words. Abstracting away from specific syntactic lexical items allows for the representation to be less language-specific making the representation attractive as a medium for machine translation and summarization.

Figure 1 shows an example TR tree, the nodes of

which represent the autosemantic words of the sentence. Each node is labeled with a morphologically reduced word-form called the lemma and a functor that describes the deep syntactic relationship to its governor (function-argument form). Additionally, the nodes are labeled with grammatemes that capture morphological and semantic information associated with the autosemantic words. For example, English verb forms are represented by the infinitive form as the lemma and the grammatemes encode the tense, aspect, and mood of the verb. For a detailed description of the TR annotation scheme see Böhmová et al. (2002). In Figure 1 we show only those features that are present in the TR structures used throughout this paper.

Both the synsemantic nodes and the left-to-right surface order[2] in the TR trees is under-specified. In the context of machine translation, we assume the TR word order carries no information with the exception of a single situation: the order of coordinated phrases is preserved in one of our models.

2.1 Analytic Representation

While it is not part of the formal TR description, the authors of the TR annotation scheme have found it useful to define an intermediate representation between the sentence and the TR tree (Böhmová et al., 2002). The analytical representation (AR) is a surface-syntactic dependency tree that encodes syntactic relationships between words (i.e., object, subject, attribute, etc.). Unlike the TR layer, the analytical layer contains all words of the sentence and their relative ordering is identical to the surface order.

2.2 Manually Annotated TR

In order to evaluate the efficacy of the generation model, we construct a dataset from both manually annotated data and automatically generated data. The information contained in the originally manually annotated TR all but specifies the surface form. We have modified the annotated data by removing all features except those that could be directly transfered across languages. Specifically, we preserve the following features: lemma, functor, verbal grammatemes, and part-of-speech tags. The **lemma** is the morphologically reduced form of the word; for verbs this is the infinitive form and for nouns this is the singular form. The **functor** is the deep-syntactic function of the node; for example, the deep functor indicates whether a node is a predicate, an actor, or a patient. Modifiers can be labeled as locative, temporal, benefactive, etc. Additionally we include a **verbal grammateme** which encodes tense and mood as well as a Penn Treebank style part-of-speech tag.

3 Generative Process

In this section we describe the generative process that inserts the synsemantic auxiliary words, reorders the trees, and produces a sentence. Our evaluation will be on English data, so we describe the models and the model features in the context of English. While the model is language independent, the specific features and the size of the necessary conditioning contexts is a function of the language.

Given a TR tree T, we wish to predict the correct auxiliary nodes A and an ordering of the words associated with $\{T \cup A\}$, defined by the function $f(\{T \cup A\})$. The functions f determine the surface word order of the words associated with nodes of the auxiliary-inserted TR tree: $N = \{T \cup A\}$. The node features that we use from the nodes in the TR and AR trees are: the word lemma, the part-of-speech (POS) tag, and the functor.[3] The objective of our model is:

$$\begin{aligned} &\arg\max_{A,f} P(A, f|T) \\ &= \arg\max_{A,f} P(f|A,T)P(A|T) \qquad (1) \\ &\approx \arg\max_{f} P(f|T, \arg\max_{A} P(A|T)) \qquad (2) \end{aligned}$$

In Equation 2 we approximate the full model with a greedy procedure. First, we predict the most likely A according to the model $P(A|T)$. Given A, we compute the best ordering of the nodes of the tree, including those introduced in A.

There is an efficient dynamic-programming solution to the objective function in Equation 1; how-

[2]In a TR tree, a subtree is always between the nodes to the left and right of its governor. More specifically, all TR trees are projective. For this reason, the relative ordering of subtrees imposes an absolute ordering for the tree.

[3]The type of functor used (deep syntactic or surface-syntactic) depends on the tree to which we are applying the model. One form of the reordering model operates on AR trees and therefore uses surface syntactic functors. The other model is based on TR trees and uses deep-syntactic functors.

ever, in this work we experiment with the greedy approximation.

3.1 Insertion Model

The specific English auxiliary nodes which are not present in TR include articles, prepositions, subordinating conjunctions, and modal verbs.[4] For each node in the TR tree, the generative process predicts which synsemantic word, if any, should be inserted as a dependent of the current node. We make the assumption that these decisions are determined independently.

Let $T = \{w_1, \ldots, w_i, \ldots, w_k\}$ be the nodes of the TR tree. For each node w_i, we define the associated node a_i to be the auxiliary node that should be inserted as a dependent of w_i. Given a tree T, we wish to find the set of auxiliary nodes $A = \{a_1, \ldots, a_k\}$ that should be inserted[5]:

$$P(A|T)$$

$$= \prod_i P(a_i|a_1, \ldots, a_{i-1}, T) \quad (3)$$

$$\approx \prod_i P(a_i|T) \quad (4)$$

$$\approx \prod_i P(a_i|w_i, w_{g(i)}) \quad (5)$$

Equation 3 is simply a factorization of the original model, Equation 4 shows the independence assumption, and in Equation 5 we make an additional conditional independence assumption that in order to predict auxiliary a_i, we need only know the associated node w_i and its governor $w_{g(i)}$.[6]

We further divide the model into three components: one that models articles, such as the English articles *the* and *a*; one that models prepositions and subordinating conjunctions; and one that models modal verbs. The first two models are of the form described by Equation 5. The modal verb insertion model is a deterministic mapping based on grammatemes expressing the verb modality of the main verb. Additionally, each model is independent of the other and therefore up to two insertions per TR node are possible (an article and another syntactic modifier). In a variant of our model, we perform a small set of deterministic transformations in cases where the classifier is relatively uncertain about the predicted insertion node (i.e., the entropy of the conditional distribution is high).

We note here that unlike the Amalgam system (Corston-Oliver et al., 2002), we do not address features which are determined (or almost completely determined) by the underlying deep-structure. For example, the task of inserting prepositions is non-trivial given we only know a node's functor (e.g., the node's valency role).

3.2 Analytical Representation Tree Generation

We have experimented with two paradigms for synthesizing sentences from TR trees. The first technique involves first generating AR trees (surface syntax). In this model, we predict the node insertions, transform the functors from TR to AR functions (deep valency relationship to surface-syntactic relationships), and then reorder the nodes. In the second framework, we reorder the nodes directly in the TR trees with inserted auxiliary nodes.

3.3 Surface-order Model

The node ordering model is used to determine a projection of the tree to a string. We assume the ordering of the nodes in the input TR trees is arbitrary, the reordering model proposed here is based only on the dependency structure and the node's attributes (words, POS tags, etc.). In a variant of the reordering model, we assume the deep order of coordinating conjunctions to be the surface order.

Algorithm 1 presents the bottom-up node reordering algorithm. In the first part of the algorithm, we determine the relative ordering of child nodes. We maximize the likelihood of a particular order via the precedence operator $\prec$. If node $c_i \prec c_{i+1}$, then the subtree of the word associated with c_i immediately precedes the subtree of the word associated with c_{i+1} in the projected sentence.

In the second half of the algorithm (starting at line 13), we predict the position of the governor within the previously ordered child nodes. Recall

[4]The function of synsemantic nodes are encoded by functors. For example, the prepositions *to, at, in, by*, and *on* may be used to indicate time or location. An autosemantic modifier will be labeled as temporal or locative, but the particular preposition is not specified.

[5]Note that we include the auxiliary node labeled NOAUX to be inserted, which in fact means a node is not inserted.

[6]In the case of nodes whose governor is a coordinating conjunction, the governor information comes from the governor of the coordination node.

Algorithm 1 Subtree Reordering Algorithm

```
procedure REORDER(T, A, O)                        ▷ Result in O
    N ←bottomUp(T ∪ A);        O ← {}
    for g ∈ N do
        bestScore ← 0;        o_g ← {}
        for C ←permutation of g's children do
            for i ← 1 . . . |C| do
                s ← s ∗ P(c_i ≺ c_{i+1}|c_i, c_{i+1}, g)
            end for
            if s > bestScore then
                bestScore ← s;        o_g ← C
            end if
        end for
        bestScore ← 0;        m ← 0
        for i ← 1 . . . |bestOrder| do
            s ← P(c_i ≺ g ≺ c_{i+1}|c_i, c_{i+1}, g)
            if s > bestScore then
                s ← bestScore ;        m ← i
            end if
        end for
        Insert governor c_g after m^th child in o_g
        O ← O ∪ o_g
    end for
end procedure
```

that this is a dependency structure; knowing the governor does not tell us where it lies on the surface with respect to its children. The model is similar to the general reordering model, except we consider an absolute ordering of three nodes (left child, governor, right child). Finally, we can reconstruct the total ordering from the subtree ordering defined in $O = \{o_1, \ldots, o_n\}$.

The procedure described here is greedy; first we choose the best child ordering and then we choose the location of the governor. We do this to minimize the computational complexity of the algorithm. The current algorithm's runtime complexity is $O(n!)$, but the complexity of the alternative algorithm for which we consider triples of child nodes is $O(n!(n-1)!)$. The actual complexity is determined by the maximum number of child nodes $k = |C|$ and is $O(\frac{n}{k}k!)$.

3.4 Morphological Generation

In order to produce true English sentences, we convert the lemma and POS tag to a word form. We use John Carroll's morphg tool[7] to generate English word forms given lemma/POS tag pairs. This is not perfect, but it performs an adequate job at recovering English inflected forms. In the complete-system evaluation, we report scores based on generated morphological forms.

3.5 Insertion Features

Features for the insertion model come from the current node being examined and the node's governor. When the governor is a coordinating conjunction, we use features from the governor of the conjunction node. The features used are the lemma, POS tag, and functor for the current node, and the lemma, POS tag, and functor of the governor.

$$\prod_i P(a_i|w_i, w_g) \quad (6)$$
$$= \prod_i P(a_i|l_i, t_i, f_i, l_g, t_g, f_g)$$

The left-hand side of Equation 6 is repeated from Equation 5 above. Equation 6 shows the expanded model for auxiliary insertion where l_i is the lemma , t_i is the POS tag, and f_i is the functor of node w_i

3.6 Reordering Features

Our reordering model for English is based primarily on non-lexical features. We use the POS tag and functor from each node as features. The two distributions in our reordering model (used in Algorithm 1) are:

$$P(c_i \prec c_{i+1}|c_i, c_{i+1}, g) \quad (7)$$
$$= (c_i \prec c_{i+1}|f_i, t_i, f_{i+1}, t_{i+1}, f_g, t_g)$$
$$P(c_i \prec g \prec c_{i+1}|c_i, c_{i+1}, g) \quad (8)$$
$$= P(c_i \prec g \prec c_{i+1}|f_i, t_i, f_{i+1}, t_{i+1}, t_g, f_g)$$

In both Equation 7 and Equation 8, only the functor and POS tag of each node is used.

4 Empirical Evaluation

We have experimented with the above models on both manually annotated TR trees and synthetic trees (i.e., automatically generated trees). The data comes from the PCEDT 1.0 corpus[8], a version of the Penn WSJ Treebank that has been been translated to Czech and automatically transformed to TR in both English and Czech. The English TR was automatically generated from the Penn Treebank's manually annotated surface syntax trees (English phrase-structure trees). Additionally, a small set of 497 sentences were manually annotated at the TR level: 248

[7] Available on the web at: http://www.informatics.susx.ac.uk/research/nlp/carroll/morph.html.

[8] LDC catalog number: LDC2004T25.

Model	Manual Data				Synthetic Data			
	Ins. Rules		No Rules		Ins. Rules		No Rules	
Model	Articles	Prep & SC	Articles	Prep & SC	Articles	Prep & SC	Articles	Prep & SC
Baseline	N/A	N/A	77.93	76.78	N/A	N/A	78.00	78.40
w/o g. functor	87.29	89.65	86.25	**89.31**	**88.07**	91.83	**87.34**	91.06
w/o g. lemma	86.77	89.48	85.68	89.02	87.53	90.95	86.55	91.16
w/o g. POS	87.29	89.45	86.10	89.14	87.68	**91.86**	86.89	**92.07**
w/o functor	86.10	85.02	84.86	84.56	86.01	85.60	84.79	85.65
w/o lemma	81.34	89.02	80.88	88.91	81.28	91.03	81.42	91.33
w/o POS	84.81	88.01	84.01	87.29	85.53	91.08	84.69	90.98
All Features	**87.49**	**89.68**	**86.45**	89.28	87.87	91.83	87.24	92.02

Table 1: Classification accuracy for insertion models on development data from PCEDT 1.0. Article accuracy is computed over the set of nouns. Preposition and subordinating conjunction accuracy (P & SC) is computed over the set of nodes that appear on the surface (excluding hidden nodes in the TR – these will not exist in automatically generated data). Models are shown for all features minus the specified feature. Features with the prefix "g." indicate governor features, otherwise the features are from the node's attributes. The Baseline model is one which never inserts any nodes (i.e., the model which inserts the most probable value – NOAUX).

for development and 249 for evaluation; results are presented for these two datasets.

All models were trained on the PCEDT 1.0 data set, approximately 49,000 sentences, of which 4,200 were randomly selected as held-out training data, the remainder was used for training. We estimate the model distributions with a smoothed maximum likelihood estimator, using Jelinek-Mercer EM smoothing (i.e., linearly interpolated backoff distributions). Lower order distributions used for smoothing are estimated by deleting the rightmost conditioning variable (as presented in the above models).

Similar experiments were performed at the 2002 Johns Hopkins summer workshop. The results reported here are substantially better than those reported in the workshop report (Hajič et al., 2002); however, the details of the workshop experiments are not clear enough to ensure the experimental conditions are identical.

4.1 Insertion Results

For each of the two insertion models (the article model and the preposition and subordinating conjunction model), there is a finite set of values for the dependent variable a_i. For example, the articles are the complete set of English articles as collected from the Penn Treebank training data (these have manual POS tag annotations). We add a dummy value to this set which indicates no article should be inserted.[9] The preposition and auxiliary model assumes the set of possible modifiers to be all those seen in the training data that were removed when modifying the manual TR trees.

The classification accuracy is the percentage of nodes for which we predicted the correct auxiliary from the set of candidate nodes for the auxiliary type. Articles are only predicted and evaluated for nouns (determined by the POS tag). Prepositions and subordinating conjunctions are predicted and evaluated for all nodes that appear on the surface. We do not report results for the modal verb insertion as it is primarily determined by the features of the verb being modified (accuracy is approximately 100%). We have experimented with different features sets and found that the model described in Equation 6 performs best when all features are used.

In a variant of the insertion model, when the classifier prediction is of low certainty (probability less than .5) we defer to a small set of deterministic rules. For infinitives, we insert "to"; for origin nouns, we insert "from", for actors we insert "of", and we attach "by" to actors of passive verbs. In the article insertion model, we do not insert anything if there is another determiner (e.g., "none" or "any") or personal pronoun; we insert "the" if the word appeared within the previous four sentences or if there is a *suggestive* adjective attached to the noun.[10]

Table 1 shows that the classifiers perform better on automatically generated data (Synthetic Data), but also perform well on the manually annotated

[9] In the classifier evaluation we consider the article *a* and *an* to be equivalent.

[10] Any adjective that is always followed by the definite article in the training data.

Model	Manual Data				Synthetic Data			
	Coord. Rules		No Rules		Coord. Rules		No Rules	
	All	Interior	All	Interior	All	Interior	All	Interior
Baseline	N/A	N/A	68.43	21.67	N/A	N/A	69.00	21.42
w/o g. functor	**94.51**	**86.44**	**92.42**	**81.27**	94.90	87.25	93.37	83.42
w/o g. tag	93.43	83.75	90.89	77.50	93.82	84.56	91.64	79.12
w/o c. functors	91.38	78.70	89.71	74.57	91.91	79.79	90.41	76.04
w/o c. tags	88.85	72.44	82.29	57.36	88.91	72.29	83.04	57.60
All Features	94.43	86.24	92.01	80.26	**95.21**	**88.04**	**93.37**	**83.42**

Table 2: Reordering accuracy for TR trees on development data from PCEDT 1.0. We include performance on the interior nodes (excluding leaf nodes) for the Manual data to show a more detailed analysis of the performance. "g." are the governor features and "c." are the child features. The baseline model sorts subtrees of each node randomly.

data. Prediction of articles is primarily dependent on the lemma and the tag of the node. The lemma and tag of the governing node and the node's functor is important to a lesser degree. In predicting the prepositions and subordinating conjunctions, the node's functor is the most critical factor.

% Errors	Reference→Hypothesis
41	the → NULL
19	a/an → NULL
16	NULL → the
11	a/an → the
11	the → a/an
2	NULL → a/an

Table 3: Article classifier errors on development data.

Manual		Synthetic	
Det.	P & SC	Det.	P & SC
85.53	89.18	85.31	91.54

Table 4: Accuracy of best models on the evaluation data.

Table 3 presents a confusion set from the best article classifier on the development data. Our model is relatively conservative, incurring 60% of the error by choosing to insert nothing when it should have inserted an article. The model requires more informed features as we are currently being overly conservative.

In Table 4 we report the overall accuracy on evaluation data using the model that performed best on the development data. The results are consistent with the results for the development data; however, the article model performs slightly worse on the evaluation set.

4.2 Reordering Results

Evaluation of the final sentence ordering was based on predicting the correct words in the correct positions. We use the reordering metric described in Hajič et al. (2002) which computes the percentage of nodes for which all children are correctly ordered (i.e., no credit for partially correct orderings).

Table 2 shows the reordering accuracy for the full model and variants where a particular feature type is removed. These results are for ordering the correct auxiliary-inserted TR trees (using deep-syntactic functors and the correctly inserted auxiliaries). In the model variant that preserves the deep order of coordinating conjunctions, we see a significant increase in performance. The child node tags are critical for the reordering model, followed by the child functors.

4.3 Combined System Results

Model	Manual	Synthetic
TR w/ Rules	**.4614**	**.4777**
TR w/o Rules	.4532	.4657
AR	.2337	.2451

Table 5: BLEU scores for complete generation system for TR trees (with and without rules applied) and the AR trees.

In order to evaluate the combined system, we used the multiple-translation dataset in the PCEDT corpus. This data contains four retranslations from Czech to English of each of the original English sentences in the development and evaluation datasets. In Table 5 we report the BLEU scores on development data for our TR generation model (including the morphological generation module) and the AR generation model. Results for the system that uses AR trees as an intermediate stage are very poor; this is likely due to the noise introduced when generating AR trees. Additionally, the results for the TR model with the additional rules are consistent with the previous results; the rules provide only a marginal improvement. Finally, we have run the complete system on the evaluation data and achieved a BLEU score of **.4633** on the manual data and **.4750** on the synthetic data. These can be interpreted as the upper-bound for Czech-English translation systems based on TR tree transduction.

5 Conclusion

We have provided a model for sentence synthesis from Tectogrammatical Representation trees. We provide a number of models based on relatively simple, local features that can be extracted from impoverished TR trees. We believe that further improvements will be made by allowing for more flexible use of the features. The current model uses simple linear interpolation smoothing which limits the types of model features used (forcing an explicit factorization). The advantage of simple models of the type presented in this paper is that they are robust to errors in the TR trees – which are expected when the TR trees are generated automatically (e.g., in a machine translation system).

Acknowledgments

This work was partially supported by U.S. NSF grants IIS–9982329 and OISE–0530118; by the project of the Czech Ministry of Education #LC536; by the Information Society Project No. 1ET201120505 of the Grant Agency of the Academy of Sciences of the Czech Republic; and Grant No. 352/2006 of the Grant Agency of Charles University.

References

Srinivas Bangalore and Owen Rambow. 2000. Exploiting a probabilistic hierarchical model for generation. In *Proceedings of the 18th International Conference on Computational Linguistics (COLING 2000)*, Saarbrücken, Germany.

Alena Böhmová, Jan Hajič, Eva Hajičová, and Barbora Vidová Hladká. 2002. The prague dependency treebank: Three-level annotation scenario. In Anne Abeille, editor, *In Treebanks: Building and Using Syntactically Annotated Corpora*. Dordrecht, Kluwer Academic Publishers, The Neterlands.

Joan Bresnan and Ronald M. Kaplan. 1982. Lexical-functional grammar: A formal system for grammatical representation. In *The Mental Representation of Grammatical Relations*. MIT Press.

Eugene Charniak and Mark Johnson. 2005. Coarse-to-fine n-best parsing and MaxEnt discriminative reranking. In *Proceedings of the 43rd Annual Meeting of the Association for Computational Linguistics*.

David Chiang. 2005. A hierarchical phrase-based model for statistical machine translation. In *Proceedings of the 43rd Annual Meeting of the Association for Computational Linguistics*, pages 263–270, Ann Arbor, MI.

Michael Collins. 2003. Head-driven statistical models for natural language processing. *Computational Linguistics*, 29(4):589–637.

Simon Corston-Oliver, Michael Gamon, Eric Ringger, and Robert Moore. 2002. An overview of Amalgam: A machine-learned generation module. In *Proceedings of the International Natural Language Generation Conference*, pages 33–40, New York, USA.

Jan Hajič, Martin Čmejrek, Bonnie Dorr, Yuan Ding, Jason Eisner, Dan Gildea, Terry Koo, Kristen Parton, Dragomir Radev, and Owen Rambow. 2002. Natural language generation in the context of machine translation. Technical report, Center for Language and Speech Processing, Johns Hopkins University, Balitmore. Summer Workshop Final Report.

Irene Langkilde and Kevin Knight. 1998. The practical value of n-grams in generation. In *Proceedings of the International Natural Language Generation Workshop*.

Irene Langkilde-Geary. 2002. An empirical verification of coverage and correctness for a general-purpose sentence generator. In *Proceedings of the International Natural Language Generation Conference*.

Carl Pollard and Ivan A. Sag. 1994. *Head-Driven Phrase Structure Grammar*. University of Chicago Press.

Chris Quirk, Arul Menezes, and Colin Cherry. 2005. Dependency treelet translation: Syntactically informed phrasal SMT. In *Proceedings of the 43rd Annual Meeting of the Association for Computational Linguistics (ACL'05)*, pages 271–279, Ann Arbor, Michigan, June. Association for Computational Linguistics.

Petr Sgall, Eva Hajičová, and Jarmila Panevová. 1986. *The Meaning of the Sentence in Its Semantic and Pragmatic Aspects*. Kluwer Academic, Boston.

Radu Soricut and Daniel Marcu. 2006. Stochastic language generation using WIDL–expressions and its application in machine translation and summarization. In *Proceedings of the 44th Annual Meeting of the Association for Computational Linguistics*.

Dekai Wu. 1997. Stochastic inversion transduction grammars and bilingual parsing of parallel corpora. *Computational Linguistics*, 23(3):377–404.

Combining Morphosyntactic Enriched Representation with n-best Reranking in Statistical Translation

H. Bonneau-Maynard, A. Allauzen, D. Déchelotte and H. Schwenk
Spoken Language Processing Group
LIMSI-CNRS, BP 133
91403 Orsay cedex, FRANCE
{maynard,allauzen,dechelot,schwenk}@limsi.fr

Abstract

The purpose of this work is to explore the integration of morphosyntactic information *into* the translation model itself, by enriching words with their morphosyntactic categories. We investigate word disambiguation using morphosyntactic categories, n-best hypotheses reranking, and the combination of both methods with word or morphosyntactic n-gram language model reranking. Experiments are carried out on the English-to-Spanish translation task. Using the morphosyntactic language model alone does not results in any improvement in performance. However, combining morphosyntactic word disambiguation with a word based 4-gram language model results in a relative improvement in the BLEU score of 2.3% on the development set and 1.9% on the test set.

1 Introduction

Recent works in statistical machine translation (SMT) shows how phrase-based modeling (Och and Ney, 2000a; Koehn et al., 2003) significantly outperform the historical word-based modeling (Brown et al., 1993). Using phrases, i.e. sequences of words, as translation units allows the system to preserve local word order constraints and to improve the consistency of phrases during the translation process. Phrase-based models provide some sort of context information as opposed to word-based models. Training a phrase-based model typically requires aligning a parallel corpus, extracting phrases and scoring them using word and phrase counts. The derived statistics capture the structure of natural language to some extent, including implicit syntactic and semantic relations.

The output of a SMT system may be difficult to understand by humans, requiring re-ordering words to recover its syntactic structure. Modeling language generation as a word-based Markovian source (an n-gram language model) discards linguistic properties such as long term word dependency and word-order or phrase-order syntactic constraints. Therefore, explicit introduction of structure in the language models becomes a major and promising focus of attention.

However, as of today, it seems difficult to outperform a 4-gram word language model. Several studies have attempted to use morphosyntactic information (also known as part-of-speech or POS information) to improve translation. (Och et al., 2004) have explored many different feature functions. Reranking n-best lists using POS has also been explored by (Hasan et al., 2006). In (Kirchhoff and Yang, 2005), a factored language model using POS information showed similar performance to a 4-gram word language model. Syntax-based language models have also been investigated in (Charniak et al., 2003). All these studies use word phrases as translation units and POS information in just a post-processing step.

This paper explores the integration of morphosyntactic information *into* the translation model itself by enriching words with their morphosyntactic cat-

Proceedings of SSST, NAACL-HLT 2007 / AMTA Workshop on Syntax and Structure in Statistical Translation, pages 65–71,
Rochester, New York, April 2007.

egories. The same idea has already been applied in (Hwang et al., 2007) to the Basic Travel Expression Corpus (BTEC). To our knowledge, this approach has not been evaluated on a large real-word translation problem. We report results on the TC-STAR task (public European Parliament Plenary Sessions translation). Furthermore, we propose to combine this approach with classical n-best list reranking. Experiments are carried out on the English-to-Spanish task using a system based on the publicly available *Moses* decoder.

This paper is organized as follows: In Section 2 we first describe the baseline statistical machine translation systems. Section 3 presents the considered task and the processing of the corpora. The experimental evaluation is summarized in section 4. The paper concludes with a discussion of future research directions.

2 System Description

The goal of statistical machine translation is to produce a target sentence $\mathbf{e}$ from a source sentence $\mathbf{f}$. Among all possible target language sentences the one with the highest probability is chosen. The use of a maximum entropy approach simplifies the introduction of several additional models explaining the translation process:

$$\begin{aligned} \mathbf{e}^* &= \arg\max \Pr(\mathbf{e}|\mathbf{f}) \\ &= \arg\max_e \{\exp(\sum_i \lambda_i h_i(\mathbf{e},\mathbf{f}))\} \end{aligned} \quad (1)$$

where the feature functions h_i are the system models characterizing the translation process, and the coefficients λ_i act as weights.

2.1 Moses decoder

Moses[1] is an open-source, state-of-the-art phrase-based decoder. It implements an efficient beam-search algorithm. Scripts are also provided to train a phrase-based model. The popular Giza++ (Och and Ney, 2000b) tool is used to align the parallel corpora.

The baseline system uses 8 feature functions h_i, namely phrase translation probabilities in both directions, lexical translation probabilities in both directions, a distortion feature, a word and a phrase penalty and a trigram target language model. Additional features can be added, as described in the following sections. The weights λ_i are typically optimized so as to maximize a scoring function on a development set (Och and Ney, 2002).

The moses decoder can output n-best lists, producing either distinct target sentences or not (as different segmentations may lead to the same sentence). In this work, distinct sentences were always used.

These n-best lists can be rescored using higher order language models (word- or syntactic-based). There are two ways to carry out the rescoring: one, by replacing the language model score or by adding a new feature function; two, by performing a log-linear interpolation of the language model used for decoding and the new language model. This latter approach was used in all the experiments described in this paper. The set of weights is systematically re-optimized using the algorithm presented below.

2.2 Weight optimization

A common criterion to optimize the coefficients of the log-linear combination of feature functions is to maximize the BLEU score (Papineni et al., 2002) on a development set (Och and Ney, 2002). For this purpose, the public numerical optimization tool *Condor* (Berghen and Bersini, 2005) is integrated in the following iterative algorithm:

0. Using good general purpose weights, the Moses decoder is used to generate 1000-best lists.
1. The 1000-best lists are reranked using the current set of weights.
2. The current hypothesis is extracted and scored.
3. This BLEU score is passed to *Condor*, which either computes a new set of weights (the algorithm then proceeds to step 1) or detects that a local maxima has been reached and the algorithm stops iterating.

The solution is usually found after about 100 iterations. It is stressed that the n-best lists are generated only once and that the whole tuning operates only on the n-best lists.

[1] http://www.statmt.org/moses/

English: I_{PP} $declare_{VVP}$ $resumed_{VVD}$ the_{DT} $session_{NN}$ of_{IN} the_{DT} $European_{NP}$ $Parliament_{NP}$

Spanish: $declaro_{VLfin}$ $reanudado_{VLadj}$ el_{ART} $perodo_{NC}$ de_{PREP} $sesiones_{NC}$ del_{PDEL} $Parlamento_{NC}$ $Europeo_{ADJ}$

Figure 1: Example of POS-tag enriched bi-text used to train the translation models

2.3 POS disambiguation

It is well-known that syntactic structures vary greatly across languages. Spanish, for example, can be considered as a highly inflectional language, whereas inflection plays only a marginal role in English.

POS language models can be used to rerank the translation hypothesis, but this requires tagging the n-best lists generated by the SMT system. This can be difficult since POS taggers are not well suited for ill-formed or incorrect sentences. Finding a method in which morphosyntactic information is used directly in the translation model could help overcome this drawback but also takes account for the syntactic specificities of both source and target languages. It seems likely that the morphosyntactic information of each word will be useful to encode linguistic characteristics, resulting in a sort of word disambiguation by considering its morphosyntactic category. Therefore, in this work we investigate a translation model which enriches every word with its syntactic category. The enriched translation units are a combination of the original word and the POS tag, as shown in Figure 1. The translation system takes a sequence of enriched units as inputs and outputs. This implies that the test data must be POS tagged before translation. Likewise, the POS tags in the enriched output are removed at the end of the process to provide the final translation hypothesis which contain only a word sequence. This approach also allows to carry out a n-best reranking step using either a word-based or a POS-based language model.

3 Task, corpus and tools

The experimental results reported in this article were obtained in the framework of an international evaluation organized by the European TC-STAR project[2] in February 2006. This project is envisaged as a long-term effort to advance research in all core technologies for speech-to-speech translation.

[2]http://www.tc-star.org/

The main goal of this evaluation is to translate public European Parliament Plenary Sessions (EPPS). The training material consists of the summary edited by the European Parliament in several languages, which is also known as the Final Text Editions (Gollan et al., 2005). These texts were aligned at the sentence level and they are used to train the statistical translation models (see Table 1 for some statistics).

	Spanish	*English*
	Whole parallel corpus	
Sentence Pairs	1.2M	
Total # Words	34.1M	32.7M
Vocabulary size	129k	74k
	Sentence length ≤ 40	
Sentence Pairs	0.91M	
Total # Words	18.5M	18.0M
Word vocabulary	104k	71k
POS vocabulary	69	59
Enriched units vocab.	115k	77.6k

Table 1: Statistics of the parallel texts used to train the statistical machine translation system.

Three different conditions are considered in the TC-STAR evaluation: translation of the Final Text Edition (*text*), translation of the transcriptions of the acoustic development data (*verbatim*) and translation of speech recognizer output (*ASR*). Here we only consider the *verbatim* condition, translating from English to Spanish. For this task, the development and test data consists of about 30k words. The test data is partially collected in the Spanish parliament. This results in a small mismatch between development and test data. Two reference translations are provided. The scoring is case sensitive and includes punctuation symbols.

3.1 Text normalization

The training data used for normalization differs significantly from the development and test data. The Final Text Edition corpus follows common orthographic rules (for instance, the first letter of the word following a full stop or a column is capitalized) and represents most of the dates, quantities, article references and other numbers in digits. Thus the text had to be "true-cased" and all numbers were verbalized using in-house language-specific tools. Numbers are not tagged as such at this stage; this is entirely left to the POS tagger.

3.2 Translation model training corpus

Long sentences (more than 40 words) greatly slow down the training process, especially at the alignment step with Giza++. As shown in Figure 2, the histogram of the length of Spanish sentences in the training corpus decreases steadily after a length of 20 to 25 words, and English sentences exhibit a similar behavior. Suppressing long sentences from the corpus reduces the number of aligned sentences by roughly 25% (see Table 1) but speeds the whole training procedure by a factor of 3. The impact on performance is discussed in the next section.

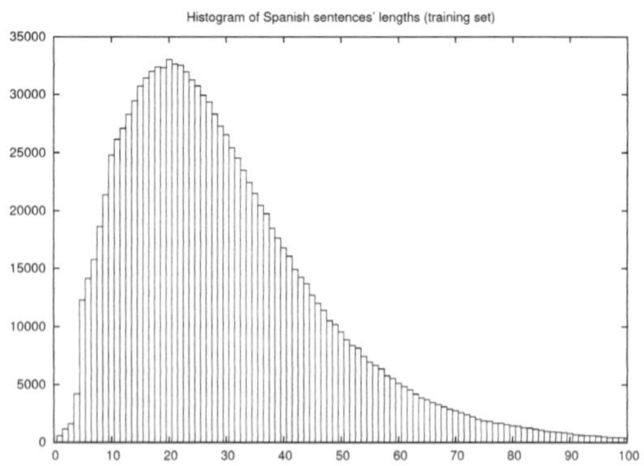

Figure 2: Histogram of the sentence length (Spanish part of the parallel corpus).

3.3 Language model training corpus

In the experiments reported below, a trigram word language model is used during decoding. This model is trained on the Spanish part of the parallel corpus using only sentences shorter than 40 words (total of 18.5M of language model training data). Second pass language models were trained on all available monolingual data (34.1M words).

3.4 Tools

POS tagging was performed with the *TreeTagger* (Schmid, 1994). This software provides resources for both of the considered languages and it is freely available. *TreeTagger* is a Markovian tagger that uses decision trees to estimate trigram transition probabilities. The English version is trained on the *PENN treebank* corpus[3] and the Spanish version on the *CRATER* corpus.[4]

Language models are built using the SRI-LM toolkit (Stolcke, 2002). Modified Knesser-Ney discounting was used for all models. In (Goodman, 2001), a systematic description and comparison of the usual smoothing methods is reported. *Modified Knesser-Ney* discounting appears to be the most efficient method.

4 Experiments and Results

Two baseline English-to-Spanish translation models were created with Moses. The first model was trained on the whole parallel text – note that sentences with more than 100 words are excluded by Giza++. The second model was trained on the corpus using only sentences with at most 40 words. The BLEU score on the development set using good general purpose weights is 48.0 for the first model and 47.0 for the second. Because training on the whole bi-text is much slower, we decided to perform our experiments on the bi-texts restricted to the "short" sentences.

4.1 Language model generation

The reranking experiments presented below use the following language models trained on the Spanish part of the whole training corpus:

- word language models,
- POS language model,
- POS language model, with a stop list used to remove the 100 most frequent words (POS-stop100 LM),
- language model of enriched units.

[3]http://www.cis.upenn.edu/ treebank

[4]http://www.comp.lancs.ac.uk/linguistics/crater/corpus.html

English :	you will be aware President that over the last few sessions in Strasbourg. ..
Baseline:	usted sabe que el Presidente *durante los últimos sesiones* en Estrasburgo ...
Enriched units:	usted sabe que el Presidente *en los últimos períodos de sesiones* en Estrasburgo ...
English :	... in this house there might be some recognition ...
Baseline:	... en esta asamblea *no puede ser un cierto reconocimiento ...*
Enriched units:	... en esta asamblea *existe un cierto reconocimiento ...*

Figure 3: Comparative translations using the baseline word system and the enriched unit system.

For each of these four models, various orders were tested ($n = 3, 4, 5$), but in this paper we only report those orders that yielded the greatest improvements. POS language models were obtained by first extracting POS sequences from the previously POS-tagged training corpus and then by estimating standard back-off language models.

As shown in Table 1, the vocabulary size of the word language model is 104k for Spanish and 74k for English. The number of POS is small: 69 for Spanish and 59 for English. We emphasize that the tagset provided by *TreeTagger* does include neither gender nor number distinction. The vocabulary size of the enriched-unit language model is 115k for Spanish and 77.6k for English. The syntactical ambiguity of words is low: the mean ambiguity ratio is 1.14 for Spanish and 1.12 for English.

4.2 Reranking the word n-best lists

The results concerning reranking experiments of the n-best lists provided by the translation model based on *words as units* are summarized in Table 2. The baseline result, with trigram word LM reranking, gives a BLEU score of 47.0 (1rst row). From the n-best lists provided by this translation model, we compared reranking performances with different target language models. As observed in the literature, an improvement can be obtained by reranking with a 4-gram word language model (47.0 $\rightarrow$ 47.5, 2d row). By post-tagging this n-best list, a POS language model reranking can be performed. However, reranking with a 5-gram POS language model alone does not give any improvement from the baseline (BLEU score of 46.9, 3rd row). This result corresponds to known work in the literature (Kirchhoff and Yang, 2005; Hasan et al., 2006), when using POS only as a post-processing step during reranking. As suggested in section 2.3, this lack of performance can be due to the fact that the tagger is not able to provide a usefull tagging of sentences included in the n-best lists. This observation is also available when reranking of the word n-best is done with a language model based on enriched units (BLEU score of 47.6, not reported in Table 2).

4.3 POS disambiguation and reranking

The results concerning reranking experiments of the n-best lists provided by the translation model based on *enriched units* are summarized in Table 3. Using a trigram language model of enriched translation units leads to a BLEU score of 47.4, a 0.4 increase over the baseline presented in section 4.2. Figure 3 shows comparative translation examples from the baseline and the enriched translation systems. In the first example, the baseline system outputs "*durante los últimos sesiones*" where the enriched translation system produces "*en los últimos períodos de sesiones*", a better translation that may be attributed to the introduction of the masculine word "*períodos*", allowing the system to build a syntactically correct sentence. In the second example, the syntactical error "*no puede ser un cierto reconocimiento*" produced by the baseline system induces an incorrect meaning of the sentence, whereas the enriched translation system hypothesis "*existe un cierto reconocimiento*" is both syntactically and semantically correct.

Reranking the enriched n-best with POS language models (either with or without a stop list) does not seem to be efficient (0.3 BLEU increasing with the POS-stop100 language model).

A better improvement is obtained when reranking is performed with the 4-gram word language model. This results in a BLEU score of 47.9, corresponding to a 0.9 improvement over the word baseline. It is interesting to observe that reranking a n-best list

	Dev.	Test
3g word LM baseline	47.0	46.0
4g word LM reranking	**47.5**	**46.5**
5g POS reranking	46.9	46.1

Table 2: BLEU scores using words as translation units.

obtained with a translation model based on enriched units with a word LM results in better performances than a enriched units LM reranking of a n-best list obtained with a translation model based on words.

The last two rows of Table 3 give results when combining word and POS language models to rerank the enriched n-best lists. In both cases, 10 features are used for reranking (8 Moses features + word language model probability + POS language model probability). The best result is obtained by combining the 5-gram word language model with the 5-gram POS-stop100 language model. In that case, the best BLEU score is observed (48.1), with a 2.3% relative increase over the trigram word baseline.

4.4 Results on the test set

The results on the test set are given in the second column of Tables 2 and 3. Although the enriched translation system is only 0.1 BLEU over the baseline system (46.0 → 46.1) when using a trigram language model, the best condition observed on the development set (word and POS-stop100 LMs reranking) results in a 46.8 BLEU score, corresponding to a 0.8 increasing.

It can be observed that rescoring with a 4-gram word language model leads to same score resulting in a 1.9% relative increase over the trigram word baseline.

5 Conclusion and future work

Combining word language model reranking of n-best lists based on syntactically enriched units seems to produce more consistent hypotheses. Using enriched translation units results in a relative 2.3% improvement in BLEU on the development set and 1.9% on the test over the trigram baseline. Over a standard translation model with 4-gram rescoring, the enriched unit translation model leads to an absolute increase in BLEU score of 0.4 both on the development and the test sets. These first results are encouraging enough to further investigate the integration of syntactic information in the translation model itself, rather than to restrict it to the post-processing pass. As follow-up experiments, it is planned to include gender and number information in the tagset, as well as the word stems to the enriched units.

	Dev.	Test
3g enriched units LM baseline	47.4	46.1
4g enriched units LM reranking	47.8	46.8
4g word LM reranking	47.9	46.9
5g POS LM reranking	47.5	46.2
5g POS-stop100 LM reranking	47.7	46.3
word + POS LMs reranking	47.9	46.9
word + POS-stop100 LMs rerank.	**48.1**	**46.8**

Table 3: BLEU scores using enriched translation units.

This work should be considered as preliminary experiments for the investigation of factored translation models, which Moses is able to handle. POS factorization is indeed a way to add some generalization capability to the enriched translation models.

6 Acknowledgments

This work has been partially funded by the European Union under the integrated project TC-STAR (IST-2002-FP6-506738), and by the French Government under the project INSTAR (ANR JCJC06_143038).

We would like to thanks Marc Ferras for his help concerning the Spanish language.

References

Frank Vanden Berghen and Hugues Bersini. 2005. CONDOR, a new parallel, constrained extension of powell's UOBYQA algorithm: Experimental results and comparison with the DFO algorithm. *Journal of Computational and Applied Mathematics*, 181:157–175.

Peter F Brown, Stephen A Della Pietra, Vincent J Della Pietra, and Robert L Mercer. 1993. The mathematics of statistical machine translation: Parameter estimation. *Computational Linguistics*, 19(2):263–311.

E. Charniak, K. Knight, and K. Yamada. 2003. Syntax-based language models for machine translation. In *Proceedings of MT Summit IX*.

C. Gollan, M. Bisani, S. Kanthak, R. Schlueter, and H̃. Ney. 2005. Cross domain automatic transcription on the TC-STAR epps corpus. In *Proceedings of ICASSP 2005*.

Joshua T. Goodman. 2001. A bit of progress in language modeling. *Computer Speech and Language*, 15(4):403–434, October.

S. Hasan, O. Bender, and H. Ney. 2006. Reranking translation hypothesis using structural properties. In *Proceedings of EACL 2006*.

Y.S. Hwang, A. Finch, and Y. Sasaki. 2007. Improving statistical machine translation using shallow linguistic knoledge. *to be published in Computer, Speech and Language*.

Katrin Kirchhoff and Mei Yang. 2005. Improved language modeling for statistical machine translation. In *Proceedings of ACL '05 workshop on Building and Using Parallel Text*, pages 125–128.

Philipp Koehn, Franz Josef Och, and Daniel Marcu. 2003. Statistical phrase-based translation. In *Proceedings of the Human Language Technology Conference 2003 (HLT-NAACL 2003)*, Edmonton, Canada, May.

Franz Josef Och and Hermann Ney. 2000a. Improved statistical alignment models. In *Proc. of the 38th Annual Meeting of the Association for Computational Linguistics*, pages 440–447, Hongkong, China, October.

Franz Josef Och and Hermann Ney. 2000b. Improved statistical alignment models. In *Proceedings of the 38th Annual Meeting of the Association for Computational Linguistics*, pages 440–447, Hong Kong, China, October.

Franz Josef Och and Hermann Ney. 2002. Discriminative training and maximum entropy models for statistical machine translation. In *Proceedings of ACL 2002*, pages 295–302.

F.-J. Och, D. Gildea, S. Khudanpur, A. Sarkar, K. Yamada, A. Fraser, S. Kumar, L. Shen, D. Smith, K. Eng, V. Jain, Z. Jin, and D. Radev. 2004. A smorgasbord of features for statistical machine translation. In *NAACL*, pages 161–168.

Kishore Papineni, Salim Roukos, Todd Ward, and Wei-Jing Zhu. 2002. Bleu: a method for automatic evaluation of machine translation. In *Proceedings of the 40th Annual Meeting of the Association for Computational Linguistics*, pages 311–318, University of Pennsylvania.

Helmut Schmid. 1994. Probabilistic part-of-speech tagging using decision trees. In *Proceedings of International Conference on New Methods in Language Processing*, September.

Andreas Stolcke. 2002. SRILM - an extensible language modeling toolkit. In *Proceedings of ICSLP*, pages II: 901–904.

A Walk on the Other Side: Adding Statistical Components to a Transfer-Based Translation System

Ariadna Font Llitjós
Carnegie Mellon University
5000 Forbes Ave.
Pittsburgh, PA, 15213
aria@cs.cmu.edu

Stephan Vogel
Carnegie Mellon University
5000 Forbes Ave.
Pittsburgh, PA, 15213
vogel+@cs.cmu.edu

Abstract

This paper seeks to complement the current trend of adding more structure to Statistical Machine Translation systems, by exploring the opposite direction: adding statistical components to a Transfer-Based MT system. Initial results on the BTEC data show significant improvement according to three automatic evaluation metrics (BLEU, NIST and METEOR).

1 Introduction

In recent years the machine translation research community has seen a remarkable paradigm shift. It is not the first one, but it has been a very dramatic one: statistical machine translation has taken the center stage. Conferences like ACL or HLT are virtually flooded with papers on various flavors of SMT. In international machine translation evaluation like NIST (NIST MT Evaluation), TC-Star (TC-STAR Evaluation) or IWSLT (IWSLT 2006) evaluations, most participating systems are SMT systems, with a few Example-Based systems sprinkled in. Rule-Based systems seem to have for the most part disappeared. There may be many reasons for this paradigm shift. One obvious reason is the comparable ease, which with data-driven systems can be built once some parallel data is available. Another reason is that the performance of statistical translation systems has dramatically improved over the last 5 to 10 years.

Does this mean that work on grammar-based systems should be stopped? Should all the insight into the structure of languages be neglected? This might be too drastic a reaction. Actually, now that SMT has reached some maturity, we see several attempts to integrate more structure into these systems, ranging from simple hierarchical alignment models (Wu 1997, Chiang 2005) to syntax-based statistical systems (Yamada and Knight 2001, Zollmann and Venugopal 2006). What can traditional Rule-Based translation systems learn from these approaches? And would it not make sense to work from both sides towards that common goal: structurally rich statistical translation models. In this paper we study some enhancements for a Transfer-Based translation system, using techniques and even components developed for statistical machine translation. While the core engine remains virtually untouched, additional features are added to re-score the n-best list generated by the transfer engine. Statistical alignment techniques are used to lower the burden in building a lexicon for a new domain. Minimum error rate training is used to optimize the system. We show that this leads to significant improvements in performance.

2 A Transfer-Based Translation System

2.1 The Lexicon and Grammar

In our Rule-Based MT (RBMT) system, translation rules include parsing, transfer, and generation information, similar to the modified transfer approach used in the early Metal system (Hutchins and Somers, 1992).

The initial lexicon (479 entries) and grammar (40 rules) used in our experiments were manually written to cover the syntactic structures and the vocabulary of the first 400 sentences of the AVENUE Elicitation Corpus (Probst et al 2001). The Elicitation Corpus contains sets of minimal pairs in English and it was designed to cover a variety of linguistic phenomena. Building these two language-dependent components took a computational linguist 2-3 months. Figures 1 and 2 show

Proceedings of SSST, NAACL-HLT 2007 / AMTA Workshop on Syntax and Structure in Statistical Translation, pages 72–79, Rochester, New York, April 2007.

examples of a translation rules in the grammar and the lexicon.

```
{S,4}
S::S : [NP VP] -> [NP VP]
( (X1::Y1) (X2::Y2)
  (x0 = x2)
  ((y2 subj) = -)
  ((y1 case) = nom)
  ((y1 agr) = (x1 agr))
  ((y2 tense) = (x2 tense))
  ((y2 agr pers) = (y1 agr pers))
  ((y2 agr num) = (y1 agr num)) )
```

Figure 1: English→Spanish translation rule with agreement constraints for subject (NP) and verb (VP).

```
V::V |: ["prefer"] -> ["prefiero"]
((X1::Y1)
((x0 form) = prefer)
((x0 tense) = pres)
((y0 agr pers) = 1)
((y0 agr num) = sg))
```

Figure 2: English→Spanish lexical entry for the verb "prefer".

2.2 Refined MT System

The original grammar and lexicon were automatically improved with an Automatic Rule Refiner, guided by a few bilingual speaker corrections (Font Llitjós & Ridmann 2007). In this approach, automatic refinements only affect the target language side of translation rules, namely transfer and generation information.

The refined MT system used in our experiments is the result of adding 30 agreement constraints to the grammar rules, which makes the grammar tighter (leading to an increase in precision), as well as adding three new rules to cover new syntactic structures and five lexical entries for new senses and forms of existing words (leading to an increase in recall).

2.3 The Transfer Engine

The Transfer Engine, or Xfer engine for short, combines the translation grammar and lexicon in order to produce translations of a source language sentence into a target language. The Xfer engine incorporates the three main processes involved in Transfer-based MT: parsing of the source language input, transfer of the parsed constituents of the source sentence to their corresponding structured constituents on the target language side, and generation of the target sentence.

The currently implemented algorithm is similar to bottom-up chart parsing as described for example in Allen (1995). A chart is first populated with all constituent structures that were created in the course of parsing the source language sentence with the source-side portion of the transfer grammar. Transfer and generation are applied to each constituent entry. The transfer rules associated with each entry in the chart are used in order to determine the corresponding constituent structure on the target language side. At the word level, lexical transfer rules are used in order to get the different lexical choices.

Often, no parse for the entire source sentence can be found. Partial parses are concatenated sequentially to generate complete translations.

In the current version of the Xfer system, the output can be a first-best translation or a n-best list, which can be used for additional n-best list rescoring. The alternatives arise from lexical ambiguity and multiple synonymous choices for lexical items in the dictionary, but also from syntactic ambiguity and multiple competing hypotheses from the grammar.

For our experiments, we used version 3 of the Xfer engine. An older version of the Xfer engine is described in detail in Peterson (2002).

2.4 Ranking Translations

The Xfer engine can generate multiple translations. This requires a quality score to be assigned to all the alternatives. Based on these scores, the 1-best translation will be selected by the system.

Fragmentation Penalty

In the original Xfer system the only score used to rank translation alternatives was a heuristic fragmentation penalty. The fragmentation penalty is essentially the number of different chunks (rules or lexical entries not embedded in another rule) that span the whole translation. The intuition behind this score is that the more partial parses are necessary to span the entire sentence the less likely the resulting translation will be a good one.

N-gram LM

The fragmentation feature is rather weak. It does not distinguish between words which are more likely to be seen in the target language and words which are less likely to be used. To generate sentences which are not only grammatically correct, but also use words and word sequences that are more natural and more common, data-driven machine translation systems use a n-gram language model. To get the same benefit in the Xfer system, an n-gram LM has been integrated with the engine.

This has the advantage that in the case of pruning, the LM score can be used to avoid pruning good hypotheses, in addition to re re-rank the final translations.

For our experiments, a suffix array language model based on the SALM toolkit (Zhang & Vogel, 2006) is used.

Length Model

To adjust for the length of the translations generated by the system, the difference between the number of words generated and the expected number of words is added as a very simple feature. The expected length is calculated by multiplying the source sentence length by the ratio of the number of target and source words in the training corpus. The effect of this feature is to balance globally the length of the translations.

2.5 Pruning

To deal with the combinatorial explosion during the parsing/translation process, pruning has to be applied. Only the *n* top-ranking hypotheses are kept in each cell of the chart. The ranking of these partial translations is based on their language model score, which at this time is only an approximation, as the true history has not been seen and cannot be taken into account.

3 Building a Xfer System for a New Domain

A major bottleneck in developing a RBMT system for a new translation task (a new language pair or a new domain) is writing the grammar and building the lexicon. Automatic grammar induction using statistical alignments has been studied in (Probst 2005).

Here, we start with an existing grammar and augment the baseline lexicon with entries to cover the new domain. We explore semi-automatic lexicon generation for fast adaptation to the travel domain (Section 3.2).

3.1 Test Data: BTEC Corpus

For initial evaluation on unseen data, we selected the Basic Travel Expression Corpus (BTEC) (Takezawa et al. 2002), which has been used in the evaluation campaigns in connection with the International Workshop on Spoken Language Translation (IWSLT 2006). Besides still being currently used to build real systems (Shimizu et al. 2006; Nakamura, et al. 2006), this corpus contains relatively simple sentences that are comparable to the ones initially corrected by users, and which are covered by the baseline manual grammar.

As our test set, we used 506 English sentences for which two sets of Spanish reference translations were available. Table 1 shows corpus statistics for the BTEC data.

Data			English
BTEC	Train	Sentences Pairs	123,416
		Sentence Length	7.3
		Word Tokens	903,525
		Word Types	12,578
	Test	Sentence Pairs	506
		Word Tokens	3,764
		Word Types	776
		Coverage Test	756 (97%)

Table 1: Corpus Statistics for the BTEC corpus

3.2 Semi-Automatic Generation of the Transfer Lexicon

The Transfer-Based system relies on a lexicon that contains POS, gender and number agreement, among other linguistic features. To adjust the system quickly to a new task, we decided to leverage from statistical alignment models to generate word and phrase alignments as candidates for the transfer lexicon.

In the first step, we trained statistical lexicons using the well-known IBM1 word alignment model: one for the directions Spanish to English, and one for the direction English to Spanish. As multi-word entries, are often needed ([valuables] → [objetos de valor], [reception desk] →[recepción], [air conditioner]→[aire acondicionado]), we used phrase alignment techniques to create translation candidates for words and 2-word phrases. The phrase alignment also generates multi-word translations for single source words. With reasonably tight pruning, a manageable phrase translation table was generated. This first step took about 5 hours.

The next step, manually cleaning the translation table, annotating them with parts-of-speech, and with agreement and tense constraints, was initially restricted to those items that overlapped with the vocabulary of our development test set, and took two days.

The statistically generated lexicon comprises 1,248 lexical entries, whereas the initial manual lexicon contained 479 lexical entries. For our BTEC experiments, we combined both lexicons.

3.3 Xfer Results with No Ranking

To determine how the Xfer system would perform only on the basis of the lexicon and grammar, we ran one translation experiment in which no language model was used. This experiment was also intended to see if the refined grammar would lead to better translations. We took the first-best translation output by the system without using any statistical components to rank alternative translations.

System	METEOR	BLEU	NIST
Baseline	0.5666	0.2745	5.88
Refined	0.5676	0.2559	5.62

Table 2: Automatic metric scores for a purely Rule-Based MT System.

Table 2 shows that, in this crude setting, different automatic metrics do not agree on the translation accuracy of both systems. On one hand, METEOR (Lavie et al. 2004), which has been shown to correlate well with human judgments (Snover et al. 2006), indicates that the refined system outperforms the baseline system (as measured by the latest version v0.5.1,). On the other hand, both BLEU (Papineni et al., 2002) and NIST (Doddington 2002) scores are higher for the baseline system (mteval-v11b.pl).

However, human inspection revealed that the refined grammar is able to augment the n-best list with correct translations that the baseline system was not able to generate. This suggests that these results reflect poor re-ranking and not n-best list quality. In the next section, we describe an oracle experiment to measure n-best list quality of both systems.

3.4 Oracle Experiment

Oracle scores provide an upper-bound in performance. For the BTEC test set, we approximated a human oracle by calculating automatic metric scores for METEOR and for BLEU and NIST.

Given 100-best lists for each source language sentence, we selected the best translation hypothesis for each automatic metric separately.

These scores reflect the fact that automatic refinements are able to feed the n-best list with better translations, as evulated by comparison against human reference translations. Even with a small set of independent user corrections, the refined system shows potential improved translation quality as indicated by higher scores for all three automatic evaluation metrics in Table 3.

System	METEOR	BLEU	NIST
Baseline	0.6863	0.4068	7.42
Refined	0.6954	0.4215	7.51

Table 3: Automatic metric oracle scores based on a 100-best list

Moreover, oracle scores provide the margin that we can gain when improving on the re-ranking of the n-best list produced by the Xfer engine.

3.5 Xfer Results with Initial Ranking

As expected, when the Xfer system is run in combination with a LM[1] as well as the fragmentation penalty, automatic metric scores for the 1-best hypothesis are significantly higher (Table 4), than when just using the first translation output by the Xfer system alone (Table 2).

System	METEOR	BLEU	NIST
Baseline	0.6176	0.3425	6.53
Refined	0.6222	0.3513	6.56

Table 4: Automatic metric scores for 1-best decoder hypothesis.

These results are lower than the oracle scores for both the baseline and the refined system (Table 3), which is also to be expected. However, the important thing to notice from these results is that, like in the oracle case, the refined system consistently outperforms the baseline MT system for all three automatic metrics.

[1] The Suffix Array Language Model (SALM) was built using the 123,416 Spanish sentences from the training data.

The difference between the baseline and the refined system in terms of 1-best scores is slightly smaller than the difference between oracle scores, which means that the decoder can not fully leverage the improvements made in the grammar. This indicates that the decoder fails to select the best translation in most cases.

4 Adding Statistical Components to a Re-Ranker

The information used in the Xfer system to rank alternative translations is limited. Essentially, it is the n-gram LM, which is the most important component, a simple sentence length model, and the fragmentation score, which measures if a completely spanning parse could be found or if the translation is glued together from partial parses. Given an n-best list of translations for each source sentence, we can apply additional models to re-rank these n-best list, hopefully pushing more good translations into the first rank. We studied the effect of adding different features to the n-best lists: lexical features and rule (type) probability features.

4.1 Word-To-Word Probabilities

In SMT systems, rescoring with an IBM1 model-like word alignment score has become a standard feature. We use two word-to-word lexicons (English→Spanish and Spanish→English) to calculate sentence translation probabilities, based on word-to-word probabilities:

$$P(e \mid s) = \frac{1}{J^I} \prod \sum p(e_i \mid s_j) \qquad \text{Eq.1}$$

and:

$$P(s \mid e) = \frac{1}{I^J} \prod \sum p(s_j \mid e_i) \qquad \text{Eq.2}$$

Here, we denote the English words with e, the Spanish words with s, the sentence lengths are given by I and J. In the IBM1 alignment model, the position alignment is a uniform distribution $p(i \mid j) = 1/I$ for Spanish to English and $p(j \mid i) = 1/J$ for English to Spanish. For Spanish to English, we have the additional factor of $(1/I)^J$, i.e. longer translations get a smaller probability, and for En-Sp we have $(1/J)^I$, which again gives a bias towards shorter translations. To compensate for this bias, we use probabilities normalized to the sentence length. Table 5 shows that adding the lexical probabilities improves the 1-best translation score. However, there is no significant difference when using different normalization of the lexicon probabilities. The length bias introduced by different lexicon features can be balanced by the decoder's length feature.

	BLEU	NIST
Refined	0.3513	6.56
+Lex Prob	0.3755	6.88

Table 5: Comparing 1-best scores with scores result of rescoring the n-best list with lexical features.

4.2 Rule Probabilities

The Xfer MT system can display the derivation tree showing the rules applied during translation. This allows rescoring the translations with rule probabilities. However, there is no annotated corpus from which the rule probabilities could be estimated. As an approximation to such a training corpus, we decided to run the Xfer system over the training data and to generate n-best lists with translations and translation trees. Overall, about 6 million parse trees were generated. Using this data to estimate rule probabilities is definitely not ideal, as the translation on the training data are far from perfect, especially as not all the vocabulary has so far been added to the Xfer lexicon. By averaging over all n-best translations a reasonable smoothing is to be expected.

We used this information in three ways. We estimated conditional probabilities rule r given rule-type R, i.e. the distribution over different VP rules or NP rules. For each derivation D the overall probability was then calculated as:

$$P(D) = \prod p(r \mid R) \qquad \text{Eq. 3}$$

As an alternative, we just build n-gram language models, one on the rule level and on the rule type level:

$$P(D) = \prod p(r \mid r_{-n} ... r_{-1}) \qquad \text{Eq. 4}$$

$$P(D) = \prod p(R \mid R_{-n} ... R_{-1}) \qquad \text{Eq. 5}$$

Overall, 1,685 different rules and 19 rule types were seen in the training data. For models 2 and 3, we used the suffix array LM once again to allow for arbitrary long histories. Even though it often backs-off to 3-gram, 2-gram or even unigram probabilities.

In Table 6, we can see the effect of adding these LMs as additional features to the system and running MER training.

	BLEU	NIST
Refined	0.3513	6.56
Lex. Prob.	0.3755	6.88
Cond. Prob.	0.3728	6.81
Rule LM	0.3717	6.74
Rule Type LM	0.3736	6.78

Table 6: BLEU scores when rescoring the n-best list with different rule probability features (as well as the n-gram LM).

5 MER Training

Like in SMT systems, in the Xfer engine translations are ranked to their total cost, which is a weighted linear combination of the individual costs. When adding more features to the translation system, a careful balancing of the individual contributions can make a significant difference. However, with each feature added, manually tuning the system becomes less and less practical, and automatic optimization becomes necessary.

Different optimization techniques are available, like the Simplex algorithm or the special Minimum Error Training as described in (Och 2003). In Minimum Error Rate (MER) training, the n-best list generated by the translation system is used to find feature weight, thereby re-ranking the n-best list. This improves the match between the 1-best translation and given reference translations. Optimization can use any metric as objective function. Typically, systems are tuned towards high BLEU or high NIST scores, more recently also towards METEOR or TER (Snover et al. 2006).

We used a MER training module (Venugopal), originally developed for an SMT system, to run MER training on the n-best lists generated by the Xfer system. This implementation allows for optimization towards BLEU and NIST mteval metrics.

5.1 Results

In Table 7, we summarize some of the results from different n-best list rescoring experiments. Using only the Xfer engine, without language model, gives a very low score, as the selection is based only on the fragmentation score.

Adding the n-gram language model gives a huge improvement. Adding additional features leads to more then 2 BLEU points improvement. However, there is not much difference when using different feature combinations. It seems that the rather small size of the n-best list is a limiting factor.

When setting the optimal weights in the Xfer engine for the LM and fragmentation penalty scores obtained from MER training, both the baseline and the refined system get higher scores, not only according to BLEU, which was used as the objective function, but also according to METEOR and NIST automatic evaluation metrics (Table 8).

	System + Statistical Components	1-best
Rule Based	Xfer	0.2559
+ Stat. Comp.	Xfer + LM + Frag	0.3513
Optimizing weights with MER training	POS LM	0.3180
	Rule Probabilities (Prob.)	0.2593
	LM + Rule Type LM	0.3736
	LM + Frag/Len + Rule Type LM	0.3737
	LM + POS + Rule LM	0.3744
	LM + Frag + Rule Type LM + Cond. Rule Prob.	0.3743
	LM + Len + Rule Type LM + Cond. Rule Prob.	0.3745
	LM + POS + Rule LM + Cond. Rule Prob.	0.3741
	LM + Frag + Len + Rule Type LM + Rule Prob.	0.3746
	LM + Frag + Len + POS + Rule LM + Rule Prob.	0.3741

Table 7: BLEU scores for the Refined MT System as the weights for the different statistical components described in Section 2.4 and 4 are optimized with MER Training.

Moreover, the difference between the Baseline and the Refined system after MER training is statistically significant[2], whereas this was not the case for the initial ranking results (Table 4).

System	METEOR	BLEU	NIST
Baseline	0.6184	0.3609	6.68
Refined	0.6231	0.3780	6.79

Table 8: Automatic metric scores for 1-best decoder hypothesis, after LM and Fragmentation weights have been optimized.

Table 9 shows a few examples from the BTEC corpus with 1-best translations output by the Refined MT system before (No Optimization) and after (With Optimization) MER training, given LM and Fragmentation penalty scores. From these examples, it can be observed that re-ranking improves after optimizing the LM and fragmentation weights. In particular, order issues get resolved (examples 1, 2 and 4), which result in correct determiner agreement (1 and 2); determiner insertion (3); correct verb form (5 and 7) and omission of incorrect pronouns (6 and 7).

6 Conclusion

Starting from a Transfer-Based translation system, we explored techniques currently used in statistical translation systems to rapidly adapt to a new domain and to improve its performance. Using word and phrase alignment techniques allowed us to quickly augment the transfer lexicon. Adding a statistical language model is crucial in selecting good translations from the n-best lists generated by the Xfer engine. Adding additional features, such as word-to-word probabilities and rule (type) probabilities, further improves performance.

While this information would ideally be used in the parsing and transfer steps of the translation system, our initial experiments were targeted at using this in an n-best list rescoring setup. As rule probabilities were estimated from noisy training data, these models are far from optimal.

To facilitate the experiments with the Xfer system, especially when adding more and more features, we added a Minimum Error Rate training component. Having such a component will definitely boost the development of the Xfer engine.

We see statistically significant improvements over the baseline system when using optimized weights for the word-level language model and the fragmentation score.

1 Source: where is the boarding gate ? NO: dónde está *el embarque puerta* ? WO: dónde está la puerta embarque ?
2 Src: where is the bus stop for city hall ? NO: dónde está *el autobús parada* para ayuntamiento ? WO: dónde está la parada autobús para ayuntamiento ?
3 Src: i would like a twin room with a bath please . NO: me gustaría habitación una cama doble con un baño por favor . WO: me gustaría una habitación cama doble con un baño por favor .
4 Src: i would like to buy some duty-free items . NO: me gustaría comprar algunos *duty-free productos*. WO: me gustaría comprar algunos artículos duty-free .
5 Src: does he speak japanese ? NO: él *hablar a* japonés ? WO: habla japonés ?
6 Src: it is just round the corner . NO: *lo* es simplemente a la vuelta de la esquina . WO: es simplemente a la vuelta de la esquina .
7 Src: do you sell duty-free items ? NO: *te* venden artículos duty-free ? WO: vendéis artículos duty-free ?

Table 9: 1-best translations from the BTEC test set output by the Refined MT system before and after MER training. NO stands for No Optimization of LM and Fragmentation weights, and WO stands for With Optimization of weights.

7 Future Work

Using rule probabilities has shown to be a promising extension to the current Xfer system. We plan to improve these models by selecting the oracle best translations from the n-best list generated on the training data. This will reduce the noise in the training stage. Ultimately, the rule probabilities should be applied not as an n-best list rescoring step, but directly in the Xfer engine decoder.

Analyzing the translation results, one important shortcoming became obvious. Currently the translation lexicon only covers about 88% of the words that appear in the reference translations. This severely limits as to what kind of BLEU score we can achieve. When we generated the phrasal lexicon from the BTEC training data, we deliberately

[2] According to the standard paired two-tailed t-Test, the decoder METEOR scores with optimized weights are statistically significant, with a p value of 0.0051.

chose to only include few alternatives, mainly to limit the manual labor when adding POS and constraint. We expect that the Xfer system will significantly benefit from further expanding the lexicon.

References

Allen, J. 1995. *Natural Language Understanding*. Second Edition ed. Benjamin Cummings.

Chiang, D. 2005. *A hierarchical phrase-based model for statistical machine translation*. In Proceedings of the 43rd Annual Meeting of the Association for Computational Linguistics (ACL), Ann Arbor, USA.

Doddington G. 2002. *Automatic evaluation of machine translation quality using n-gram co-occurrence statistics*. In Proc. of the HLT 2002, San Diego, USA.

Hutchins, W. J., and H. L. Somers. 1992. *An Introduction to Machine Translation*. London: Academic Press.

Font Llitjós, A. and W. Ridmann. 2007 *The Inner Works of an Automatic Rule Refiner for Machine Translation*. METIS-II Workshop, Leuven, Belgium.

IWSLT 2006: http://www.slt.atr.jp/IWSLT2006/

Lavie, A., K. Sagae and S. Jayaraman. 2004. *The Significance of Recall in Automatic Metrics for MT Evaluation*. AMTA, Washington DC, USA.

Nakamura, S., K. Markov, H. Nakaiwa, G. Kikui, H. Kawai, T. Jitsuhiro, J. Zhang, H. Yamamoto, E. Sumita, and S. Yamamoto. 2006. *The ATR multilingual speech-to-speech translation system*. IEEE Trans. on Audio, Speech, and Language Processing, 14, No.2:365–376.

NIST MT Evaluations:
http://www.nist.gov/speech/tests/mt/

Och, F. J. 2003. *Minimum error rate training in statistical machine translation*. In Proc. of the 41st Annual Meeting of the Association for Computational Linguistics (ACL), Sapporo, Japan.

Papineni, K, S. Roukos, T. Ward, and W. Zhu. 2002. *BLEU: a method for automatic evaluation of machine translation*. In Proc. of the 40th ACL, Philadelphia, USA.

Peterson, E. 2002. *Adapting a transfer engine for rapid machine translation development*. M.S. Thesis, Georgetown University.

Probst, K., Brown, R., Carbonell, J., Lavie, A. Levin, and L., Peterson, E., 2001. *Design and Implementation of Controlled Elicitation for Machine Translation of Low density Languages*. Proceedings of the MT2001 workshop at MT Summit, Santiago de Compostela, Spain.

SALM Toolkit:
http://projectile.is.cs.cmu.edu/research/public/tools/salm/salm.htm

Shimizu T., Y. Ashikari, E. Sumita, H. Kashioka and S. Nakamura. 2006. *Development of client-server speech translation system on a multi-lingual speech communication platform*. IWSLT, Kyoto, Japan.

Snover, M; B. Dorr, R. Schwartz, L. Micciulla, 2006. *Targeted Human Annotation*. AMTA, Boston, USA.

Takezawa, T, E. Sumita, F. Sugaya, H. Yamamoto, and S. Yamamoto, 2002. *Toward a Broad-Coverage Bilingual Corpus for Speech Translation of Travel Conversations in the Real World.* In Proceedings of 3rd LREC, Las Palmas, Spain.

TC-STAR Evaluations: http://www.tc-star.org/

Venugopal, A.: MER Training Toolkit.
http://www.cs.cmu.edu/~ashishv/mer.html

Wu, D. 1997. *Stochastic inversion transduction grammars and bilingual parsing of parallel corpora*. Computational Linguistics, 23:377–404.

Yamada, Kenji and Kevin Knight. 2001. *A syntax-based statistical translation model*. In Proceedings of the 39th Annual Meeting of the ACL, Toulouse, France.

Zhang, Y and S. Vogel. 2006. *Suffix Array and its Applications in Empirical Natural Language Processing,*. Technical Report CMU-LTI-06-010, Pittsburgh PA, USA.

Zhang, Y, A. S. Hildebrand and S. Vogel. 2006. *Distributed Language Modeling for N-best List Reranking*. Empirical Methods in Natural Language Processing (EMNLP), Sydney, Australia.

Zollmann A. and A. Venugopal. 2006. *Syntax Augmented Machine Translation via Chart Parsing*. In Proc. of NAACL 2006 - Workshop on Statistical Machine Translation, New York, USA.

Dependency-Based Automatic Evaluation for Machine Translation

Karolina Owczarzak **Josef van Genabith** **Andy Way**
National Centre for Language Technology
School of Computing, Dublin City University
Dublin 9, Ireland

{owczarzak,josef,away}@computing.dcu.ie

Abstract

We present a novel method for evaluating the output of Machine Translation (MT), based on comparing the dependency structures of the translation and reference rather than their surface string forms. Our method uses a treebank-based, wide-coverage, probabilistic Lexical-Functional Grammar (LFG) parser to produce a set of structural dependencies for each translation-reference sentence pair, and then calculates the precision and recall for these dependencies. Our dependency-based evaluation, in contrast to most popular string-based evaluation metrics, will not unfairly penalize perfectly valid syntactic variations in the translation. In addition to allowing for legitimate syntactic differences, we use paraphrases in the evaluation process to account for lexical variation. In comparison with other metrics on 16,800 sentences of Chinese-English newswire text, our method reaches high correlation with human scores. An experiment with two translations of 4,000 sentences from Spanish-English Europarl shows that, in contrast to most other metrics, our method does not display a high bias towards statistical models of translation.

1 Introduction

Since their appearance, string-based evaluation metrics such as BLEU (Papineni et al., 2002) and NIST (Doddington, 2002) have been the standard tools used for evaluating MT quality. Both score a candidate translation on the basis of the number of *n*-grams shared with one or more reference translations. Automatic measures are indispensable in the development of MT systems, because they allow MT developers to conduct frequent, cost-effective, and fast evaluations of their evolving models.

These advantages come at a price, though: an automatic comparison of *n*-grams measures only the string similarity of the candidate translation to one or more reference strings, and will penalize any divergence from them. In effect, a candidate translation expressing the source meaning accurately and fluently will be given a low score if the lexical and syntactic choices it contains, even though perfectly legitimate, are not present in at least one of the references. Necessarily, this score would differ from a much more favourable human judgement that such a translation would receive.

The limitations of string comparison are the reason why it is advisable to provide multiple references for a candidate translation in BLEU- or NIST-based evaluations. While Zhang and Vogel (2004) argue that increasing the size of the test set gives even more reliable system scores than multiple references, this still does not solve the inadequacy of BLEU and NIST for sentence-level or small set evaluation. In addition, in practice even a number of references do not capture the whole potential variability of the translation. Moreover, when designing a statistical MT system, the need for large amounts of training data limits the researcher to collections of parallel corpora such as Europarl (Koehn, 2005), which provides only one reference, namely the target text; and the cost of creating additional reference translations of the test set, usually a few thousand sentences long, is often prohibitive. Therefore, it would be desirable to find an evaluation method that accepts legitimate syntactic and lexical differences

Proceedings of SSST, NAACL-HLT 2007 / AMTA Workshop on Syntax and Structure in Statistical Translation, pages 80–87,
Rochester, New York, April 2007.

between the translation and the reference, thus better mirroring human assessment.

In this paper, we present a novel method that automatically evaluates the quality of translation based on the dependency structure of the sentence, rather than its surface form. Dependencies abstract away from the particulars of the surface string (and CFG tree) realization and provide a "normalized" representation of (some) syntactic variants of a given sentence. The translation and reference files are analyzed by a treebank-based, probabilistic Lexical-Functional Grammar (LFG) parser (Cahill et al., 2004), which produces a set of dependency triples for each input. The translation set is compared to the reference set, and the number of matches is calculated, giving the precision, recall, and f-score for that particular translation.

In addition, to allow for the possibility of valid lexical differences between the translation and the references, we follow Kauchak and Barzilay (2006) and Owczarzak et al. (2006) in adding a number of paraphrases in the process of evaluation to raise the number of matches between the translation and the reference, leading to a higher score.

Comparing the LFG-based evaluation method with other popular metrics: BLEU, NIST, General Text Matcher (GTM) (Turian et al., 2003), Translation Error Rate (TER) (Snover et al., 2006)[1], and METEOR (Banerjee and Lavie, 2005), we show that combining dependency representations with paraphrases leads to a more accurate evaluation that correlates better with human judgment.

The remainder of this paper is organized as follows: Section 2 gives a basic introduction to LFG; Section 3 describes related work; Section 4 describes our method and gives results of two experiments on different sets of data: 4,000 sentences from Spanish-English Europarl and 16,800 sentences of Chinese-English newswire text from the Linguistic Data Consortium's (LDC) Multiple Translation project; Section 5 discusses ongoing work; Section 6 concludes.

[1] As we focus on purely automatic metrics, we omit HTER (Human-Targeted Translation Error Rate) here.

2 Lexical-Functional Grammar

In Lexical-Functional Grammar (Bresnan, 2001) sentence structure is represented in terms of c(onstituent)-structure and f(unctional)-structure. C-structure represents the surface string word order and the hierarchical organisation of phrases in terms of CFG trees. F-structures are recursive feature (or attribute-value) structures, representing abstract grammatical relations, such as *subj*(ect), *obj*(ect), *obl*(ique), *adj*(unct), approximating to predicate-argument structure or simple logical forms. C-structure and f-structure are related in terms of functional annotations (attribute-value structure equations) in c-structure trees, describing f-structures.

While c-structure is sensitive to surface word order, f-structure is not. The sentences *John resigned yesterday* and *Yesterday, John resigned* will receive different tree representations, but identical f-structures, shown in (1).

(1) *C-structure:* *F-structure:*

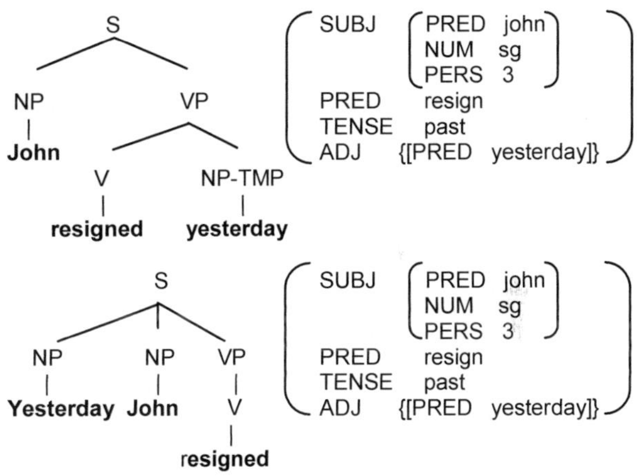

Notice that if these two sentences were a translation-reference pair, they would receive a less-than-perfect score from string-based metrics. For example, BLEU with add-one smoothing[2] gives this pair a score of barely 0.3781.

The f-structure can also be described as a flat set of triples. In triples format, the f-structure in (1) could be represented as follows: {*subj*(resign, john), *pers*(john, 3), *num*(john, sg), *tense*(resign,

[2] We use smoothing because the original BLEU gives zero points to sentences with fewer than one four-gram.

past), *adj*(resign, yesterday), *pers*(yesterday, 3), *num*(yesterday, sg)}.

Cahill et al. (2004) presents Penn-II Treebank-based LFG parsing resources. Her approach distinguishes 32 types of dependencies, including grammatical functions and morphological information. This set can be divided into two major groups: a group of predicate-only dependencies and non-predicate dependencies. Predicate-only dependencies are those whose path ends in a predicate-value pair, describing grammatical relations. For example, for the f-structure in (1), predicate-only dependencies would include: {*subj*(resign, john), *adj*(resign, yesterday)}.[3]

In parser evaluation, the quality of the f-structures produced automatically can be checked against a set of gold standard sentences annotated with f-structures by a linguist. The evaluation is conducted by calculating the precision and recall between the set of dependencies produced by the parser, and the set of dependencies derived from the human-created f-structure. Usually, two versions of f-score are calculated: one for all the dependencies for a given input, and a separate one for the subset of predicate-only dependencies.

In this paper, we use the parser developed by Cahill et al. (2004), which automatically annotates input text with c-structure trees and f-structure dependencies, reaching high precision and recall rates.[4]

3 Related work

The insensitivity of BLEU and NIST to perfectly legitimate syntactic and lexical variation has been raised, among others, in Callison-Burch et al. (2006), but the criticism is widespread. Even the creators of BLEU point out that it may not correlate particularly well with human judgment at the sentence level (Papineni et al., 2002). A side effect of this phenomenon is that BLEU is less reliable for smaller data sets, so the advantage it provides in the speed of evaluation is to some extent counterbalanced by the time spent by developers on producing a sufficiently large test set in order to obtain a reliable score for their system.

Recently a number of attempts to remedy these shortcomings have led to the development of other automatic MT evaluation metrics. Some of them concentrate mainly on word order, like General Text Matcher (Turian et al., 2003), which calculates precision and recall for translation-reference pairs, weighting contiguous matches more than non-sequential matches, or Translation Error Rate (Snover et al., 2005), which computes the number of substitutions, inserts, deletions, and shifts necessary to transform the translation text to match the reference. Others try to accommodate both syntactic and lexical differences between the candidate translation and the reference, like CDER (Leusch et al., 2006), which employs a version of edit distance for word substitution and reordering; or METEOR (Banerjee and Lavie, 2005), which uses stemming and WordNet synonymy. Kauchak and Barzilay (2006) and Owczarzak et al. (2006) use paraphrases during BLEU and NIST evaluation to increase the number of matches between the translation and the reference; the paraphrases are either taken from WordNet[5] in Kauchak and Barzilay (2006) or derived from the test set itself through automatic word and phrase alignment in Owczarzak et al. (2006). Another metric making use of synonyms is the linear regression model developed by Russo-Lassner et al. (2005), which makes use of stemming, WordNet synonymy, verb class synonymy, matching noun phrase heads, and proper name matching. Kulesza and Schieber (2004), on the other hand, train a Support Vector Machine using features like proportion of n-gram matches and word error rate to judge a given translation's distance from human-level quality.

Nevertheless, these metrics use only string-based comparisons, even while taking into consideration reordering. By contrast, our dependency-based method concentrates on utilizing linguistic structure to establish a comparison between translated sentences and their reference.

---

[3] Other predicate-only dependencies include: *apposition*, *complement*, *open complement*, *coordination*, *determiner*, *object*, *second object*, *oblique*, *second oblique*, *oblique agent*, *possessive*, *quantifier*, *relative clause*, *topic*, *relative clause pronoun*. The remaining non-predicate dependencies are: *adjectival degree*, *coordination surface form*, *focus*, complementizer forms: *if*, *whether*, and *that*, *modal*, *number*, *verbal particle*, *participle*, *passive*, *person*, *pronoun surface form*, *tense*, *infinitival clause*.

[4] http://lfg-demo.computing.dcu.ie/lfgparser.html

[5] http://wordnet.princeton.edu/

4 LFG f-structure in MT evaluation

The process underlying the evaluation of f-structure quality against a gold standard can be used in automatic MT evaluation as well: we parse the translation and the reference, and then, for each sentence, we check the set of translation dependencies against the set of reference dependencies, counting the number of matches. As a result, we obtain the precision and recall scores for the translation, and we calculate the f-score for the given pair. Because we are comparing two outputs that were produced automatically, there is a possibility that the result will not be noise-free.

To assess the amount of noise that the parser may introduce we conducted an experiment where 100 English Europarl sentences were modified by hand in such a way that the position of adjuncts was changed, but the sentence remained grammatical and the meaning was not changed. This way, an ideal parser should give both the source and the modified sentence the same f-structure, similarly to the case presented in (1). The modified sentences were treated like a translation file, and the original sentences played the part of the reference. Each set was run through the parser. We evaluated the dependency triples obtained from the "translation" against the dependency triples for the "reference", calculating the f-score, and applied other metrics (TER, METEOR, BLEU, NIST, and GTM) to the set in order to compare scores. The results, inluding the distinction between f-scores for all dependencies and predicate-only dependencies, appear in Table 1.

	baseline	modified
TER	0.0	6.417
METEOR	1.0	0.9970
BLEU	1.0000	0.8725
NIST	11.5232	11.1704 (96.94%)
GTM	100	99.18
dep f-score	100	96.56
dep_preds f-score	100	94.13

Table 1. Scores for sentences with reordered adjuncts

The baseline column shows the upper bound for a given metric: the score which a perfect translation, word-for-word identical to the reference, would obtain.[6] In the other column we list the scores that the metrics gave to the "translation" containing reordered adjunct. As can be seen, the dependency and predicate-only dependency scores are lower than the perfect 100, reflecting the noise introduced by the parser.

To show the difference between the scoring based on LFG dependencies and other metrics in an ideal situation, we created another set of a hundred sentences with reordered adjuncts, but this time selecting only those reordered sentences that were given the same set of dependencies by the parser (in other words, we simulated having the ideal parser). As can be seen in Table 2, other metrics are still unable to tolerate legitimate variation in the position of adjuncts, because the sentence surface form differs from the reference; however, it is not treated as an error by the parser.

	baseline	modified
TER	0.0	7.841
METEOR	1.0	0.9956
BLEU	1.0000	0.8485
NIST	11.1690	10.7422 (96.18%)
GTM	100	99.35
dep f-score	100	100
dep_preds f-score	100	100

Table 2. Scores for sentences with reordered adjuncts in an ideal situation

4.1 Initial experiment – Europarl

In the first experiment, we attempted to determine whether the dependency-based measure is biased towards statistical MT output, a problem that has been observed for *n*-gram-based metrics like BLEU and NIST. Callison-Burch et al. (2006) report that BLEU and NIST favour *n*-gram-based MT models such as Pharaoh (Koehn, 2004), so the translations produced by rule-based systems score lower on the automatic evaluation, even though human judges consistently rate their output higher than Pharaoh's translation. Others repeatedly

[6] Two things have to be noted here: (1) in case of NIST the perfect score differs from text to text, which is why we provide the percentage points as well, and (2) in case of TER the lower the score, the better the translation, so the perfect translation will receive 0, and there is no upper bound on the score, which makes this particular metric extremely difficult to directly compare with others.

observed this tendency in previous research as well; in one experiment, reported in Owczarzak et al. (2006), where the rule-based system Logomedia[7] was compared with Pharaoh, BLEU scored Pharaoh 0.0349 points higher, NIST scored Pharaoh 0.6219 points higher, but human judges scored Logomedia output 0.19 points higher (on a 5-point scale).

4.1.1 Experimental design

In order to check for the existence of a bias in the dependency-based metric, we created a set of 4,000 sentences drawn randomly from the Spanish-English subset of Europarl (Koehn, 2005), and we produced two translations: one by a rule-based system Logomedia, and the other by the standard phrase-based statistical decoder Pharaoh, using alignments produced by GIZA++[8] and the refined word alignment strategy of Och and Ney (2003). The translations were scored with a range of metrics: BLEU, NIST, GTM, TER, METEOR, and the dependency-based method.

4.1.2 Adding synonyms

Besides the ability to allow syntactic variants as valid translations, a good metric should also be able to accept legitimate lexical variation. We introduced synonyms and paraphrases into the process of evaluation, creating new best-matching references for the translations using either paraphrases derived from the test set itself (following Owczarzak et al. (2006)) or WordNet synonyms (as in Kauchak and Barzilay (2006)).

Bitext-derived paraphrases

Owczarzak et al. (2006) describe a simple way to produce a list of paraphrases, which can be useful in MT evaluation, by running word alignment software on the test set that is being evaluated. Paraphrases derived in this way are specific to the domain at hand and contain low-level syntactic variants in addition to word-level synonymy.

Using the standard GIZA++ software and the refined word alignment strategy of Och and Ney (2003) on our test set of 4,000 Spanish-English sentences, the method generated paraphrases for just over 1100 items. These paraphrases served to create new individual best-matching references for the Logomedia and Pharaoh translations. Due to the small size of the paraphrase set, only about 20% of reference sentences were actually modified to better reflect the translation. This, in turn, led to little difference in scores.

WordNet synonyms

To maximize the number of matches between a translation and a reference, Kauchak and Barzilay (2006) use WordNet synonyms during evaluation. In addition, METEOR also has an option of including WordNet in the evaluation process. As in the case of bitext-derived paraphrases, we used WordNet synonyms to create new best-matching references for each of the two translations. This time, given the extensive database containing synonyms for over 150,000 items, around 70% of reference sentences were modified: 67% for Pharaoh, and 75% for Logomedia. Note that the number of substitutions is higher for Logomedia; this confirms the intuition that the translation produced by Pharaoh, trained on the domain which is also the source of the reference text, will need fewer lexical replacements than Logomedia, which is based on a general non-domain-specific model.

4.1.3 Results

Table 3 shows the difference between the scores which Pharaoh's and Logomedia's translations obtained from each metric: a positive number shows by how much Pharaoh's score was higher than Logomedia's, and a negative number reflects Logomedia's higher score (the percentages are absolute values). As can be seen, all the metrics scored Pharaoh higher, inlcuding METEOR and the dependency-based method that were boosted with WordNet. The values in the table are sorted in descending order, from the largest to the lowest advantage of Pharaoh over Logomedia.

Interestingly, next to METEOR boosted with WordNet, it is the dependency-based method, and especially the predicates-only version, that shows the least bias towards the phrase-based translation. In the next step, we selected from this set smaller subsets of sentences that were more and more similar in terms of translation quality (as determined by a sentence's BLEU score). As the similarity of the translation quality increased, most metrics lowered their bias, as is shown in Table 4.

The first column shows the case where the sentences chosen differed at the most by 0.05

[7] http://www.lec.com/

[8] http://www.fjoch.com/GIZA++

points BLEU score; in the second column the difference was lowered to 0.01; and in the third column to 0.005. The numbers following the hash signs in the header row indicate the number of sentences in a given set.

metric	PH score – LM score
TER	1.997
BLEU	7.16%
NIST	6.58%
dep	4.93%
dep+paraphr	4.80%
GTM	3.89%
METEOR	3.80%
dep_preds	3.79%
dep+paraphr_preds	3.70%
dep+WordNet	3.55%
dep+WordNet_preds	2.60%
METEOR+WordNet	1.56%

Table 3. Difference between scores assigned to Pharaoh and Logomedia. Positive numbers show by how much Pharaoh's score was higher than Logomedia's. Legend: dep = dependency f-score, paraph = paraphrases, _preds = predicate-only f-score.

~ 0.05	#1692	~ 0.01	#567	~ 0.005	#335
NIST	2.29%	NIST	1.76%	NIST	1.48%
BLEU	0.95%	BLEU	0.42%	BLEU	0.59%
GTM	0.94%	GTM	0.29%	GTM	-0.09%
d+p	0.67%	d	0.04%	d+p	-0.15%
d	0.61%	d+p	0.02%	d	-0.24%
d+WN	-0.29%	d+WN	-0.78%	d+WN	-0.99%
d+p_pr	-0.70%	M	-0.99%	d+p_pr	-1.30%
d_pr	-0.75%	d_pr	-1.37%	d_pr	-1.43%
M	-1.03%	d+p_pr	-1.38%	M	-1.57%
d+WN_pr	-1.43%	d+WN_pr	-1.97%	d+WN_pr	-1.94%
M+WN	-2.51%	M+WN	-2.21%	M+WN	-2.74%
TER	-1.579	TER	-1.228	TER	-1.739

Table 4. Difference between scores assigned to Pharaoh and Logomedia for sets of increasing similarity. Positive numbers show Pharaoh's advantage, negative numbers show Logomedia's advantage. Legend: d = dependency f-score, p = paraphrases, _pr = predicate-only f-score, M = METEOR, WN = WordNet.

These results confirm earlier suggestions that the predicate-only version of the dependency-based evaluation is less biased in favour of the statistical MT system than the version that includes all dependency types. Adding a sufficient number of lexical choices reduces the bias even further; although again, paraphrases generated from the test set only are too few to make a significant difference. Similarly to METEOR, the dependency-based method shows on the whole lower bias than other metrics. However, we cannot be certain that the underlying scores vary linearly with each other and with human judgements, as we have no framework of reference such as human segment-level assessment of translation quality in this case. Therefore, the correlation with human judgement is analysed in our next experiment.

4.2 Correlation with human judgement – MultiTrans

To calculate how well the dependency-based method correlates with human judgement, and how it compares to the correlation shown by other metrics, we conducted an experiment on Chinese-English newswire text.

4.2.1 Experimental design

We used the data from the Linguistic Data Consortium Multiple Translation Chinese (MTC) Parts 2 and 4. The data consists of multiple translations of Chinese newswire text, four human-produced references, and segment-level human scores for a subset of the translation-reference pairs. Although a single translated segment was always evaluated by more than one judge, the judges used a different reference every time, which is why we treated each translation-reference-human score triple as a separate segment. In effect, the test set created from this data contained 16,800 segments. As in the previous experiment, the translation was scored using BLEU, NIST, GTM, TER, METEOR, and the dependency-based method.

4.2.2 Results

We calculated Pearson's correlation coefficient for segment-level scores that were given by each metric and by human judges. The results of the correlation are shown in Table 5. Note that the correlation for TER is negative, because in TER zero is the perfect score, in contrast to other metrics where zero is the worst possible score; however, this time the absolute values can be easily compared to each other. Rows are ordered by the highest value of the (absolute) correlation with the human score.

First, it seems like none of the metrics is very good at reflecting human fluency judgments; the correlation values in the first column are significantly lower than the correlation with accuracy. However, the dependency-based method in almost all its versions has decidedly the highest correlation in this area. This can be explained by the method's sensitivity to the grammatical structure of the sentence: a more grammatical translation is also a translation that is more fluent.

H_FL		H_AC		H_AVE	
d+WN	0.168	M+WN	0.294	M+WN	0.255
d	0.162	M	0.278	d+WN	0.244
d+WN_pr	0.162	NIST	0.273	M	0.242
BLEU	0.155	d+WN	0.266	NIST	0.238
d_pr	0.154	GTM	0.260	d	0.236
M+WN	0.153	d	0.257	GTM	0.230
M	0.149	d+WN_pr	0.232	d+WN_pr	0.220
NIST	0.146	d_pr	0.224	d_pr	0.212
GTM	0.146	BLEU	0.199	BLEU	0.197
TER	-0.133	TER	-0.192	TER	-0.182

Table 5. Pearson's correlation between human scores and evaluation metrics. Legend: d = dependency f-score, _pr = predicate-only f-score, M = METEOR, WN = WordNet, H_FL = human fluency score, H_AC = human accuracy score, H_AVE = human average score.[9]

Second, and somewhat surprisingly, in this detailed examination the relative order of the metrics changed. The predicate-only version of the dependency-based method appears to be less adequate for correlation with human scores than its non-restricted versions. As to the correlation with human evaluation of translation accuracy, our method currently falls short of METEOR and even NIST. This is caused by the fact that both METEOR and NIST assign relatively little importance to the position of a specific word in a sentence, therefore rewarding the translation for content rather than linguistic form. For our dependency-based method, the noise introduced by the parser might be the reason for low correlation: if even one side of the translation-reference pair contains parsing errors, this may lead to a less reliable score. An obvious solution to this problem, which we are examining at the moment, is to include a number of best parses for each side of the evaluation.

High correlation with human judgements of fluency and lower correlation with accuracy results in a high second place for our dependency-based method when it comes to the average correlation coefficient. The WordNet-boosted dependency-based method scores only slightly lower than METEOR with WordNet. These results are very encouraging, especially as we see a number of ways the dependency-based method could be further developed.

5 Current and future work

While the idea of a dependency-based method is a natural step in the direction of a deeper linguistic analysis for MT evaluation, it does require an LFG grammar and parser for the target language. There are several obvious areas for improvement with respect to the method itself. First, we would also like to adapt the process of translation-reference dependency comparison to include *n*-best parsers for the input sentences, as well as some basic transformations which would allow an even deeper logical analysis of input (e.g. passive to active voice transformation).

Second, we want to repeat both experiments using a paraphrase set derived from a large parallel corpus, rather than the test set, as described in Owczarzak et al. (2006). While retaining the advantage of having a similar size to a corresponding set of WordNet synonyms, this set will also capture low-level syntactic variations, which can increase the number of matches and the correlation with human scores.

Finally, we want to take advantage of the fact that the score produced by the dependency-based method is the proportional average of f-scores for a group of up to 32 (but usually far fewer) different dependency types. We plan to implement a set of weights, one for each dependency type, trained in such a way as to maximize the correlation of the final dependency f-score with human evaluation.

6 Conclusions

In this paper we present a novel way of evaluating MT output. So far, all metrics relied on

[9] In general terms, an increase of 0.015 between any two scores is significant with a 95% confidence interval.

comparing translation and reference on a string level. Even given reordering, stemming, and synonyms for individual words, current methods are still far from reaching human ability to assess the quality of translation. Our method compares the sentences on the level of their grammatical structure, as exemplified by their f-structure dependency triples produced by an LFG parser. The dependency-based method can be further augmented by using paraphrases or WordNet synonyms, and is available in full version and predicate-only version. In our experiments we showed that the dependency-based method correlates higher than any other metric with human evaluation of translation fluency, and shows high correlation with the average human score. The use of dependencies in MT evaluation is a rather new idea and requires more research to improve it, but the method shows potential to become an accurate evaluation metric.

Acknowledgements

This work was partly funded by Microsoft Ireland PhD studentship 2006-8 for the first author of the paper. We would also like to thank our reviewers for their insightful comments. All remaining errors are our own.

References

Satanjeev Banerjee and Alon Lavie. 2005. METEOR: An Automatic Metric for MT Evaluation with Improved Correlation with Human Judgments. *Proceedings of the ACL 2005 Workshop on Intrinsic and Extrinsic Evaluation Measures for MT and/or Summarization*: 65-73.

Joan Bresnan. 2001. *Lexical-Functional Syntax*, Blackwell, Oxford.

Aoife Cahill, Michael Burke, Ruth O'Donovan, Josef van Genabith, and Andy Way. 2004. Long-Distance Dependency Resolution in Automatically Acquired Wide-Coverage PCFG-Based LFG Approximations, In *Proceedings of ACL-04*: 320-327

Chris Callison-Burch, Miles Osborne and Philipp Koehn. 2006. Re-evaluating the role of BLEU in Machine Translation Research. *Proceedings of EACL 2006*: 249-256

George Doddington. 2002. Automatic Evaluation of MT Quality using N-gram Co-occurrence Statistics. *Proceedings of HLT 2002*: 138-145.

David Kauchak and Regina Barzilay. 2006. Paraphrasing for Automatic Evaluation. *Proceedings of HLT-NAACL 2006*: 45-462.

Philipp Koehn. 2004. Pharaoh: a beam search decoder for phrase-based statistical machine translation models. *Proceedings of the AMTA 2004 Workshop on Machine Translation: From real users to research*: 115-124.

Philipp Koehn. 2005. Europarl: A Parallel Corpus for Statistical Machine Translation. *Proceedings of MT Summit 2005*: 79-86.

Alex Kulesza and Stuart M. Shieber. 2004. A learning approach to improving sentence-level MT evaluation. In *Proceedings of the TMI 2004*: 75-84.

Gregor Leusch, Nicola Ueffing and Hermann Ney. 2006. CDER: Efficient MT Evaluation Using Block Movements. *Proceedings of EACL 2006*: 241-248.

Franz Josef Och and Hermann Ney. 2003. A Systematic Comparison of Various Statistical Alignment Modes. *Computational Linguistics*, 29:19-51.

Karolina Owczarzak, Declan Groves, Josef van Genabith, and Andy Way. 2006. Contextual Bitext-Derived Paraphrases in Automatic MT Evaluation. *Proceedings of the HLT-NAACL 2006 Workshop on Statistical Machine Translation*: 86-93.

Kishore Papineni, Salim Roukos, Todd Ward, and WeiJing Zhu. 2002. BLEU: a method for automatic evaluation of machine translation. In *Proceedings of ACL 2002*: 311-318.

Grazia Russo-Lassner, Jimmy Lin, and Philip Resnik. 2005. A Paraphrase-based Approach to Machine Translation Evaluation. Technical Report LAMP-TR-125/CS-TR-4754/UMIACS-TR-2005-57, University of Maryland, College Park, MD.

Mathew Snover, Bonnie Dorr, Richard Schwartz, John Makhoul, Linnea Micciula. 2006. A Study of Translation Error Rate with Targeted Human Annotation. *Proceedings of AMTA 2006*: 223-231.

Joseph P. Turian, Luke Shen, and I. Dan Melamed. 2003. Evaluation of Machine Translation and Its Evaluation. *Proceedings of MT Summit 2003*: 386-393.

Ying Zhang and Stephan Vogel. 2004. Measuring confidence intervals for the machine translation evaluation metrics. *Proceedings of TMI 2004*: 85-94.

Probabilistic Synchronous Tree-Adjoining Grammars for Machine Translation: The Argument from Bilingual Dictionaries

Stuart M. Shieber
School of Engineering and Applied Sciences
Harvard University
Cambridge, MA 02138
shieber@seas.harvard.edu

Abstract

We provide a conceptual basis for thinking of machine translation in terms of synchronous grammars in general, and probabilistic synchronous tree-adjoining grammars in particular. Evidence for the view is found in the structure of bilingual dictionaries of the last several millennia.

1 Introduction

In this paper, we provide a conceptual basis for thinking of machine translation in terms of synchronous grammars in general, and probabilistic synchronous tree-adjoining grammars in particular. The basis is conceptual in that the arguments are based on generalizations about the translation relation at a conceptual level, and not on empirical results at an engineering level. Nonetheless, the conceptual idea is consistent with current efforts in MT, and in fact may be seen as underlying so-called syntax-aware MT.

We will argue that the nature of the translation relation is such that an appropriate formalism for realizing it should have a set of properties — expressivity, trainability, efficiency — that we will characterize more precisely below. There may be multiple formalisms that can achieve these ends, but one, at least, is probabilistic synchronous tree-adjoining grammar, and to our knowledge, no other qualitatively distinct formalism has been argued to display all of the requisite properties.

Below, we will discuss the various properties, with particular attention to an examination of a particular source of data about the translation relation, namely bilingual dictionaries. Multilingual lexicography has a history of some four millennia or more. In that time, a great deal of knowledge about particular translation relations has been explicitly codified in multilingual dictionaries. More interestingly for our present purposes, multilingual dictionaries through their own structuring implicitly express information about translation relations in general.

In Section 2, we introduce the Construction Principle, a property of the translation relation implicit in the structure of bilingual dictionaries throughout their four millennium history. Section 3 provides a review of synchronous tree-adjoining grammars showing that this formalism directly incorporates the Construction Principle and allows the formal implementation of bilingual dictionary relations. In Section 4, we argue that the probabilistic variant of STAG (PSTAG) inherits the expressivity advantages of STAG while adding the trainability of statistical MT. Section 5 concerns the practical efficacy of STAG. We conclude (Section 6) with an overall proposal for the use of PSTAG in a statistical MT system. By virtue of its fundamentality to the modeling of the translation relation, PSTAG or its formal relatives merits empirical examination as a basis for statistical MT.

2 Expressivity

Of course, a formalism for describing the translation relation must be able to capture the relations between words in the two languages: *acqua* means *water*, *dormire* means *sleep*, and so forth. Indeed, the stereotype of a bilingual dictionary is just such a relation; the HarperCollins Italian College Dictionary (HCICD) (Clari and Love, 1995) contains en-

Proceedings of SSST, NAACL-HLT 2007 / AMTA Workshop on Syntax and Structure in Statistical Translation, pages 88–95,
Rochester, New York, April 2007.

tries ⟨*acqua / water*⟩$_{10}$ and ⟨*dormire / sleep*⟩$_{191}$.[1] This property doesn't distinguish among any of the formal means for capturing these direct lexical relationships. Finite-state string transducers naturally capture these simple relationships, but so do more (and less) expressive formalisms.

Simple word-by-word replacement is not a viable translation method; this was noted even as early as Weaver's famous memorandum (Weaver, 1955). Systems based on word-to-word lexicons, such as the IBM systems (Brown et al., 1990; Brown et al., 1993), incorporate further devices that allow reordering of words (a "distortion model") and ranking of alternatives (a monolingual language model). Together, these allow for the possibility that

The Word Principle:
> Words translate differently when adjacent to other words.

This property of the translation relation is patently true.

Even a word-to-word system with the ability to reorder words and rank alternatives has obvious limitations, which have motivated the machine translation research community toward progressively more expressive formalisms. Again, we see precedent for the move in bilingual dictionaries, which provide phrasal translations in addition to simple word translations: ⟨*by and large / nel complesso*⟩$_{86}$, ⟨*full moon / luna piena*⟩$_{406}$. The insight at work here is

The Phrase Principle:
> Phrases (not words) translate differently when adjacent to other phrases.

And again, we see this insight informing statistical machine translation systems, for instance, in the phrase-based approaches of Och (2003) and Koehn et al. (2003). These two principles, while true, do not exhaust the insights implicit in the structure of bilingual dictionaries. A fuller view is accomplished by moving from words and phrases to constructions.

2.1 The construction principle

The phenomenon that underlies the use of synchronous grammars for MT is simply this:

[1]Throughout, we notate entries in HCICD with the notation ⟨*entry form / translation form*⟩$_{page}$, providing the Italian and English forms, along with the page number of the cited entry.

The Construction Principle:
> Words and phrases translate differently in construction with other words.

The notion of *in construction with* is a structural notion. A word is in construction with another if they are related by a structural relation of some sort dependent on the identity or role of the word.

For example, the English word *take* is prototypically translated with a form of the Italian *prendere* ⟨*take / prendere*⟩$_{661}$. But when its object is a *bath*, as in the sentence "I like to take several long bubble baths every day", the word is translated with a form of *fare*. More accurately, the *construction* typified by the phrase *take a bath* is translated by the corresponding construction typified by the phrase *fare un bagno* (⟨*take a bath / fare un bagno*⟩$_{662}$).

One may think that we are still in the realm of the Phrase Principle; the phrase *take a bath* translates as the phrase *fare un bagno*. But the generalization is clearly much more general than that in several ways.

First, the notion of *in construction with* does not necessarily lead to contiguous phrases because of *variability* within the constructions. Bilingual dictionaries have developed notational conventions for such cases. When freely variable objects can intervene between the words in construction, a kind of variable word is used in dictionary entries, such as SB (*somebody*), STH (*something*), QN (*qualcuno*), QC (*qualcosa*). The word *take* participates in another construction ⟨*take* SB *by surprise / cogliere [literally "catch"]* QN *di sorpresa*⟩. The phenomenon is widespread. We find entries for light verb phrases such as *take* SB *by surprise*, idiomatic constructions such as ⟨*pull* SB*'s leg / prendere in giro* QN⟩$_{507}$, and particle constructions such as ⟨*call* SB *up / chiamare* QN⟩$_{86}$. These variable notations not only stand in for variable textual material and categorize that material (as specifying an entity (QC) or human (QN)) but also provide links between the portions of the two constructions. Whatever lexical material instantiates a SB variable on the English side, its translation instantiates the QN in the Italian. Thus translations require not only structure in the monolingual representations, but structure bilingually across them.[2]

[2]The linking of the subject roles in these constructions is typically left implicit in these entries, following from an as-

Second, even constructions that are in and of themselves contiguous may become discontiguous by *intervention* of other lexical material: modifiers, appositives, and the like. An example has already been seen in the example "I like to take several long bubble baths every day". There is no contiguity between *take* and *bath* here. A formalism based purely on concatenation of contiguous phrases will be unable to model such constructions.

These two aspects of variability and intervention within and between constructions preclude simple concatenative formalisms such as finite-state or context-free formalisms.

2.2 Prevalence of bilingual constructions

A natural question arises as to the prevalence of such nontrivial bilingual constructions. Presumably, if they are sufficiently rare and exotic, it may be acceptable, and in fact optimal, from an engineering point of view to ignore them and stay with simpler formalisms.

We can ask the prevalence question at the level of types or tokens. At the type level, a simple examination of a comprehensive modern bilingual dictionary reveals a quite high frequency of non-word-for-word translations. Analysis of a small random subsample of HCICD yielded only 34% of entries of the ⟨*acqua / water*⟩$_{10}$ sort. In contrast, 52% were contiguous multi-word translations, e.g., ⟨*guarda caso / strangely enough*⟩$_{100}$. An additional 11% of entries had variable content, split about equally between entries with overt marking of variability (⟨*prendere* QN *in castagna / to catch* SB *in the act*⟩$_{100}$) and implicit variability (⟨*hai fatto caso al suo cappello? / did you notice his hat?*⟩$_{100}$, in which the ⟨*suo cappello / his hat*⟩ pair serves as a placeholder for other translates. (The remaining 3% is accounted for by entries providing monolingual equivalences and untranslated proper names.) The line between implicit variability and multi-word translations is quite permeable, so that many of the 54% of entries classified as the latter might in fact be better thought of as the former, and in any case many of the multi-word entries would be subject to noncontiguity through insertion of other lexical material. At the type level, then, there is plenty of evidence for the Phrase Principle and the Construction Principle.

At the token level, the general interest in so-called syntax-aware statistical MT approaches is itself evidence that researchers believe that the tokens accounting for the performance gap in current systems based on the Word and Phrase Principles transcend those principles in some way, presumably because they manifest the Construction Principle.[3] Only time will tell if such syntax-aware systems are able to display performance improvements over their nonstructural alternatives. Successful experiments such as those of Chiang (2005) using synchronous context-free grammar are a good first start.[4]

2.3 Heritage of the construction principle

We have argued that a formalism expressive enough to model the translation relation implicit in bilingual dictionaries must be based on relations over constructions, the primitive relations found in such bilingual dictionaries and founded by the Construction Principle. The fundamentality of this principle is evidenced by the fact that it has informed bilingual dictionaries literally *since their inception*. The earliest known bilingual dictionaries are those incorporated in the so-called lexical texts of ancient Mesopotamia from four millennia ago. Even there, we find evidence of the Construction Principle in entries that describe translation of words dependent upon words they are in construction with. Civil (1995) cites an example of the Akkadian word *nakāpu* (to gore, to knock down) whose translation into Sumerian is given differentially dependent on the nature of "grammatical constructions with particular subjects or objects":

sumption that subjects are typically linked across these languages. Where this assumption fails, however, explicit marking is found in the dictionary, either by using a passive alternation ⟨*piacere a* QN */ to be liked by* SB⟩$_{424}$, or implicit linking ⟨*mi piace / I like it*⟩$_{424}$.

[3] A reviewer objects that this point is vacuous: "Is the fact that researchers aren't building large-scale statistical semantic transfer models evidence for the fact that they don't believe in semantics?" This is an instance of the logical fallacy of denying the antecedent. If researchers act on a premise, they believe the premise. From this it does not follow that if they fail to act on a premise, they deny the premise.

[4] It would be more convincing to have empirical token-level statistics on the prevalence of constructions found in bilingual dictionaries. Unfortunately, this would require much of the effort of building an MT system on a construction basis itself.

Translation	When said of
sag-ta-dug$_4$-ga	the head
du$_7$	oxen
ru$_5$	rams
si-tu$_{10}$	oxen/bulls
kur-ku	a flood
ru-gú	a finger
si-ga	a garment

3 Synchronous Grammars Reviewed

To summarize, the translation relation in evidence implicitly in bilingual dictionaries requires a formalism expressive enough to directly represent *relations* between *constructions*, appropriately *linked*, and to do so in a way that allows these constructions to be realized *noncontiguously* by virtue of *variability* and *intervention*. As we will show, the former requirement is exactly the idea underlying synchronous grammars. The latter requirement of noncontiguity in its two aspects further implicates operations of substitution and adjunction (respectively) to combine constructions. The requirements lead naturally to a consideration of synchronous tree-adjoining grammar as the direct embodiment of the bilingual dictionaries of the last four millennia.

A synchronous grammar formalism is built by synchronizing grammars from some base formalism. A grammar in the base formalism consists of a set of elementary tree structures along with one or more combining operations. All of the familiar monolingual formalisms—finite-state grammars, context-free grammars, tree-substitution and -adjoining grammars, categorial grammars, inter alia—can be thought of in this way. A synchronous grammar consists of a set of pairs of elementary trees from the base formalism together with a linking relation between nodes in the trees at which combining operations can perform. Derivation proceeds as in the base formalism, whatever that is, except that a pair of trees operate at a pair of linked nodes in an elementary tree pair. An operation performed at one end of a link must be matched by a corresponding operation at the other end of the link. For example, the tree pair in Figure 1 might be appropriate for use in translating the sentence *Eli took his father by surprise*. The links between the NP nodes play the same role as the linked variables SB and QN in the bilingual dictionary entry. They allow for substitution of tree pairs for *Eli* and its translation and *his father* and its. The additional links allow for further modification, as in *Eli recently took his father by surprise by preparing dinner*, the modifiers *recently* and *by preparing dinner* adjoining at the VP and S links, respectively.

Expressing this relation in other frameworks involves either limiting its scope (for instance, to particular objects and intervening material), expanding its scope (by separating the translations of the contiguous portions of the constructions), or mimicking the structure of the STAG (as described at the end of Section 5).

The basic idea of using synchronous TAG for machine translation dates from the original definition (Shieber and Schabes, 1990), and has been pursued by several researchers (Abeille et al., 1990; Dras, 1999; Prigent, 1994; Palmer et al., 1999), but only recently in its probabilistic form (Nesson et al., 2006). The directness with which the formalism follows from the structure of bilingual dictionaries has not to our knowledge been previously noted. It leads to the possibility of making direct use of bilingual dictionary material in a statistical machine translation system.[5] But even if the formalism is not used in that way, there is import to the fact that its expressivity matches that thought by lexicographers of the last several millennia to be needed for capturing the translation relation; this fact indicates at least that STAG's use as a substrate for MT systems may be a promising research direction to pursue, should other necessary properties be satisfiable as well. We turn next to two of these properties: trainability and efficiency.

4 Trainability

The mere ability to formally represent the contents of manually developed bilingual dictionaries is not sufficient for the building of robust machine translation systems. The last decade and a half of MT research has demonstrated the importance of trainability of the models based on statistical evidence found in corpora. Without such training, manually

[5]For construction-based MT, reconstruction of tree alignments from data is much more difficult than for phrase-based MT, and hence extracting them from a dictionary becomes much more appealing.

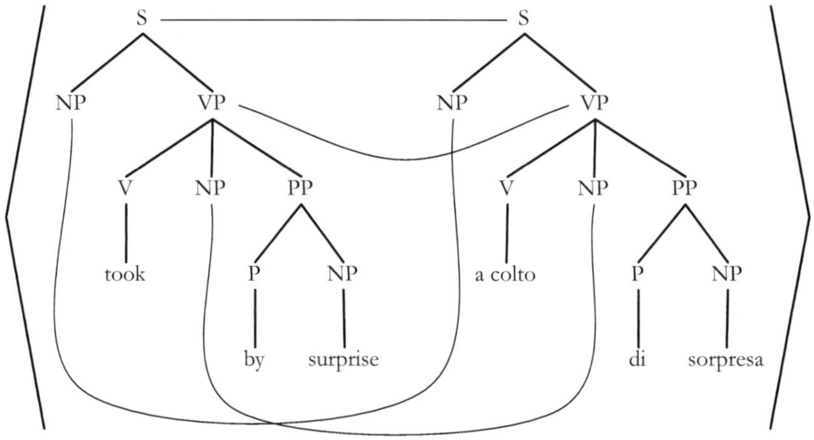

Figure 1: A synchronous tree pair.

developed models are too brittle to be seriously considered as a basis for machine translation.

It may also be the case that *with* such training, the manually generated materials are redundant. Certainly, it has been difficult to show the utility of manually generated annotations in improving MT performance. But this may be because the means by which the materials are represented is not yet appropriate; it does not articulate well with the statistical substrate used by the training methodology.

A further property, then, for the formalism is that it be trainable based on bilingual corpora. Consider training of the sort that underlies the IBM-style word models and their phrase-based offshoots, or statistical parsing based on probabilistic CFGs (Lari and Young, 1990) or other generative formalisms. Such methods use an underlying probabilistic formalism, typically structuring the parameters based on a universal parametric normal form (as *n*-gram probabilities are for finite-state grammars and Chomsky-normal form is for PCFGs), and applying an efficient training algorithm to set values for the parameters.

A full system based on STAG would use the formalism to express both the detailed bilingual constructional relationships as found in a bilingual dictionary and a backbone in the form of the universal normal form. Trained together, the normal form would serve to smooth the brittle construction-specific part, while the construction-specific part would relieve the burden on the universal learned portion to allocate parameters to rare constructions.

How do synchronous tree-adjoining grammars fare in this area? Do they admit of the kind of universal normal-form training that might serve as a smoothing method for the more highly articulated but brittle lexicographic relation?

A probabilistic variant of synchronous TAG is straightforward to specify, given that the formalism itself has a natural generative interpretation (Shieber, 1994). A universal parametric normal form has been provided by Nesson et al. (2006) (see Figure 2), who show that, at least on small training sets, a synchronous TAG in this normal form performs at a level comparable to standard word- and phrase-based systems. Synchronous TAGs thus seem to have the best of both worlds: They can directly express the types of ramified bilingual constructions as codified in bilingual dictionaries, and they can also express the types of universal assumption-free normal forms that underlie modern statistical MT. Importantly, they can do so *at one and the same time*, as both types of information are expressed in the same way, as sets of tree pairs. Both can therefore be trained together based on bilingual corpora.

We emphasize that the advantage that we find for STAGs in displaying well the necessary properties for statistical machine translation systems implicit in bilingual dictionaries is not that they are able to code efficiently all generalizations about the translation relation. Indeed, STAG is not able to do so (Shieber, 1994), which has motivated more expressive exten-

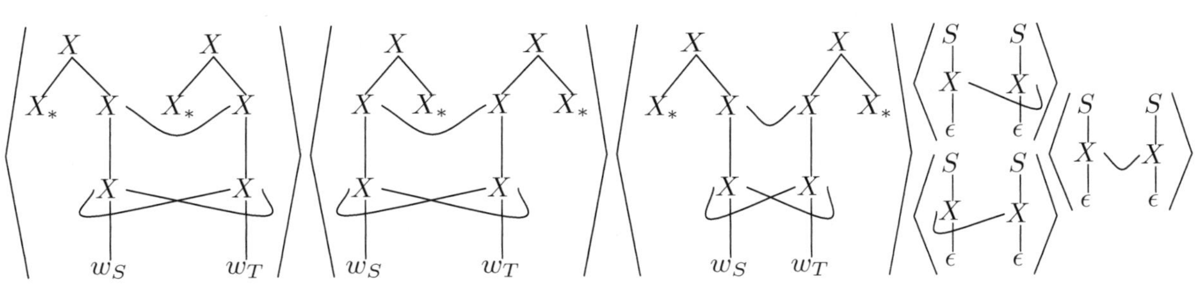

Figure 2: A normal form for synchronous tree-insertion grammar. (Reproduced from Nesson et al. (2006).)

sions of the formalism (Chiang et al., 2000). For example, STAG might express the construction relation ⟨*attraversare* QC *di corsa* / *run across* ST⟩ and similar relations between Italian verbs of direction with modifiers of motion and English verbs of motion with directional modifiers. However, the generalization that directional verbs with motion-manner adverbials translate as motion-manner verbs with directional adverbials is not expressed or expressible by STAG. Each instance of the generalization must be specified or learned separately.[6] Nonetheless, we are content (in the spirit of statistical MT) to have lots of such particular cases missing a generalization, so long as the parts from which they are constructed are pertinent, that is, so long as we do not need to specify ⟨*attraversare la strada di corsa* / *run across the road*⟩$_{51}$ separately from all of the other things one might run across.

5 Efficiency

A final set of considerations has to do with the efficiency of the formalism. Is it practical to use STAG for the purposes we have outlined? It is important not to preclude a formalism merely based on impracticality of its current use (given the constant increases in computer speed), but inherent intractability is another matter.[7]

Here, the STAG situation is equivocal. Bilingual parsing of a corpus relative to an STAG is a necessary first step in parameter training. The recognition problem for STAG, like that for synchronous context-free grammar (SCFG) is NP-hard (Satta and Peserico, 2005). Under appropriate restrictions of binarizability, SCFG parsing can be done in $O(n^6)$ time, doubling the exponent of CFG parsing. Similarly, STAG parsing under suitable limitations (Nesson et al. (2005)) can be done in $O(n^{12})$ time doubling the exponent of monolingual TAG parsing. On the positive side, recent work exploring the automatic binarization of synchronous grammars (Zhang et al., 2006) has indicated that non-binarizable constructions seem to be relatively rare in practice. Nonetheless, such a high-degree polynomial makes the complete algorithm impractical.

Nesson et al. (2006) use synchronous tree-insertion grammar (STIG) (Schabes and Waters, 1995) rather than STAG for this very reason. STIG retains the ability to express a universal normal form, while allowing $O(n^6)$ bilingual parsing. (Again, limitations on the formalism are required to achieve this complexity.) Even this complexity may be too high. Methods such as those of Chiang (2005) have been proposed for further reducing the complexity of SCFG parsing; they may be applicable to STIG (and STAG) parsing as well.

The STIG formalism can be shown to be expressively equivalent to synchronous tree-substitution grammar (STSG) and even SCFG. Does this vitiate the argument for STIG as a natural formalism for MT? No. The reductions of STIG to these other formalisms operate by introducing additional nodes

[6] Palmer et al. (1999) provide an approach to STAG that attempts to address this particular problem as does the extension of Dras (1999). It is unclear to what extent such extensions are amenable to trainable probabilistic variants.

[7] Of course, too much might be made of this question of computational complexity. The algorithms used for decoding of statistical MT systems almost universally incorporate heuristics for efficiency reasons, even those that are polynomial. One reviewer notes that "the admittedly perplexing reality is that exponential decoders run much faster than polynomial ones, presumably because they prune more intelligently."

in the elementary trees that extend the size of those trees and hence the complexity of their parsing, unless subtle tricks are used to take advantage of the special structure of these added nodes. These tricks essentially amount to treating the formalism as an STIG, not an SCFG. That is, even if an SCFG were to be used, its structure would best be built on the observations found here.

For example, the method of Cowan et al. (2006) synchronizes elementary trees of a prescribed form to handle translation of clauses (verbs plus their arguments) essentially implementing a kind of STSG. However, because modifiers can make these trees discontiguous, they augment the model by allowing for free insertion of modifiers in certain locations. One view of this is as an implementation of the principle that motivates adjoining, without using adjoining itself. Thus, systems that are designed to take account of the principles adduced in this paper are likely to be implementing aspects of STAG implicitly, even if not explicitly.

Similarly, recent research is beginning to unify synchronous grammar formalisms and tree transducers (Shieber, 2004; Shieber, 2006). There may well be equally direct transducer formalisms that elegantly express construction-based translation relations. This would not be a denial of the present thesis but a happy acknowledgment of it.

6 Conclusion

We have argued that probabilistic synchronous TAG or some closely related formalism possesses a constellation of properties—expressivity, trainability, and efficiency—that make it a good candidate at a conceptual level for founding a machine translation system. What would such a system look like? It would start with a universal normal form subgrammar serving as the robust "backoff" relation to which additional more articulated bilingual material could be added in the form of additional tree pairs. These tree pairs might be manually generated, automatically reconstructed from repurposed bilingual dictionaries, or automatically induced from aligned bilingual treebanks (Groves et al., 2004; Groves and Way, 2005) or even unannotated bilingual corpora (Chiang, 2005). In fact, since all of these sources of data yield interacting tree pairs, more than one of these techniques might be used. In any case, further training would automatically determine the interactions of these information sources.

The conclusions of this paper are admittedly programmatic. But plausible arguments for a program of research may be just the thing for clarifying a research direction and even promoting its pursual. In that sense, this paper can be read as a kind of manifesto for the use of probabilistic synchronous TAG as a substrate for MT research.

Acknowledgments

We thank Rani Nelken, Rebecca Nesson, and Alexander Rush for helpful discussion and the anonymous reviewers for their insightful comments. This work was supported in part by grant IIS-0329089 from the National Science Foundation.

References

Anne Abeille, Yves Schabes, and Aravind K. Joshi. 1990. Using lexicalized tags for machine translation. In *Proceedings of the 13th International Conference on Computational Linguistics*.

Peter F. Brown, John Cocke, Stephen Della Pietra, Vincent J. Della Pietra, Frederick Jelinek, John D. Lafferty, Robert L. Mercer, and Paul S. Roossin. 1990. A statistical approach to machine translation. *Computational Linguistics*, 16(2):79–85.

Peter F. Brown, Stephen Della Pietra, Vincent J. Della Pietra, and Robert L. Mercer. 1993. The mathematics of statistical machine translation: Parameter estimation. *Computational Linguistics*, 19(2):263–311.

David Chiang, William Schuler, and Mark Dras. 2000. Some remarks on an extension of synchronous TAG. In *Proceedings of the 5th International Workshop on Tree Adjoining Grammars and Related Formalisms (TAG+5)*, Paris, France, 25–27 May.

David Chiang. 2005. A hierarchical phrase-based model for statistical machine translation. In *Proceedings of the 43rd Annual Meeting of the Association for Computational Linguistics (ACL'05)*, pages 263–270, Ann Arbor, Michigan, June. Association for Computational Linguistics.

Miguel Civil. 1995. Ancient Mesopotamian lexicography. In Jack M. Sasson, editor, *Civilizations of the Ancient Near East*, volume 4, pages 2305–14. Scribners, New York.

Michela Clari and Catherine E. Love, editors. 1995. *HarperCollins Italian College Dictionary*. HarperCollins Publishers, Inc., New York, NY.

Brooke Cowan, Ivona Kucerov, and Michael Collins. 2006. A discriminative model for tree-to-tree translation. In *Proceedings of EMNLP 2006*.

Mark Dras. 1999. A meta-level grammar: Redefining synchronous TAG for translation and paraphrase. In *Proceedings of the 37th Annual Meeting of the Association for Computational Linguistics*, pages 80–87, Morristown, NJ, USA. Association for Computational Linguistics.

Declan Groves and Andy Way. 2005. Hybrid example-based SMT: the best of both worlds? In *Workshop on Building and Using Parallel Texts: Data-Driven Machine Translation and Beyond*, Ann Arbor, MI, June. ACL '05.

Declan Groves, Mary Hearne, and Andy Way. 2004. Robust sub-sentential alignment of phrase-structure trees. In *COLING '04, Geneva Switzerland.*

Philipp Koehn, Franz Josef Och, and Daniel Marcu. 2003. Statistical phrase-based translation. In *Proceedings of HLT/NAACL.*

Karim Lari and Steve J. Young. 1990. The estimation of stochastic context-free grammars using the inside-outside algorithm. *Computer Speech and Language*, 4:35–56.

Rebecca Nesson, Alexander Rush, and Stuart M. Shieber. 2005. Induction of probabilistic synchronous tree-insertion grammars. Technical Report TR-20-05, Division of Engineering and Applied Sciences, Harvard University, Cambridge, MA.

Rebecca Nesson, Stuart M. Shieber, and Alexander Rush. 2006. Induction of probabilistic synchronous tree-insertion grammars for machine translation. In *Proceedings of the 7th Conference of the Association for Machine Translation in the Americas (AMTA 2006)*, Boston, Massachusetts, 8-12 August.

Franz Josef Och. 2003. *Statistical Machine Translation: From Single-Word Models to Alignment Templates*. Ph.D. thesis, Technical University of Aachen, Aachen, Germany.

Martha Palmer, Joseph Rosenzweig, and William Schuler. 1999. Capturing motion verb generalizations in synchronous tree-adjoining grammar. In Patrick Saint-Dizier, editor, *Predicative Forms in Natural Language and in Lexical Knowledge Bases*. Kluwer Press.

Gilles Prigent. 1994. Synchronous TAGs and machine translation. In *Proceedings of the Third International Workshop on Tree Adjoining Grammar and Related Formalisms (TAG+3)*, Université Paris 7.

Giorgio Satta and Enoch Peserico. 2005. Some computational complexity results for synchronous context-free grammars. In *Proceedings of the Conference on Human Language Technology and Empirical Methods in Natural Language Processing (HLT/EMNLP 05)*, pages 803–810, Morristown, NJ, USA. Association for Computational Linguistics.

Yves Schabes and Richard C. Waters. 1995. Tree insertion grammar: A cubic time, parsable formalism that lexicalizes context-free grammars without changing the trees produced. *Computational Linguistics*, 21(3):479–512.

Stuart M. Shieber and Yves Schabes. 1990. Synchronous tree-adjoining grammars. In *Proceedings of the 13th International Conference on Computational Linguistics*, volume 3, pages 253–258, Helsinki, Finland.

Stuart M. Shieber. 1994. Restricting the weak-generative capacity of synchronous tree-adjoining grammars. *Computational Intelligence*, 10(4):371–385, November. Also available as cmp-lg/9404003.

Stuart M. Shieber. 2004. Synchronous grammars as tree transducers. In *Proceedings of the Seventh International Workshop on Tree Adjoining Grammar and Related Formalisms (TAG+ 7)*, Vancouver, Canada, May 20-22.

Stuart M. Shieber. 2006. Unifying synchronous tree-adjoining grammars and tree transducers via bimorphisms. In *Proceedings of the 11th Conference of the European Chapter of the Association for Computational Linguistics (EACL-06)*, Trento, Italy, 3–7 April.

Warren Weaver. 1955. Translation. In W.N. Locke and A. D. Booth, editors, *Machine Translation of Languages: Fourteen Essays*, pages 15–23. Technology Press of the Massachusetts Institute of Technology, Cambridge, Massachusetts.

Hao Zhang, Liang Huang, Daniel Gildea, and Kevin Knight. 2006. Synchronous binarization for machine translation. In *Proceedings of the Conference on Human Language Technology and Annual Meeting of the North American Chapter of the Association of Computational Linguistics (HLT/NAACL 2006)*, pages 256–263, Morristown, NJ, USA. Association for Computational Linguistics.

Three models for discriminative machine translation using Global Lexical Selection and Sentence Reconstruction

Sriram Venkatapathy
Language Technologies Research Centre, IIIT-Hyderabad
Hyderabad - 500019, India.
sriram@research.iiit.ac.in

Srinivas Bangalore
AT&T Labs - Research
Florham Park, NJ 07932
USA
srini@research.att.com

Abstract

Machine translation of a source language sentence involves selecting appropriate target language words and ordering the selected words to form a well-formed target language sentence. Most of the previous work on statistical machine translation relies on (local) associations of target words/phrases with source words/phrases for lexical selection. In contrast, in this paper, we present a novel approach to lexical selection where the target words are associated with the entire source sentence (global) without the need for local associations. This technique is used by three models (Bag–of–words model, sequential model and hierarchical model) which predict the target language words given a source sentence and then order the words appropriately. We show that a hierarchical model performs best when compared to the other two models.

1 Introduction

The problem of machine translation can be viewed as consisting of two subproblems: (a) lexical selection, where appropriate target language lexical items are chosen for each source language lexical item and (b) lexical reordering, where the chosen target language lexical items are rearranged to produce a meaningful target language string. Most of the previous work on statistical machine translation, as exemplified in (Brown et al., 1993), employs word–alignment algorithm (such as GIZA++ (Och et al., 1999)) that provides local associations between source words and target words. The source–to–target word–alignments are sometimes augmented with target–to–source word alignments in order to improve the precision of these local associations. Further, the word–level alignments are extended to phrase–level alignments in order to increase the extent of local associations. The phrasal associations compile some amount of (local) lexical reordering of the target words—those permitted by the size of the phrase. Most of the state–of–the–art machine translation systems use these phrase–level associations in conjunction with a target language model to produce the target sentence. There is relatively little emphasis on (global) lexical reordering other than the local re-orderings permitted within the phrasal alignments. A few exceptions are the hierarchical (possibly syntax–based) transduction models (Wu, 1997; Alshawi et al., 1998; Yamada and Knight, 2001; Chiang, 2005) and the string transduction models (Kanthak et al., 2005).

In this paper, we present three models for doing discriminative machine translation using *global lexical selection* and *lexical reordering*.

1. **Bag–of–Words model** : Given a source sentence, each of the target words are chosen by looking at the entire source sentence. The target language words are then permuted in various ways and then, the best permutation is chosen using the language model on the target side. The size of the search space of these permutations can be set by a parameter called the permutation window. This model does not allow long distance re-orderings of target words unless a very large permutation window chosen which is very expensive.

2. **Sequential Lexical Choice model** : Given a source sentence, the target words are predicted in an order which is faithful to the or-

Proceedings of SSST, NAACL-HLT 2007 / AMTA Workshop on Syntax and Structure in Statistical Translation, pages 96–102,
Rochester, New York, April 2007.

der of words in the source sentence. Now, the number of permutations that need to be examined to obtain the best target language strings are much less when compared to the Bag–of–Words model. This model is expected to give good results for language pairs such as English–French for which only local word order variations exist between sentences.

3. **Hierarchical lexical association and reordering model** : For language pairs such as English–Hindi or English–Japanese where there is a high degree of global reordering (Figure 1), it is necessary to be able to handle long distance movement of words/phrases. In this approach, the target words predicted through global lexical selection are associated with various nodes of the source dependency tree and then, hierarchical reordering is done to obtain the order of words in the target sentence. Hierarchical reordering allows phrases to distort to longer distances than the previous two models.

Figure 1: Sample distortion between English–Hindi

The outline of the paper is as follows. In Section 2, we talk about the global lexical selection. Section 3 describes three models for global lexical selection and reordering. In Section 4, we report the results of the translation models on English–Hindi language pair and contrast the strengths and limitations of the models.

2 Global lexical selection

For global lexical selection, in contrast to the local approaches of associating target words to the source words, the target words are associated to the entire source sentence. The intuition is that there may be lexico–syntactic features of the source sentence (not necessarily a single source word) that might trigger the presence of a target word in the target sentence. Furthermore, it might be difficult to exactly associate a target word to a source sentence in many situations - (a) when translations are not exact but paraphrases (b) the target language does not have one lexical item to express the same concept that is expressed in the source word. The extensions of word alignments to phrasal alignments attempt to address some of these situations in additional to alleviating the noise in word–level alignments.

As a consequence of the global lexical selection approach, we no longer have a tight association between source language words/phrases and target language words/phrases. The result of lexical selection is simply a bag of words(phrases) in the target language and the target sentence has to be reconstructed using this bag of words.

The target words in the bag, however, might be enhanced with rich syntactic information that could aid in the reconstruction of the target sentence. This approach to lexical selection and sentence reconstruction has the potential to circumvent the limitations of word–alignment based methods for translation between significantly different word order languages. However, in this paper, to handle large word order variations, we associate the target words with source language dependency structures to enable long distance reordering.

3 Training the discriminative models for lexical selection and reordering

In this section, we present our approach for a global lexical selection model which is based on discriminatively trained classification techniques. Discriminant modeling techniques have become the dominant method for resolving ambiguity in speech and natural language processing tasks, outperforming generative models for the same task. We expect the discriminatively trained global lexical selection models to outperform generatively trained local lexical selection models as well as provide a framework for incorporating rich morpho–syntactic information.

Statistical machine translation can be formulated as a search for the best target sequence that maximizes $P(T \mid S)$, where S is the source sentence and T is the target sentence. Ideally, $P(T \mid S)$ should be estimated directly to maximize the conditional likelihood on the training data (discriminant model). However, T corresponds to a sequence with a exponentially large combination of possible labels, and traditional classification approaches cannot be used directly. Although

Conditional Random Fields (CRF) (Lafferty et al., 2001) train an exponential model at the sequence level, in translation tasks such as ours the computational requirements of training such models are prohibitively expensive.

3.1 Bag-of-Words Lexical Choice Model

This model doesn't require the sentences to be word aligned in order to learn the local associations. Instead, we take the sentence aligned corpus as before but we treat the target sentence as a bag–of–words or BOW assigned to the source sentence. The goal is, given a source sentence S, to estimate the probability that we find a given word (t_j) in its translation ie.., we need to estimate the probabilities $P(true|t_j, S)$ and $P(false|t_j, S)$. To train such a model, we need to build binary classifiers for all the words in the target language vocabulary. The probability distributions of these binary classifiers are learnt using maximum entropy model (Berger et al., 1996; Haffner, 2006). For the word t_j, the training sentence pairs are considered as positive examples where the word appears in the target, and negative otherwise. Thus, the number of training examples for each binary classifier equals the number of training examples. In this model, classifiers are training using n–gram features (BOgrams(S)).

During decoding, instead of producing the target sentence directly, what we initially obtain is the target bag of words. Each word in the target vocabulary is detected independently, so we have here a very simple use of binary static classifiers. Given a sentence S, the bag of words ($BOW(T)$ contains those words whose distributions have the positive probability greater than a threshold (τ).

$$BOW(T) = \{t \mid P(true \mid t, BOgrams(S)) > \tau\} \quad (1)$$

In order to reconstruct the proper order of words in the target sentence, we consider various permutations of words in $BOW(T)$ and weight them by a target language model. Considering all possible permutations of the words in the target sentence is computationally not feasible. But, the number of permutations examined can be reduced by using heuristic forward pruning or by constraining the permutations to be within a local window of adjustable size (also see (Kanthak et al., 2005)). We have chosen to constrain permutations here. Constraining the permutation using a local window can provide us some very useful local reorderings.

The bag–of–words approach can also be modified to allow for length adjustments of target sentences, if we add optional deletions in the final step of permutation decoding. The parameter τ and an additional word deletion penalty δ can then be used to adjust the length of translated outputs.

3.2 Sequential Lexical Choice Model

The previous approach gives us a predetermined order of words initially which are then permuted to obtain the best target string. Given that we would not be able to search the entire space, it would be a helpful if we could start searching various permutations using a more definite string. One such definite order in which the target words can be placed is the order of source words itself. In this model, during the lexical selection, we try to place the target words in an order which is faithful to the source sentence.

This model associates sets of target words with every position in the source sentence and yet retains the power of global lexical selection. For every position (i) of the source sentence, a prefix string is formed which consists of the sequence of words from positions 1 to i. Each of these prefix strings are used to predict bags of target words using the global lexical selection. Now, these bags generated using the prefix strings are processed in the order of source positions. Let T_i be the bag of target words generated by prefix string i (Figure 2).

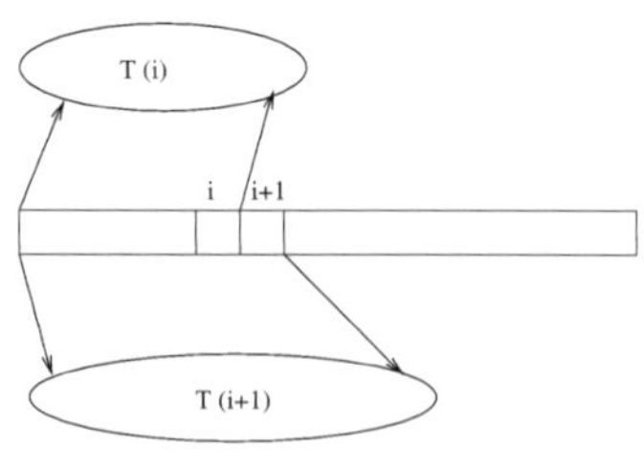

Figure 2: The generation of target bags associated with source sentence position

The goal is to associate a set of target words with every source position. A target word t is attached to the ith source position if it is present in T_i but not in T_{i-1} and the probability $P(true|t, T_i) > \tau$. The intuition behind this approach is that a word t is associated with a position i if there was some information present at the ith source position that triggered the probability of the t to exceed the threshold τ.

Hence, the initial target string is the sequence of target language words associated with the sequence of source language positions. This string is now permuted in all possible ways (section 3.1) and the best target string is chosen using the language model.

3.3 Hierarchical lexical association and reordering model

The *Sequential Lexical Choice Model* presented in the last section is expected to work best for language pairs for which there are mostly local word order variations. For language pairs with significant word order variation, the search for the target string may still fail examine the best target language string given the source sentence. The model proposed in this section should be able to handle such long distance movement of words/phrases.

In this model, the goal is to search for the best target string T which maximizes the probability $P(T|S, D(S))$, where S is the source sentence and $D(S)$ is the dependency structure associated with the source sentence S. The probabilities of the target words given the source sentence are estimated in the same way as the bag–of–words model. The only main difference during the estimation stage is that we consider the dependency tree based features apart from the n-gram features.

The decoding of the source sentence S takes place in three steps,

1. Predict the bag–of–words : Given a source sentence S, predict the bag of words BOW(T) whose distributions have a positive probabilities greater than a threshold (τ).

2. Attachment to Source nodes : These target words are now attached to the nodes of source dependency trees. For making the attachments, the probability distributions of target words conditioned on features local to the source nodes are used.

3. Ordering the target language words : Traverse the source dependency tree in a bottom-up fashion to obtain the best target string.

3.3.1 Predict the bag–of–words

Given a source sentence S, all the target words whose positive probability distributions are above τ are included in the bag.

$$BOW(T) = \{t \mid P(true|t, f(S))\} \quad (2)$$

In addition to the n–gram features, this model uses cues provided by the dependency structure to predict the target bag–of–words.

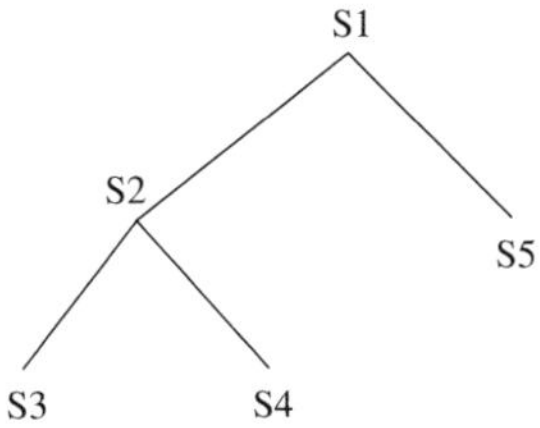

Figure 3: Dependency tree of a source sentence with words s1, s2, s3, s4 and s5

Hence, the features that we have considered in the model are (Figure 3),

1. N-grams. For example, in Figure 2, 's1', 's2 s3 s4', 's4 s5' etc.

2. Dependency pair (The pair of nodes and its parents). Example in Figure 2., 's2 s1', 's4 s2' etc.

3. Dependency treelet (The triplet of a node, it's parent and sibling). For example, 's3 s2 s4', 's2 s1 s5' etc.

3.3.2 Attachment to Source nodes

For every target word t_j in the bag, the most likely source nodes are determined by measuring the positive distribution of the word t_j given the features of the particular node (Figure 4). Let $S(t_j)$ denote the set of source nodes to which the word t_j can be attached to, then $S(t_j)$ is determined as,

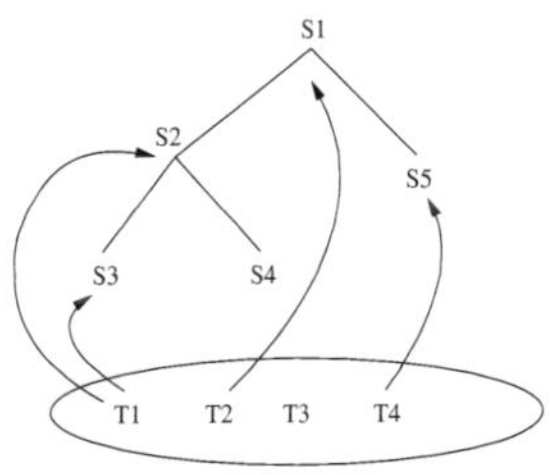

Figure 4: Dependency tree of a source sentence with words S1, S2, S3, S4 and S5

$$S(t_j) = argmax_s(P(true|t_j, f(s)) \quad (3)$$

where $f(s)$ denotes the features of S in which only those features are active which contain the lexical item representing the node s. The target words are in the global bag are processed in the order of their global probabilities $p(t|S)$. While attaching the target words, it is ensured that no source node had more than ρ target words attached to it. Also, a target word should not be attached to more to more than σ number of times. There is another constraint that can be applied to ensure that the ratio of the total target words (which are attached to source nodes) to the total number of words in the source sentence does exceed a value (μ).

3.4 Ordering the target language words

In this step, the source sentence dependency tree is traversed in a bottom–up fashion. At every node, the best possible order of target words associated with the sub-tree rooted at the node is determined. This string is then used as a cohesive unit by the superior nodes.

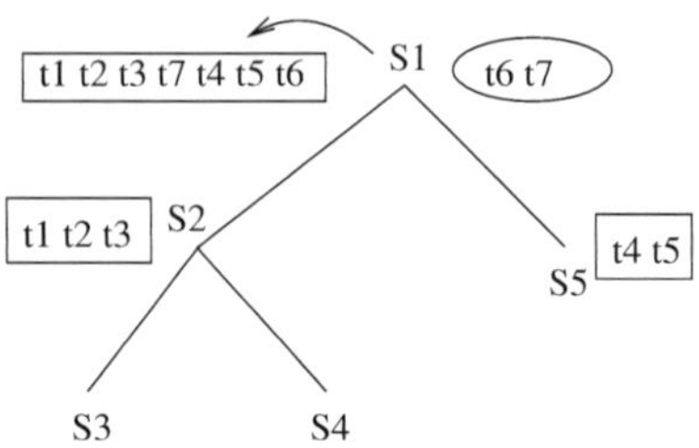

Figure 5: The target string associated with node S1 is determined by permuting strings attached to the children (in rectangular boxes, to signify that they are frozen) and the lexical items attached to S1

For example, in Figure 5, let 't1 t2 t3', 't4 t5' be the best strings associated with the children of nodes s2 and s3 respectively. Let t6 and t7 be the words that are attached to node s1. The best string for the node s1 is determined by permuting the strings 't1 t2 t3', 't4 t5', 't6' 't7' in all possible ways and then choosing the best string using the language model.

4 Dataset

The language pair that we considered for our experiments are English–Hindi. The training set consists of 37967 sentence pairs, the development set contains 819 sentence pairs and the test set has 699 sentence pairs. The dataset is from the newspaper domain with topics ranging from politics to tourism. The sentence pairs have a maximum source sentence length of 30 words. The average length of English sentences is 18 while that of Hindi sentences is 20.

The source language vocabulary is 41017 and target sentence vocabulary is 48576. The token/type ratio of English in the dataset is 16.70 and that of Hindi is 15.64. This dataset is relatively sparse. So, the translation accuracies on this dataset would be relatively less when compared to those on much larger datasets. In the target side of the development corpus, the percentage of unseen tokens is 13.48%(3.87% types) while in the source side, the percentage of unseen tokens is 10.77%(3.20% types). On furthur inspection of a small portion of the dataset, we found that the maximum percentage of the unseen words on the target side are the named entities.

5 Results

5.1 Bag-of-Words model

The quality of the bag–of–words obtained is governed by the parameter τ (probability threshold). To determine the best τ value, we experiment with various values of τ and measure the lexical accuracies (F-score) of the bags generated on the development set (See Figure 6). The total number of features used for training this model are 53166 (with count-cutoff of 2).

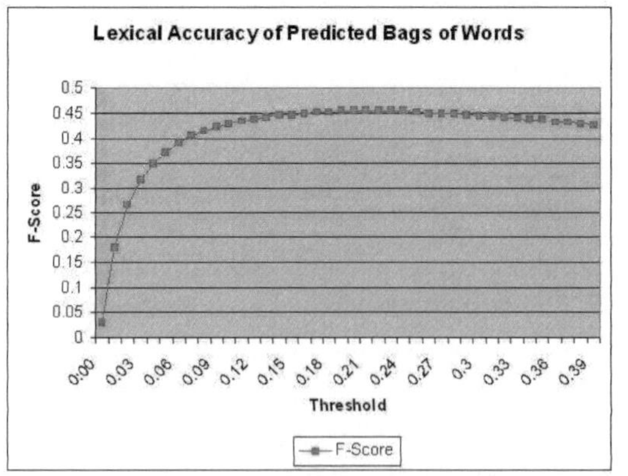

Figure 6: Lexical Accuracies of the Bags-of-words

Now, we order the bags of words obtained through global selection to get the target language strings. While reordering using the language model, some of the noisy words from the bag can be deleted by setting a deletion cost (δ). We experimented with various deletion costs, and tuned it according to the best BLEU score that we obtained on the development set. Figure 7 shows the best BLEU scores obtained by reordering the bags associated with various threshold values.

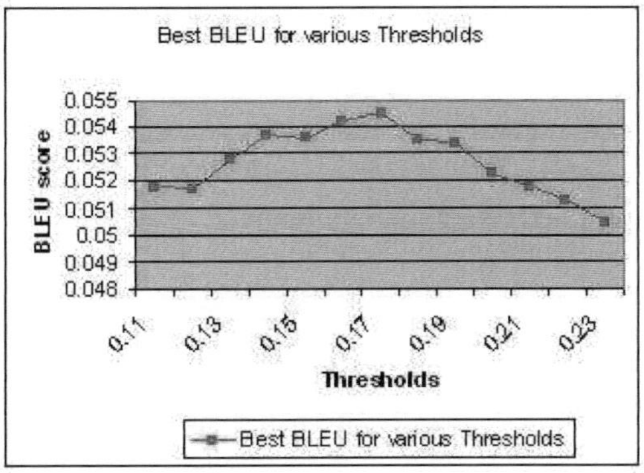

Figure 7: Lexical Accuracies of the Bags-of-words

We can see that we obtained the best BLEU when we choose a threshold of 0.17 to obtain the bag–of–words, when the deletion cost is set to 19.

The reference target strings of the development set has 15986 tokens. So, while tuning the parameters, we should ensure that the bags (obtained using the global lexical selection) that we consider have more tokens than 15986 to allow some deletions during reordering, and in effect obtain the target strings whose total token count is approximately equal to 15986. Figure 8 shows the variation in BLEU scores for various deletion costs by fixing the threshold at 0.17.

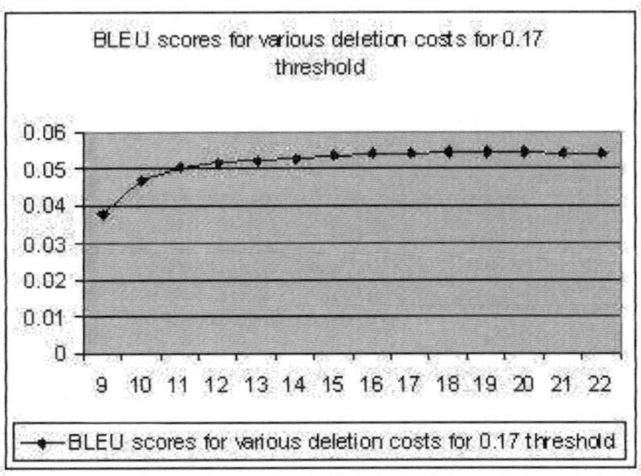

Figure 8: BLEU scores for various deletion costs when the threshold for global lexical selection is set to 0.17

On the test set, we now fix the threshold at 0.17 (τ) and the deletion cost (δ) at 19 to obtain the target language strings. The BLEU score that we obtained for this set is 0.0428.

5.2 Sequential Lexical Choice Model

The lexical accuracy values of the sequence of words obtained by the sequential lexical choice model are comparable to those obtained using the bag–of–words model. The real difference comes for the BLEU score. The best BLEU score obtained on the development set was **0.0586** when τ was set to 0.14 and deletion cost was 15. On the test set, the BLEU score obtained was 0.0473.

5.3 Tree based model

The lexical accuracy values of the words obtained in this model are comparable to the lexical accuracy values of the bag of words model. The total number of features used for training this model are 118839 (with count-cutoff of 2). On the development set, we obtained a BLEU score of **0.0650** for τ set at 0.17 and the deletion cost set at 20. On the test set, we obtained a BLEU score of 0.0498. We can see that the BLEU scores are now better than the ones obtained using any of the other models discussed before. This is because the Tree based model has both the strengths of the global lexical selection that ensures high quality lexical items in the target sentences and that of an efficient reconstruction model which takes care of long distance reordering. The table summarizes the BLEU scores obtained by the three models on the development and test sets.

	Devel. Set	Test. Set
Bag-of-Words	0.0545	0.0428
Sequential	0.0586	0.0473
Hierarchical	0.0650	0.0498

Table 1: Summary of the results

6 Conclusion

In this paper, we present a novel approach to lexical selection where the target words are associated with the entire source sentence (global) without the need for local associations. This technique is used by three models (Bag–of–words model, sequential model and hierarchical model) which predict the target language words given a source sentence and then order the words appropriately. We show that a hierarchical model performs best when compared to the other two models. The hierarchical model presented in this paper has both the strengths of the global lexical selection and efficient reconstruction model.

In the future, we are planning to improve the hierarchical model by making two primary additions

- Handling cases of structural non-isomorphism between source and target sentences.
- Obtaining K-best target string per node of the source dependency tree instead of just one per node. This would allow us to explore more possibilities without having to compromise much on computational complexity.

References

Hiyan Alshawi, Srinivas Bangalore, and Shona Douglas. 1998. Automatic acquisition of hierarchical transduction models for machine translation. In *Proceedings of the 36th Annual Meeting Association for Computational Linguistics*, Montreal, Canada.

A.L. Berger, Stephen A. D. Pietra, D. Pietra, and J. Vincent. 1996. A Maximum Entropy Approach to Natural Language Processing. *Computational Linguistics*, 22(1):39–71.

P. Brown, S.D. Pietra, V.D. Pietra, and R. Mercer. 1993. The Mathematics of Machine Translation: Parameter Estimation. *Computational Linguistics*, 16(2):263–312.

David Chiang. 2005. A hierarchical phrase-based model for statistical machine translation. In *Proceedings of the 43rd Annual Meeting of the Association for Computational Linguistics (ACL'05)*, pages 263–270, Ann Arbor, Michigan, June. Association for Computational Linguistics.

P. Haffner. 2006. Scaling large margin classifiers for spoken language understanding. *Speech Communication*, 48(iv):239–261.

S. Kanthak, D. Vilar, E. Matusov, R. Zens, and H. Ney. 2005. Novel reordering approaches in phrase-based statistical machine translation. In *Proceedings of the ACL Workshop on Building and Using Parallel Texts*, pages 167–174, Ann Arbor, Michigan.

J. Lafferty, A. McCallum, and F. Pereira. 2001. Conditional random fields: Probabilistic models for segmenting and labeling sequence data. In *Proceedings of ICML*, San Francisco, CA.

Franz Och, Christoph Tillmann, and Herman Ney. 1999. Improved alignment models for statistical machine translation. In *In Proc. of the Joint Conf. of Empirical Methods in Natural Language Processing and Very Large Corpora*, pages 20–28.

Dekai Wu. 1997. Stochastic Inversion Transduction Grammars and Bilingual Parsing of Parallel Corpora. *Computational Linguistics*, 23(3):377–404.

K. Yamada and K. Knight. 2001. A syntax-based statistical translation model. In *Proceedings of* 39th *ACL.*

Comparing Reordering Constraints for SMT Using Efficient BLEU Oracle Computation

Markus Dreyer, Keith Hall, and Sanjeev Khudanpur
Center for Language and Speech Processing
Johns Hopkins University
3400 North Charles Street, Baltimore, MD 21218 USA
{dreyer,keith_hall,khudanpur}@jhu.edu

Abstract

This paper describes a new method to compare reordering constraints for Statistical Machine Translation. We investigate the best possible (oracle) BLEU score achievable under different reordering constraints. Using dynamic programming, we efficiently find a reordering that approximates the highest attainable BLEU score given a reference and a set of reordering constraints. We present an empirical evaluation of popular reordering constraints: local constraints, the IBM constraints, and the Inversion Transduction Grammar (ITG) constraints. We present results for a German-English translation task and show that reordering under the ITG constraints can improve over the baseline by more than 7.5 BLEU points.

1 Introduction

Reordering the words and phrases of a foreign sentence to obtain the target word order is a fundamental, and potentially the hardest, problem in machine translation. The search space for all possible permutations of a sentence is factorial in the number of words/phrases; therefore a variety of models have been proposed that constrain the set of possible permutations by allowing certain reorderings while disallowing others. Some models (Brown et al. (1996), Kumar and Byrne (2005)) allow words to change place with their local neighbors, but disallow global reorderings. Other models (Wu (1997), Xiong et al. (2006)) explicitly allow global reorderings, but do not allow all possible permutations, including some local permutations.

We present a novel technique to compare achievable translation accuracies under different reordering constraints. While earlier work has trained and tested instantiations of different reordering models and then compared the translation results (Zens and Ney, 2003) we provide a more general mechanism to evaluate the *potential* efficacy of reordering constraints, independent of specific training paradigms. Our technique attempts to answer the question: *What is the highest* BLEU *score that a given translation system could reach when using reordering constraints X?* Using this oracle approach, we abstract away from issues that are not inherent in the reordering constraints, but may nevertheless influence the comparison results, such as model and feature design, feature selection, or parameter estimation. In fact, we compare several sets of reordering constraints empirically, but do not train them as models. We merely decode by efficiently searching over possible translations allowed by each model and choosing the reordering that achieves the highest BLEU score.

We start by introducing popular reordering constraints (Section 2). Then, we present dynamic-programming algorithms that find the highest-scoring permutations of sentences under given reordering constraints (Section 3). We use this technique to compare several reordering constraints empirically. We combine a basic translation framework with different reordering constraints (Section 4) and

Proceedings of SSST, NAACL-HLT 2007 / AMTA Workshop on Syntax and Structure in Statistical Translation, pages 103–110,
Rochester, New York, April 2007.

present results on a German-English translation task (Section 5). Finally, we offer an analysis of the results and provide a review of related work (Sections 6–8).

2 Reordering Constraints

Reordering constraints restrict the movement of words or phrases in order to reach or approximate the word order of the target language. Some of the constraints considered in this paper were originally proposed for reordering words, but we will describe all constraints in terms of reordering phrases. Phrases are units of consecutive words read off a phrase translation table.

2.1 Local Constraints

Local constraints allow phrases to swap with one another only if they are adjacent or very close to each other. Kumar and Byrne (2005) define two local reordering models for their Translation Template Model (TTM): In the first one, called MJ-1, only adjacent phrases are allowed to swap, and the movement has to be done within a window of 2. A sequence consisting of three phrases *abc* can therefore become *acb* or *bac*, but not *cba*. One phrase can jump at most one phrase ahead and cannot take part in more than one swap. In their second strategy, called MJ-2, phrases are allowed to swap with their immediate neighbor or with the phrase next to the immediate neighbor; the maximum jump length is 2. This allows for all six possible permutations of *abc*. The movement here has to take place within a window of 3 phrases. Therefore, a four-phrase sequence *abcd* cannot be reordered to *cadb*, for example. MJ-1 and MJ-2 are shown in Figure 1.

2.2 IBM Constraints

First introduced by Brown et al. (1996), the IBM constraints are among the most well-known and most widely used reordering paradigms. Translation is done from the beginning of the sentence to the end, phrase by phrase; at each point in time, the constraints allow one of the first k still untranslated phrases to be selected for translation (see Figure 1d, for k=2). The IBM constraints are much less restrictive than local constraints. The first word of the input, for example, can move all the way to the end, independent of the value of k. Typically, k is set to 4 (Zens and Ney, 2003). We write IBM with k=4 as IBM(4). The IBM constraints are supersets of the local constraints.

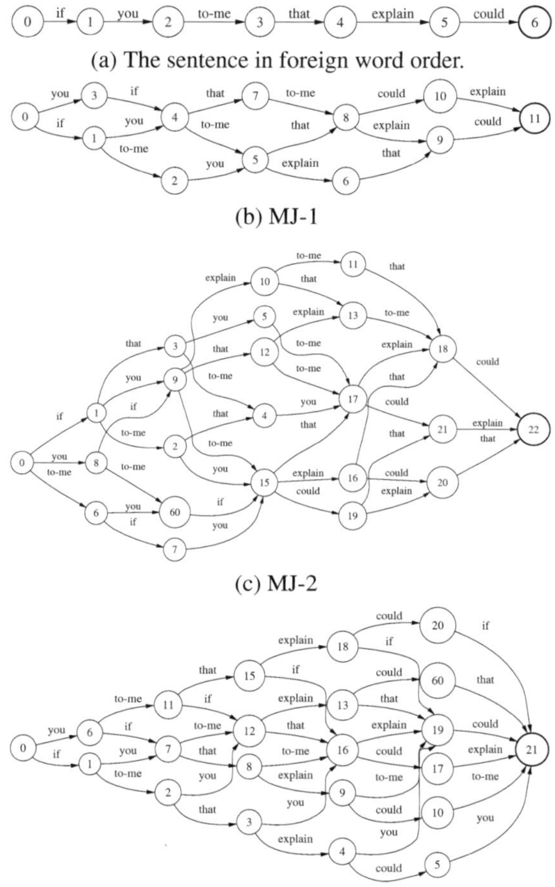

(a) The sentence in foreign word order.

(b) MJ-1

(c) MJ-2

(d) IBM(2)

Figure 1: The German word order *if you to-me that explain could* ('wenn Sie mir das erklären könnten') and all possible reorderings under different constraints, represented as lattices. None of these lattices contains the correct English order *if you could explain that to-me*. See also Table 1.

2.3 ITG Constraints

The Inversion Transduction Grammar (ITG) (Wu, 1997), a derivative of the Syntax Directed Transduction Grammars (Aho and Ullman, 1972), constrains the possible permutations of the input string by defining rewrite rules that indicate permutations of the string. In particular, the ITG allows all permutations defined by all binary branching structures where the children of any constituent may be swapped in order. The ITG constraint is different from the other reordering constraints presented in that it is not based on finite-state operations. An

Model	# perm.	"Best" sentence	n-gram precisions	BLEU
MJ-1	13	if you that to-me could explain	100.0/66.7/20.0/0.0	0.0
MJ-2	52	to-me if you could explain that	100.0/83.3/60.0/50.0	70.71
IBM(2)	32	if to-me that you could explain	100.0/50.0/20.0/0.0	0.0
IBM(4)	384	if you could explain that to-me	100.0/100.0/100.0/100.0	100.0
IBM(4) (prune)	42	if you could explain that to-me	100.0/100.0/100.0/100.0	100.0
ITG	394	if you could explain that to-me	100.0/100.0/100.0/100.0	100.0
ITG (prune)	78	if you could explain that to-me	100.0/100.0/100.0/100.0	100.0

Table 1: Illustrating example: The number of permutations (# perm.) that different reordering paradigms consider for the input sequence *if you to-me that explain could*, and the permutation with highest BLEU score. The sentence length is 7, but there are only 6! possible permutations, since the phrase *to-me* counts as one word during reordering. ITG (prune) is the ITG BLEU decoder with the pruning settings we used in our experiments (beam threshold 10^{-4}). For comparison, IBM(4) (prune) is the lattice BLEU decoder with the same pruning settings, but we use pruning only for ITG permutations in our experiments.

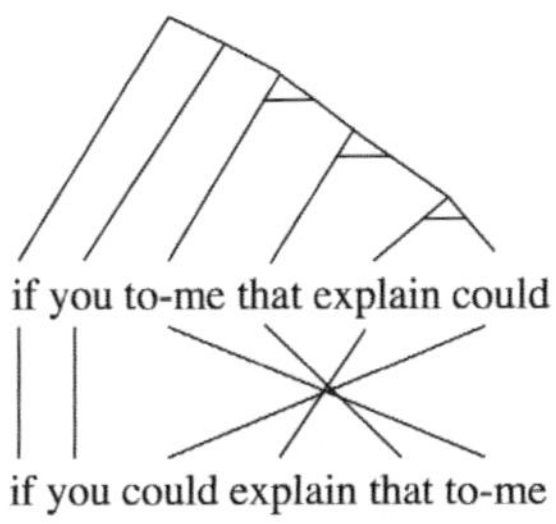

Figure 2: The example *if you to-me that explain could* and its reordering to *if you could explain that to-me* using an ITG. The alignments are added below the tree, and the horizontal bars in the tree indicate a swap.

ITG decoder runs in polynomial time and allows for long-distance phrasal reordering. A phrase can, for example, move from the first position in the input to the last position in the output and vice versa, by swapping the topmost node in the constructed binary tree. However, due to the binary bracketing constraint, some permutations are not modeled. A four-phrase sequence *abcd* cannot be permuted into *cadb* or *bdac*. Therefore, the ITG constraints are not supersets of the IBM constraints. IBM(4), for example, allows *abcd* to be permuted into *cadb* and *bdac*.

3 Factored BLEU Computation

The different reordering strategies described allow for different permutations and restrict the search space in different ways. We are concerned with the maximal achievable accuracy under given constraints, independent of feature design or parameter estimation. This is what we call the *oracle* accuracy under the reordering constraints and it is computed on a dataset with reference translations.

We now describe algorithms that can be used to find such oracle translations among unreordered translation candidates. There are two equivalent strategies: The reordering constraints that are being tested can be expressed as a special dynamic-programming decoder which, when applied to an unreordered hypothesis, searches the space of permutations defined by the reordering constraints and returns the highest-scoring permutation. We employ this strategy for the ITG reorderings (Section 3.2). For the other reordering constraints, we employ a more generic strategy: Given the set of reordering constraints, all permutations of an unreordered translation candidate are precomputed and explicitly represented as a lattice. This lattice is passed as input to a Dijkstra-style decoder (Section 3.1) which traverses it and finds the solution that reachest the highest BLEU score.[1]

3.1 Dijkstra BLEU Decoder

The Dijkstra-style decoder takes as input a lattice in which each path represents one possible permutation of an unreordered hypothesis under a given reordering paradigm, as in Figure 1. It traverses the lattice and finds the solution that has the highest approximate BLEU score, given the reference. The dynamic-programming algorithm divides the problem into subproblems that are solved independently, the solutions of which contribute to the solutions of other subproblems. The general procedure is sketched in Figure 3: for each subpath of the lattice containing the precomputed permutations, we store the three most recently attached words (Fig-

[1]For both strategies, several unreordered translation candidates do not have to be regarded separately, but can be represented as a weighted lattice and be used as input to the special dynamic program or to the process that precomputes possible permutations.

$$\beta([0, k, len+1, w_2, w_3, w_{new}]) = \max_{w_1} (\text{ get\_bleu } ([0, j, len, w_1, w_2, w_3], [j, k, w_{new}])) \quad (1)$$

$$\begin{aligned} &\text{function get\_bleu } ([0, j, len, w_1, w_2, w_3], [j, k, w_{new}]) := \\ &\quad \text{update\_ngrams } (0, j, k, len, w_1, w_2, w_3, w_{new}) \, ; \\ &\quad \text{return } exp \left(\frac{1}{4} \sum_{n=1}^{4} log \left(\frac{\text{ngrams}_i([0, k, len+1, w_2, w_3, w_{new}])}{len - n + 1} \right) \right) ; \end{aligned} \quad (2)$$

Figure 3: **Top:** The BLEU score is used as inside score for a subpath from 0 to k with the rightmost words w_2, w_3, w_{new} in the Dijkstra decoder. **Bottom:** Pseudo code for a function `get_bleu` which updates the n-gram matches $\text{ngrams}_1(\dots)$, $\text{ngrams}_2(\dots)$, $\text{ngrams}_3(\dots)$, $\text{ngrams}_4(\dots)$ for the resulting subpath in a hash table $[0, k, len+1, w_2, w_3, w_{new}]$ and returns its approximate BLEU score.

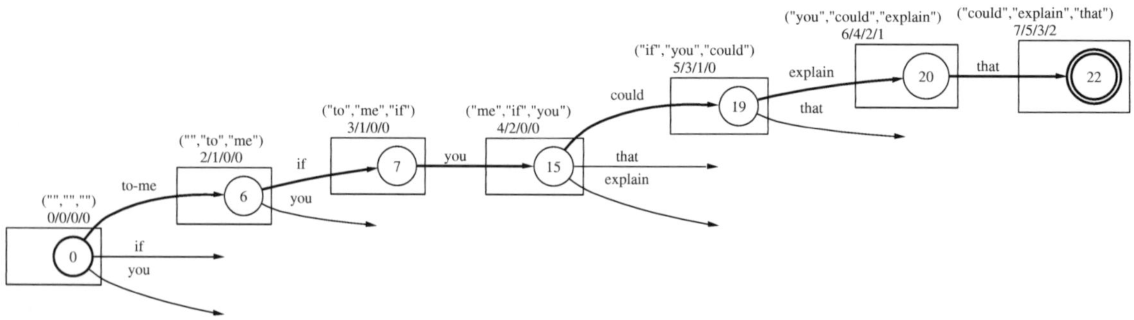

Figure 4: Three right-most words and n-gram matches: This shows the best path for the MJ-2 reordering of *if you to-me that explain could*, along with the words stored at each state and the progressively updated n-gram matches. The full path *to-me if you could explain that* has 7 unigram matches, 5 bigram, 3 trigram, and 2 fourgram matches. See the full MJ-2 lattice in Figure 1c.

ure 4). A context of three words is needed to compute fourgram precisions used in the BLEU score. Starting from the start state, we recursively extend a subpath word by word, following the paths in the lattice. Whenever we extend the path by a word to the right we incorporate that word and use `update_ngrams` to update the four n-gram counts for the subpath. The function `update_ngrams` has access to the reference string[2] and stores the updated n-gram counts for the resulting path in a hash table.[3] The inside score of each subpath is the approximate BLEU score, calculated as the average of the four n-gram log precisions. An n-gram precision is always the number of n-gram matches divided by the length len of the path minus $(n-1)$. A path of length 4 with 2 bigram matches, for example, has a bigram precision of $^2/_3$. This method is similar to Dijkstra's algorithm (Dijkstra, 1959) composed with a fourgram finite-state language model, where the scoring is done using n-gram counts and precision scores. We call this the Dijkstra BLEU decoder.

3.2 ITG BLEU Decoder

For the ITG reordering constraints, we use a dynamic program that computes the permutations implicitly. It takes only the unreordered hypothesis as input and creates the possible reorderings under the ITG constraints during decoding, as it creates a parse chart. The algorithm is similar to a CKY parsing algorithm in that it proceeds bottom-up and combines smaller constituents into larger ones recursively. Figure 5 contains details of the algorithm. The ITG BLEU decoder stores the three leftmost and the three rightmost words in each constituent. A constituent from position i to position k, with w_a, w_b, and w_c as leftmost words, and w_x, w_y, w_z as rightmost words is written as $[i, k, (w_a, w_b, w_c), (w_x, w_y, w_z)]$. Such a constituent can be built by straight or inverted rules. Using an inverted rule means swapping the order of the children in the built constituent. The successive bottom-up combinations of adjacent constituents result in hierarchical binary bracketing with swapped and non-

[2] Multiple reference strings can be used if available.

[3] An epsilon value of 1^{-10} is used for zero precisions.

$$\beta\left([i,k,(w_a,w_b,w_c),(w_x,w_y,w_z)]\right) = \max\left(\begin{array}{l}\beta_{()}\left([i,k,(w_a,w_b,w_c),(w_x,w_y,w_z)]\right),\\ \beta_{<>}\left([i,k,(w_a,w_b,w_c),(w_x,w_y,w_z)]\right)\end{array}\right) \quad (3)$$

$$\beta_{<>}([i,k,(w_a,w_b,w_c),(w_x,w_y,w_z)]) = \max_{j,w_{a'},w_{b'},w_{c'},w_{x'},w_{y'},w_{z'}}\left(\text{get\_bleu}\left(\begin{array}{l}[j,k,(w_a,w_b,w_c),(w_{x'},w_{y'},w_{z'})],\\ [i,j,(w_{a'},w_{b'},w_{c'}),(w_x,w_y,w_z)]\end{array}\right)\right) \quad (4)$$

Figure 5: Equations for the ITG oracle BLEU decoder. $[i, k, (w_a, w_b, w_c), (w_x, w_y, w_z)]$ is a constituent from i to k with leftmost words w_a,w_b,w_c and rightmost words w_x,w_y,w_z. Top: A constituent can be built with a straight or a swapped rule. Bottom: A swapped rule. The `get_bleu` function can be adapted from Figure 3

swapped constituents. Our ITG BLEU decoder uses standard beam search pruning. As in Zens and Ney (2003), phrases are not broken up, but every phrase is, at the beginning of reordering, stored in the chart as one lexical token together with the precomputed n-gram matches and the n-gram precision score.

In addition to standard ITG we run experiments with a constrained ITG, in which we impose a bound ρ on the maximum length of reordered constituents, measured in phrases. If the combined length of two constituents exceeds this bound they can only be combined in the given monotone order. Experiments with this ITG variant give insight into the effect that various long-distance reorderings have on the final BLEU scores (see Table 3). Such bounds are also effective speedup techniques(Eisner and Tromble, 2006).

3.3 BLEU Approximations

BLEU is defined to use the *modified* n-gram precision, which means that a correct n-gram that occurs once in the reference, but several times in the system translation will be counted only once as correct. The other occurrences are clipped. We do not include this global feature since we want a dynamic-programming solution with polynomial size and runtime. The decoder processes subproblems independently; words are attached locally and stored only as boundary words of covered paths/ constituents. Therefore we cannot discount a locally attached word that has already been attached elsewhere to an alternative path/constituent. However, clipping affects most heavily the unigram scores which are constant, like the length of the sentence.[4]

We also adopt the approximation that treats every sentence with its reference as a separate corpus (Tillmann and Zhang, 2006) so that ngram counts are not accumulated, and parallel processing of sentences becomes possible. Due to these two approximations, our method is not guaranteed to find the best reordering defined by the reordering constraints. However, we have found on our heldout data that an oracle that does not accumulate n-gram counts is only minimally worse than an oracle that does accumulate them (up to 0.25 BLEU points).[5] If, in addition, clipping is ignored, the resulting oracle stays virtually the same, at most 0.02 BLEU points worse than the oracle found otherwise. All results in this paper are computed with the original BLEU formula on the sentences found by the oracle algorithms.

4 Creating a Monotone Translation Baseline

To compare the reordering constraints under oracle conditions we first obtain unreordered candidate translations from a simple baseline translation model. For each reordering paradigm, we take the candidate translations, get the best oracle reorderings under the given reordering constraints and pick the best sentence according to the BLEU score.

The baseline translation system is created using probabilistic word-to-word and phrase-to-phrase ta-

[4]Since the sentence lengths are constant for all reorderings of a given sentence we can in our experiments also ignore the brevity penalty which cancels out. If the input consists of several sentences of different lengths (see fn. 1) then the brevity penalty can be built in by keeping track of length ratios of attached phrases.

[5]The accumulating oracle algorithm makes a greedy decision for every sentence given the ngram counts so far accumulated (Zens and Ney, 2005). The result of such a greedy oracle method may depend on the order of the input sentences. We tried 100 shuffles of these and received 100 very similar results, with a variance of under 0.006 BLEU points. The non-accumulating oracles use an epsilon value (1^{-10}) for zero counts.

bles. Using the translation probabilities, we create a lattice that contains word and phrase translations for every substring of the source sentence. The resulting lattice is made of English words and phrases of different lengths. Every word or phrase translation probability p is a mixture of $p(f|e)$ and $p(e|f)$. We discard short phrase translations exponentially by a parameter that is trained on heldout data. Insertions and deletions are handled exclusively by the use of a phrase table: an insertion takes place wherever the English side of a phrase translation is longer than the foreign side (e.g. English *presidential candidate* for German *Präsidentschaftskandidat*), and vice versa for deletions (e.g. *we discussed* for *wir haben diskutiert*). Gaps or discontinuous phrases are not handled. The baseline decoder outputs the n-best paths through the lattice according to the lattice scores[6], marking consecutive phrases so that the oracle reordering algorithms can recognize them and keep them together. Note that the baseline system is trained on real data, while the reordering constraints that we want to test are not trained.

5 Empirical Comparison of Reordering Constraints

We use the monotone translation baseline model and the oracle BLEU computation to evaluate different popular reordering strategies. We now describe the experimental settings. The word and phrase translation probabilities of the baseline model are trained on the Europarl German-English training set, using GIZA++ and the Pharaoh phrase extraction algorithm. For testing we use the NAACL 2006 SMT Shared Task test data. For each sentence of the test set, a lattice is created in the way described in Section 4, with parameters optimized on a small heldout set.[7] For each sentence, the 1000-best candidates according to the lattice scores are extracted. We take the 10-best oracle candidates, according to the reference, and use a BLEU decoder to create the best permutation of each of them and pick the best one. Using this procedure, we make sure that we get the highest-scoring unreordered candidates and choose the best one among their oracle reorderings. Table 2 and Figure 6 show the resulting BLEU scores for different sentence lengths. Table 3 shows results of the ITG runs with different length bounds ρ. The average phrase length in the candidate translations of the test set is 1.42 words.

Oracle decodings under the ITG and under IBM(4) constraints were up to 1000 times slower than under the other tested oracle reordering methods in our implementations. Among the faster methods, decoding under MJ-2 constraints was up to 40% faster than under IBM(2) constraints in our implementation.

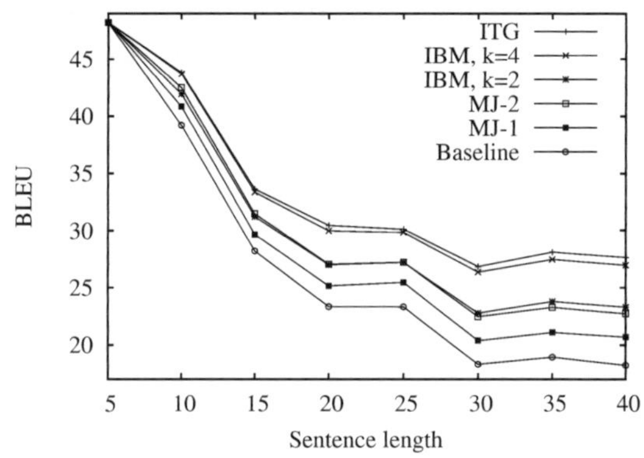

Figure 6: Reordering oracle scores for different sentence lengths. See also Table 2.

6 Discussion

The empirical results show that reordering under sufficiently permissive constraints can improve a monotone baseline oracle by more than 7.5 BLEU points. This gap between choosing the best unreordered sentences versus choosing the best optimally reordered sentences is small for short sentences and widens dramatically (more than nine BLEU points) for longer sentences.

The ITG constraints and the IBM(4) constraints both give very high oracle translation accuracies on the German-English translation task. Overall, their BLEU scores are about 2 to more than 4 points better than the BLEU scores of the best other methods. This gap between the two highest-scoring constraints and the other methods becomes bigger as the sentence lengths grow and is greater than 4

[6]We use a straightforward adaption of Algorithm 3 in Huang and Chiang (2005)

[7]We fill the initial phrase and word lattice with the 20 best candidates, using phrases of 3 or less words.

Sentence length	# of test sentences	ITG (prune)	IBM, k=4	IBM, k=2	MJ-2	MJ-1	No reordering
		BLEU (NIST) scores					
1–5	61	48.21 (5.35)	48.21 (5.35)	48.21 (5.35)	48.21 (5.35)	48.21 (5.35)	48.17 (5.68)
6–10	230	43.83 (6.75)	43.71 (6.74)	41.94 (6.68)	42.50 (6.71)	40.85 (6.66)	39.21 (6.99)
11–15	440	33.66 (6.71)	33.37 (6.71)	31.23 (6.62)	31.49 (6.64)	29.67 (6.56)	28.21 (6.76)
16–20	447	30.47 (6.66)	29.99 (6.65)	27.00 (6.52)	27.06 (6.50)	25.15 (6.45)	23.34 (6.52)
21–25	454	30.13 (6.80)	29.83 (6.79)	27.21 (6.67)	27.22 (6.65)	25.46 (6.58)	23.32 (6.63)
26–30	399	26.85 (6.42)	26.36 (6.42)	22.79 (6.25)	22.47 (6.22)	20.38 (6.12)	18.31 (6.11)
31–35	298	28.11 (6.45)	27.47 (6.43)	23.79 (6.25)	23.28 (6.21)	21.09 (6.12)	18.94 (6.06)
36–40	242	27.65 (6.37)	26.97 (6.35)	23.31 (6.19)	22.73 (6.16)	20.70 (6.06)	18.22 (5.94)
1–40	2571	29.63 (7.48)	29.17 (7.46)	26.07 (7.24)	25.89 (7.22)	23.95 (7.08)	21.89 (7.07)

Table 2: BLEU and NIST results for different reordering methods on binned sentence lengths. The ITG results are, unlike the other results, with pruning (beam 10^{-4}). The BLEU results are plotted in Figure 6. All results are computed with the original BLEU formula on the sentences found by the oracle algorithms.

BLEU scores for sentences longer than 30 sentences. This advantage in translation accuracy comes with high computational cost, as mentioned above.

Among the computationally more lightweight reordering methods tested, IBM(2) and MJ-2 are very close to each other in translation accuracy, with IBM(2) obtaining slightly better scores on longer sentences, while MJ-2 is more efficient. MJ-1 is less successful in reordering, improving the monotone baseline by only about 2.5 BLEU points at best, but is the best choice if speed is an issue.

As described above, the reorderings defined by the local constraints MJ-1 and MJ-2 are subsets of IBM(2) and IBM(3). We did not test IBM(3), but the values can be interpolated between IBM(2) and IBM(4). The ITG constraints do not belong in this family of finite-state contraints; they allow reorderings that none of the other methods allow, and vice versa. The fact that ITG constraints can reach such high translation accuracies supports the findings in Zens et al. (2004) and is an empirical validation of the ITG hypothesis.

The experiments with the constrained ITG show the effect of reorderings spanning different lengths (see Table 3). While most reorderings are short-distance ($<$5 phrases) a lot of improvements can still be obtained when ρ is increased from length 5 to 10 and even from 10 to 20 phrases.

Len.	ρ=0	ρ=5	ρ=10	ρ=20	ρ=30	ρ=40
26–30	18.31	24.07	26.40	26.79	26.85	26.85
31–35	18.94	25.10	27.21	28.00	28.09	28.11
36–40	18.22	24.46	26.66	27.53	27.64	27.65
26–40	18.49	24.74	26.74	27.41	27.50	27.51

Table 3: BLEU results of ITGs that are constrained to reorderings not exceeding a certain span length ρ. Results shown for different sentence lengths.

7 Related Work

There exist related algorithms that search the space of reorderings and compute BLEU oracle approximations. Zens and Ney (2005) describe a dynamic-programming algorithm in which at every state the number of n-gram matches is stored, along with a multiset that contains all words from the reference that have not yet been matched. This makes it possible to compute the *modified* ngram precision, but the search space is exponential. Tillmann and Zhang (2006) use a BLEU oracle decoder for discriminative training of a local reordering model. No details about the algorithm are given. Zens and Ney (2003) perform a comparison of different reordering strategies. Their study differs from ours in that they use reordering models trained on real data and may therefore be influenced by feature selection, parameter estimation and other training-specific issues. In our study, only the baseline translation model is trained on data. Zens et al. (2004) conduct a study similar to Zens and Ney (2003) and note that the results for the ITG reordering constraints were quite dependent on the very simple probability model used. Our study avoids this issue by using the

BLEU oracle approach. In Wellington et al. (2006), hand-aligned data are used to compare the standard ITG constraints to ITGs that allow gaps.

8 Conclusions

We have presented a training-independent method to compare different reordering constraints for machine translation. Given a sentence in foreign word order, its reference translation(s) and reordering constraints, our dynamic-programming algorithms efficiently find the oracle reordering that has the approximately highest BLEU score. This allows evaluating different reordering constraints experimentally, but abstracting away from specific features, the probability model or training methods of the reordering strategies. The presented method evaluates the theoretical capabilities of reordering constraints, as opposed to more arbitrary accuracies of specifically trained instances of reordering models.

Using our oracle method, we presented an empirical evaluation of different reordering constraints for a German-English translation task. The results show that a good reordering of a given monotone translation can improve the translation quality dramatically. Both short- and long-distance reorderings contribute to the BLEU score improvements, which are generally greater for longer sentences. Reordering constraints that allow global reorderings tend to reach better oracles scores than ones that search more locally. The ITG constraints and the IBM(4) constraints both give the highest oracle scores.

The presented BLEU decoder algorithms can be useful in many ways: They can generally help decide what reordering constraints to choose for a given translation system. They can be used for discriminative training of reordering models (Tillmann and Zhang, 2006). Furthermore, they can help detecting insufficient parameterization or incapable training algorithms: If two trained reordering model instances show similar performances on a given task, but the oracle scores differ greatly then the training methods might not be optimal.

Acknowledgments

This work was partially supported by the National Science Foundation via an ITR grant (No 0121285), the Defense Advanced Research Projects Agency via a GALE contract (No HR0011-06-2-0001), and the Office of Naval Research via a MURI grant (No N00014-01-1-0685). We thank Jason Eisner, David Smith, Roy Tromble and the anonymous reviewers for helpful comments and suggestions.

References

A. V. Aho and J. D. Ullman. 1972. *The Theory of Parsing, Translation, and Compiling*. Prentice Hall.

A.L. Berger P. F. Brown, S. A. Della Pietra, V. J. Della Pietra, J. R. Gillett, J. D. Lafferty, R. L. Mercer, H. Printz, and L. Ures. 1996. Language translation apparatus and method using context-based translation models. United States Patent No. 5,510,981.

E.W. Dijkstra. 1959. A note on two problems in connexion with graphs. *Numerische Mathematik.*, 1:269–271.

J. Eisner and R. W. Tromble. 2006. Local search with very large-scale neighborhoods for optimal permutations in Machine Translation. In *Proc. of the Workshop on Computationally Hard Problems and Joint Inference*, New York.

L. Huang and D. Chiang. 2005. Better k-best parsing. In *Proc. of IWPT*, Vancouver, B.C., Canada.

S. Kumar and W. Byrne. 2005. Local phrase reordering models for Statistical Machine Translation. In *Proc. of HLT/EMNLP*, pages 161–168, Vancouver, B.C., Canada.

C. Tillmann and T. Zhang. 2006. A discriminative global training algorithm for Statistical MT. In *Proc. of ACL*, pages 721–728, Sydney, Australia.

B. Wellington, S. Waxmonsky, and D. Melamed. 2006. Empirical lower bounds on the complexity of translational equivalence. In *Proc. of COLING-ACL*, pages 977–984, Sydney, Australia.

D. Wu. 1997. Stochastic inversion transduction grammars and bilingual parsing of parallel corpora. *Computational Linguistics*, 23(3):377–404.

D. Xiong, Q. Liu, and S. Lin. 2006. Maximum entropy based phrase reordering model for Statistical Machine Translation. In *Proc. of COLING-ACL*, pages 521–528, Sydney, Australia.

R. Zens and H. Ney. 2003. A comparative study on reordering constraints in Statistical Machine Translation. In *Proc. of ACL*, pages 144–151, Sapporo, Japan.

R. Zens and H. Ney. 2005. Word graphs for Statistical Machine Translation. In *Proc. of the ACL Workshop on Building and Using Parallel Texts*, pages 191–198, Ann Arbor, MI.

R. Zens, H. Ney, T. Watanabe, and E. Sumita. 2004. Reordering constraints for phrase-based Statistical Machine Translation. In *Proc. of CoLing*, pages 205–211, Geneva.

Author Index

Association for Computational Linguistics
209 N. Eighth Street
Stroudsburg, Pennsylvania 18360